T0330187

RESEARCHING AND WRITING DIFFERENTLY

Ilaria Boncori

First published in Great Britain in 2023 by

Policy Press, an imprint of
Bristol University Press
University of Bristol
1–9 Old Park Hill
Bristol
BS2 8BB
UK
t: +44 (0)117 374 6645
e: bup-info@bristol.ac.uk

Details of international sales and distribution partners are available at
policy.bristoluniversitypress.co.uk

British Library Cataloguing in Publication Data
A catalogue record for this book is available from the British Library

ISBN 978-1-4473-6814-4 hardcover
ISBN 978-1-4473-6816-8 ePub
ISBN 978-1-4473-6815-1 ePdf

Cover design: Liam Roberts Design
Front cover image: Alamy/WD6469 Justin Lee
Bristol University Press and Policy Press use environmentally responsible
print partners.
Printed in Great Britain by CPI Group (UK) Ltd, Croydon, CR0 4YY

Contents

About the author

Ilaria Boncori is Professor in Management and Marketing at the University of Essex (UK). Her current research is concerned with the articulation of inequality in organizations, and particularly regarding experiences located at the intersections of gender, race, foreignness and sexual orientation. She is a critical management scholar and a qualitative researcher with a strong interest in the exploration of embodied and affective dynamics in the workplace, investigated mainly through ethnographic and narrative methods.

Acknowledgements

This book means a lot to me and, as for everything I care deeply about, I am not sure I have done it justice. I hope it will be a small brick contributing to the community building and practice development of people who want to inhabit today's academia differently. This book stems from other academics' work, approaches and practices of researching and writing differently. Writing Differently has brought to me much joy as a scholar – a reader, author and reviewer. It has sparked reflection not only on how to write and publish differently, but also on how to foster caring approaches to researching and doing academic work. I wholeheartedly hope that in a decade the background information, practical guidelines, and pleas for development and inclusion made in this volume will have become obsolete and redundant due to the widespread valuing and visibility of the Writing Differently type of research.

I owe a deep debt of gratitude to many colleagues. In particular to Alison Pullen, Jenny Helin, Sarah Gilmore, Nancy Harding, and Monika Kostera for reigniting and keeping alive the Writing Differently fire in management and organization studies, and for inspiring me with their work to believe that a different type of scholarship is possible. Their formal and informal contributions to our field, together with research by many other colleagues, make a difference. I would not be writing this book without the map of the path they have charted in my field of inquiry.

A special thanks to Heather Höpfl, a colleague and a friend who was my doctoral supervisor many moons ago. I wish I had developed enough intellectual maturity and knowledge back then to understand her work like I now do. I wish we could sit again for a coffee and have one of our long chats. I wish I could have shown her the draft of this book and received some of her insightful and supportive feedback. But even though she is no longer with us, I find her often in my research; her whispers filter across my thoughts; her words are interspersed through my work; and the portion of her vast book collection that I was lucky enough to be gifted surrounds me like an embrace both in my office and in my living room. I keep finding unexpected treasures and little handwritten notes.

This book would not have been possible without Paul Stevens (senior commissioning editor at Bristol University Press). I met Paul's warm smile at the Bristol University Press table during the 2019 Critical Management Studies Conference at the Open University. I was, as always, looking for new interesting book finds to take home. We started an informal conversation about the experience of writing books, the current prohibitive cost of monographs, the great social topics covered in the BUP publications, and the potential idea of writing about writing differently. I said I didn't have enough to say, and this book was just a remote nebulous idea in my head. Within a few months, with Paul's practical support, kindness and guidance, what I thought would materialize in a few years' time became a book proposal that resulted in the commissioning of a book where no words had yet been written. I am very grateful for the type of support Paul and BUP have provided throughout the lifespan of this book, and I cannot recommend this publisher enough to colleagues and students.

A heartfelt thanks to the amazing colleagues who provided feedback on an early draft of this manuscript – Emmanouela Manadalaki, Astrid Huopalainen, Noortje van Amsterdam, Saoirse Caitlin O'Shea and Monika Kostera – and others who have informally discussed ideas with me. This collegial support is especially appreciated as my request came during a global pandemic, which caused many personal and professional challenges. Many thanks also to Andrew Priest – our lovely weekly cross-disciplinary writing sessions during lockdown have (re)ignited writing when I thought I had really nothing left to say.

I would also like to extend loving thanks to my colleague, friend and husband Haji Yakubu, whose undying trust in my abilities helps me to dare when my own confidence falters.

Finally, I would like to dedicate this book to my daughter Livia, who is a toddler still – and a feminist *ante litteram* if ever I have seen one. And to our little Gaia. I hope that one day they will read and feel my work, and be proud of their *mamy*.

Introduction

The inspiration for this book was born out of my engagement with texts, approaches, collaborations and practices connected with 'writing differently' – a phrase which has become increasingly common and has accrued a plethora of meanings. The starting ground for the reflections provided in this manuscript are today's neoliberal academic context, and feminist perspectives on researching and being an academic.

In the spirit of embracing difference and opening up possibilities of researching and writing that go against rigid preconceptions of what academic research and publishing must look like, this book is written to blur traditional boundaries of academic volumes. As such, this book is both an academic monograph and a volume on methods; it engages with theory while being firmly rooted in a practical approach. It is not intended to provide a review of the writing differently literature, but it offers several contemporary and *ante litteram* exemplars to help the reader engage with the relevant conversations. Borrowing from Heather Höpfl (2007, 619) these are the intention, the spirit and the execution of this book:

> And so this piece of writing attempts to undermine the extravagance of masculine forms of writing; of writing to produce the codpiece, writing as conceit; writing which is antagonistic to fragmented experience. It will not satisfy some, it will irritate others. The article is unbalanced, unresolved: like life itself. It is about stories, illustrations, asides, observations. It is also, with all its attempts to sub-vert (with all its attempts to make it 'dirty'), a piece of male writing.

The aims of this volume are: to discuss why researching and writing differently are important in today's academic context; to frame researching and writing differently as a political and feminist project; to offer an exploration of the meanings of 'writing differently', together with some examples; to provide reflections on various academic processes that can be done differently in line with feminist approaches; to investigate some of the qualitative methods and approaches that are often used in researching and writing differently; and finally to discuss some practical aspects linked with researching and publishing differently.

Rooted in the social sciences, this book is heavily influenced by approaches in the humanities and interdisciplinary perspectives. As such, although it pivots around conversations in management and organization studies, this approach to researching and writing differently is relevant to other fields of inquiry. I am a critical management scholar, and as such I am interested in critical perspectives that interrogate both the theory and practice of management and organization studies, challenge the status quo, problematize phenomena and perspectives at different levels, and surface power dynamics in organizing. To me, a crucial aspect of critical management studies is also about the (re)imagining of ways forward and new structures for organizations and organizing. These two aspects are particularly linked to feminist approaches. I strive to achieve 'radical reflexivity' (Cunliffe, 2003) and to consciously elaborate the complexities behind my positionality and my work as a researcher – this approach helps me understand the dynamics behind my interpretation and research practice, for instance, and it is also a political choice in writing and scholarly activity. I am, of course, aware that to a certain extent the distinction between 'mainstream' and 'critical' research is in itself problematic and rather blurred. There is ample evidence of many mainstream business organizations being far more critical in practice than the theoretical critical work done in some scholarly corners, and some of the critical management theory has already become well known and mainstreamed (for example, in the context of business schools education). However, at a time when critical approaches to management and business research are being challenged, silenced and even used to threaten the livelihood of academics worldwide, I feel that it is important to continue to highlight the value and strength of critical work both in theory and in practice.

In line with qualitative approaches and some of the methods linked to Writing Differently that I discuss in the book, I write this monograph in the first person, up close and personal. Perhaps due to my kinship with autoethnography, this book is written as a conversation, exploring what researching and writing differently means to me. My perspective is by no means intended to be an 'expert' one, a 'leading' one in the field, or one of 'authority' on the topic, even though that is usually what is expected by a book author.[1] Alongside theoretical and methodological discussions, this book also includes some personal narratives that speak of how I came to writing differently in my personal and academic life. I feel that a book premised on the value of researching and writing differently must be approached in a way that sets it apart from the disembodied, depersonalized academic research which is still often presented as the gold standard in the social sciences. As such, in line with writing differently approaches that value individual experiences regardless of their status, hierarchy and tenure, my embodied personal voice has become an integral part of this book in an effort to avoid alienating and depersonalized business approaches, and to find the author hidden behind the complexity of academic language. I write in a conversational style scattered with reflections and personal examples, anecdotes and emotional engagement. I hope that my style will not be perceived as self-congratulatory or self-absorbed, but that it will instead make this work approachable and easy to enter into dialogue with for both scholars and students.

In this book I connect theory, epistemology and social engagement to practical strategies for engaging with researching and writing differently. It is, to a certain extent, what I would have liked someone to teach me at the start of my writing differently journey. Instead, I have learned through an iterative and non-linear process of (mis)understanding, reading, trying, reflecting and doing – I am still engaged with this learning path. Therefore, this book does not stem from a place of absolute and monolithic knowing, but from a place of learning *in itinere*. I wish for my perspective to be heard as one small piece contributing to larger feminist collective projects. I draw on different theories, exemplars, disciplines and methods to engage with researching and writing differently in a way I hope will be useful to others. As such, while not aiming to provide a comprehensive list of all authors and texts that can be associated with researching and writing differently, I cite numerous sources that could help others in their writing differently. This selection of specific theories, authors and contributions that I have found particularly meaningful in my journey through researching and writing differently is by no means exhaustive, and can be further integrated, interrogated and critiqued. Given the limited word count available, I inevitably exclude more than I can include here, and my editorial choices of what to focus on may miss work that is considered seminal by others.

Throughout the book, I will use the term 'writing differently' to describe different things: a process, a perspective, an ethos, a methodology, a type of scholarship and a movement. The latter will be capitalized, intended as a collective impetus made up of many examples of how we, as scholars, can drive forward the writing differently agenda. Writing Differently is not per se necessarily linked to Feminism(s), but it is for me, which I will further explore in the book. Some of the publications I cite and engage with will be 'formally' part of Writing Differently – for instance, through their inclusion in the homonymous special issue in the journal *Management Learning* (Gilmore et al, 2019), in the three seminars that led to the birth of that special issue, in conference presentations, or in related edited volumes (Pullen, Helin and Harding, 2020; Kostera, 2022). Some studies may not have been defined by their authors as part of Writing Differently, but will be included here as examples of what I consider types of researching and writing differently.

I would also like to qualify my use of the term 'Feminism', although I will discuss this more in detail in Part I of this book. My acception of the term Feminism is not exclusively inclusive to women and their rights, but it has a strong focus on them. When I speak about women, I do not just refer to those who were assigned a biologically female gender at birth: I speak about all women. My understanding of Feminism is intersectional across categories of being and being seen. These categories include but are not restricted to race, sexual orientation, disability, class and nationality. Although I could use the plural term 'feminisms' instead, I have chosen to adopt 'Feminism' as a collective uncountable noun that includes the nuances of meaning mentioned above and different schools of thought or strands of feminism. As an advocate for feminist perspectives, I pride myself in calling myself a Feminist, although I am not claiming to be a 'typical' one (is there even such a person?) or a representative for all feminist scholars in the field of management and organization studies. This book, however, is firmly rooted in feminist values and care-ful approaches to researching and inhabiting academia.

Also, it is important to explain that in using the adjectives masculine and feminine, I do not merely refer to biological differences between people. Instead, I use these throughout this book in their broader sense referring to behaviour, approaches and sociocultural understandings traditionally associated with men or women. Although my studies in what was called 'oriental languages and cultures' over two decades ago have opened up a myriad of meanings and understandings of the word 'masculine' from different sociocultural perspectives, my use of 'masculine' and its counterpart in this book is deeply affected by my original European roots and centred around white Western patriarchal contexts. As such, these two adjectives are not used to reinforce a binary view of gender identity, but to question such traditional perspectives in a broader sense.

Other interconnected and contested terms such as equality, equity, diversity and inclusion are used in different ways across different fields of research, national contexts and languages. The word 'equality' can be understood as referring exclusively to the feminist agenda of providing equal opportunities to everyone through the provision of equal treatment within a given system, which often links to the 'sameness perspective' (see Rees, 2005; Walby, 2005); on the other hand, 'equity' is often used to reject the idea of 'equal opportunities' as discriminatory itself, and promote instead the aim of providing equal outcomes through differential treatment that helps individuals flourish and achieve (see Phillips, 2004; Simpson et al, 2010). In this book I will use the word 'equality' in a broader sense that includes both positions above, unless specified otherwise. The word 'diversity' is used to draw attention 'to the multiplicity of strands of difference' (Özbilgin, 2009, 2), and I use the term 'inclusion' in a positive way, meaning the design, creation and redevelopment of structures that are inclusive of difference and perspectives. This is in contrast with the use of the word 'inclusion' to mean a form of assimilation and the opening of structural doors contingent to the need for people who are seen as 'different' to become similar or in line with those in positions of power in order to be 'allowed' to join the existing structure. The latter is clearly an ethically compromised position and one that reinforces exclusion.

In writing this book I do not intend to speak for others, but to offer an opportunity for the reader to engage with different ways of listening to, feeling, sensing and understanding researching and academic writing. My primary intended readers are doctoral students, early career academics and other scholars who may be interested in exploring different ways of writing and being in academia. This is reflected in the structure of the book, which combines theoretical argument and subject content with more practice-based considerations and discussions around publishing, methodology and methods.

Here I also advocate for change in management and organization studies that is not predicated on people who want to write differently becoming assimilated into the system that rejects this type of research and relegates it to 'second tier', belittled, marginalized spaces and publications. I argue that we need structural and systemic changes to challenge the barriers we have created and reproduced. These contemporary academic structures still sustain a hegemonic masculine normative culture of doing and writing research, and of being (or performing) a specific type of academic identity in order to be accepted within networks, professional communities and editorial teams. I call for individual differences to be embraced, for equality to be genuinely implemented, and for privilege to be surfaced and questioned. For those who do not follow the prescribed mainstream way, it is especially important to explore how a different path can be pursued, how to foster sharing and understanding, researching and writing differently. I feel that as academics 'we' have a responsibility to move the agenda forward, call out what we recognize as barriers and limitations in our field in support of early-career researcher, doctoral students and the next generations of scholars in our field. Of course, this is a necessarily generalized 'we', masking some voices and homogenizing others like tinted glass: not all academics hear this 'call', and not everyone sees barriers. Some people do not want to engage with movements or collective projects, and many do not see the need for change.

As I began to write this book, we found ourselves in the middle of a global COVID-19 pandemic. In the UK, we were about six months in, with no end in sight. I was due to start writing on 1 March 2020, but the pandemic took over our professional and personal lives in ways that could not have been foreseen. Therefore, the background reading went on during scraps of time between meetings that ended earlier, my child's naps, and cooking dinner on the stove. I described my experience of this early stage of the pandemic in an essay published by the journal *Gender, Work and Organization,* the first in an open call special issue in the Feminist Frontiers section of the Journal (Boncori, 2020a). That paper, like this book and some of my previous and ongoing research work, is an example of writing differently. This has definitely been a different writing experience than the one I had with my first monograph or my edited volumes. Multiple coronavirus-related lockdowns and waves followed, which added complexities to life and work, but also allowed me to collaborate online with colleagues around the world and forge links with academic communities like never before.

This volume is written differently in the following ways:

1) The nature and structure of the book cut across academic genres by bringing theory on writing differently and feminist perspectives together with an exploration of the methods through which one can write differently – most books do one or the other, but not both.
2) The tone of the book is personal and conversational, aimed at doctoral students as well as scholars, to enhance accessibility and foster understanding.
3) Unlike some recent excellent edited books on Writing Differently (Pullen, Helin and Harding, 2020) and on how to write differently (Kostera, 2022), this project stems from the perspective and experience of one author.

Mary Phillips, Alison Pullen and Carl Rhodes (2014) noted that 'by writing in a genre suitable for academic publication we inevitably find ourselves participating [...] in the very forms of writing that we seek to contest' (Phillips et al, 2014, 315) – this volume is written in a way that goes against the aerodynamics of traditional masculine writing for publication in management and organization studies. I hope you will find it interesting.

The book is structured as an inverted pyramid, a journey from the broader theoretical aspects of researching and writing to the practical and the particular levels of academic activity. While this project is inspired by the Writing Differently movement and related work, it builds on it to consider not only aspects of writing per se, but also more broadly ways in which the ethos and spirit of Writing Differently can permeate various aspects of researching and being in academia. Part I is entitled 'Researching and Writing Differently today', and the two chapters therein provide an overview of the contemporary neoliberal academic context (Chapter 1) and of why researching and Writing Differently can be considered a political and feminist project (Chapter 2). This contextualization is important in understanding why different approaches to inhabiting academia have become urgent. In this brief discussion of the neoliberal contemporary academic context – which is becoming increasingly pervasive worldwide – I explore how masculine ways of understanding and measuring academic work have generated a metric-driven professional context that dictates who has the right to speak (publish), what content is appropriate, and how research should be quantified to be considered 'appropriate' or 'good enough'. Further, I offer a brief excursus into Feminism, articulating why this can be seen as a fertile locus for changing the status quo, and researching and writing differently.

Part II, entitled 'Daring to research and write differently', is focused on an exploration of different types of writing and content that lend themselves to be approached differently (Chapter 3) and some key traits of researching differently, such as vulnerability, exposure and failure (Chapter 4). Framed through intersectional and interdisciplinary perspectives, researching and writing differently is here explored in terms of time and movement, embodiment, emotions, inequality and discrimination. This part is closed by a section on the value of approaching research from a vulnerable position that allows exposure and connection with the reader.

Part III delves into the practicalities of researching and writing differently, in terms of methods (Chapter 5) and praxis (Chapter 6). Starting from the positioning of research within the realm of qualitative inquiry, I provide an overview of some methodologies and methods that better lend themselves to the creation of scholarship written differently. In particular, I will consider ethnographic and arts-based methods (both narrative and visual methods). Here I also explore other research practices that can be done differently – like data collection and the use of citations – that are discussed critically through a feminist lens. I also explore the importance of embracing failure and creating a conducive space of individual and collaborative engagement with researching and writing differently (noting that even enabling spaces are not safe or caring for all at the same level and in the same ways). Finally, before drawing my conclusions, I explore some aspects of researching and writing differently from the perspective of doctoral students. This includes a discussion on writing doctoral theses differently, and some explicit reflections of publishing and other academic practices that are often taken for granted but that may be useful to acknowledge for PhD students and early-career researchers.

PART I

Researching and writing differently today

1

The contemporary neoliberal academic context

In this first section, contemporary academic discourses are located within the neoliberal landscape. The particular juncture of time, space and status of academia today is generating or reinforcing competitive and masculine approaches to researching, which I believe have made the need to rethink the way we inhabit academia even more urgent. It is important to consider this landscape, because when we write it is never in isolation, even when we do it on our own – we write against the backdrop of a specific system and its sociocultural, professional or financial implications. Within this context, I offer an overview of the main characteristics of contemporary neoliberal academia and focus on some key factors – for example, the need to perform and publish according to traditional masculine understandings of research and the overarching hegemony of masculine metrics. From this discussion will emerge why researching and writing differently can be considered and used as a tool for challenging the status quo, and why it is a particularly important project now.

Neoliberal academia

Neoliberalism can be understood as a system guided by market principles, which are then reinforced and given a legitimate space. In its interface and interlacing with academia, neoliberalism stems from a 'form of reason that configures all aspects of existence in economic terms' (Brown, 2015, 17). Hence, in an increasing number of countries worldwide, even higher education institutions founded on non-economic principles and focusing on education and research are now conceived of as market players serving customers through the creation and promotion of products, aiming to maximize income, and valuing 'enterprise and investment' (Rhodes, 2017, 25). Indeed, due to lack of governmental funding and other sociopolitical dynamics at the national and international level, many universities are today run like businesses (Tuchman, 2009). In 'Education in the liquid-modern setting' (2009) and 'Educational challenges of the liquid-modern era' (2003), Zygmunt Bauman provides an outline of 'liquid modernity', and explores the particular issues that it raises for education and academics. One of the key concerns in contemporary neoliberal 'liquid academia' is the notion of what universities, education and research are for, and whether these should be considered as an investment that students make to improve their future currency in the job market, and as products that students as customers are able to consume. Although this phenomenon has, luckily, yet to become completely pervasive on a global level, it is definitely felt in the UK, Australia and other countries worldwide.

As investigated elsewhere (Strauß and Boncori, 2020; Boncori, Sicca and Bizjak, 2020), it seems clear that the neoliberal approach has reconfigured the nature of academic work and academic identities, with significant and often disastrous consequences (Clegg, 2008; Fleming, 2021). Today's expectations on academic work are permeated by a constellation of metric-driven expectations: publishing in the 'right' journals that have a high ranking and strong impact factors; teaching on courses in a manner that generates high student satisfaction scores (Szwabowski and Wężniejewska, 2017); raising funds for research through grant applications; engaging in 'smart' networking within profile-raising groups; and marketing academic profiles through websites and social media. These, or similar iterations and combinations of measurable outputs, have become *conditio sine qua non* of today's neoliberal academia. Academics are thus required not only to produce publications that advance knowledge and contribute to the development of education and research, but also to make themselves available and visible. This visibility is increasingly expected as it brings benefits not only to their own careers, but also to their universities through rankings, status, branding and so on. By highlighting certain aspects which are considered more valuable than others (for example, number of publications, citations, and grant funding), higher education institutions implicitly set an expectation for the type of work that academics should focus on, and ignite a competitive approach towards one another. While this has allowed some to flourish and operate in a more criteria-driven environment that in some cases has improved transparency, for others it has meant a marked worsening of their professional lives. An academic landscape of 'collective depression' has been explored, for instance, in Maria do Mar Pereira's insightful book, which provides an ethnography of academia inspired by feminist epistemology (2017). Productivity, often narrowly defined, reigns supreme in many academic contexts, allowing the continuous (re)production of inequality and forms of academic masculinity in academic labour. Have academics themselves become a (by-)product of the neoliberal academic environment, requiring branding (Who are you? What's your specialism? Are you easily identifiable? Tell me your uniqueness in two minutes! How attractive is your name on a conference programme or on a book cover? Are you a good return on investment as 'the big name' for grant applications?), self-marketing (for example, visibility enhanced via academic publications; broader profile-raising via non-specialist articles that have a wide reach to influence international reputation; promotional activities with networks to increase social media indexes; personal websites;

public CVs shared on academic sites), and optimization (for example, strategies to raise one's *h*-index; altmetrics;[1] keyword optimization; strategic co-authoring and so on)?

According to the neoliberal approach, academics' 'value' and output production have become increasingly measurable in a quantitative manner computed across different metrics – for example, research assessments, citations, publications of a certain level/band, and editorial appointments (Strathern, 2000; Craig et al, 2014; Shore and Wright, 2015). These criteria are no longer considered desirable achievements or an added form of recognition, but are instead deemed necessary requirements for probation, promotion and job safety. What is more important, these metrics are used to decide what 'counts' as writing, and what counts as good quality research and writing too. Mittelman (2018, 2019) contends that due to today's obsession in academia with rankings, globalization and metrics, 'the means have become the ends' (2019, 708), as 'universities are *repurposing* at the expense of their high principles' (2019, 708, emphasis in original):

> As they strive to be 'world-class,' higher education institutions are shifting away from their core missions of cultivating democratic citizenship, fostering critical thinking, and safeguarding academic freedom. A new form of utilitarianism is gaining ground, one that favours market power over academic values. It stresses rationalist thinking rather than other modes of reasoning, as in the arts, classical languages, history, and philosophy. (Mittelman, 2019, 708)

These quantifications of quality not only standardize and stigmatize what is acceptable in terms of content, but also with regards to the style we use and how we communicate or disseminate our research. The issue of writing style and register, which will be further explored later in this book, is particularly prominent for researching and writing differently, since it is often both dismissed on the grounds of being inappropriate or not 'scientific enough' while also having to be 'stylish' (evocative, different, with resonance and so on). This policing of research content, type, style and level of formality in academic language has a political charge, because it restricts access to what is discussed and disseminated and perpetuates white, Western-centric notions of what is acceptable to research and write about, and by whom.

The reason for this increasing control over what is researched, and how, is that these metrics ultimately contribute to universities' national and global rankings, which bring in financial rewards in the form of funding or student registrations (Butler and Spoelstra, 2012; Münch, 2014). So here the vicious circle of neoliberalism is closed through a self-perpetuating motion of economic interest, supply and demand. Locked in a domino effect known as 'organizational isomorphism' (Powell and DiMaggio, 1991), organizations come to mirror each other and change together (in the case of neoliberal academia, to avoid being cut off from funding and to gain other benefits), thus solidifying a specific set of expectations and continuing to 'move the goalposts' by reinscribing codes of behaviour and modifying shared values and professional aims to suit neoliberal goals.

In an autoethnographic paper, Zawadzki and Jensen (2020) highlight important points regarding the academic environment experienced within a neoliberal context. They consider how hyper-performativity, questionable ethical practices, lack of wellbeing and bullying have become normalized experiences:

> the neoliberal university – characterized by excessive pressures of job performance ('in search of excellence'), a masculine culture of competition, a division of labour based on control and punishment (management and administration) and achievement (academics), scarce resources and cutbacks, and pressure on workers to succeed (Branch and Murray, 2015; Hollis, 2017; Twale, 2018) – seems to be fertile ground for bullying. (Zawadzki and Jensen, 2020, 400)

This 'greedy university' has become an increasingly toxic 'new normal', which has further exacerbated gendered and racialized inequalities and magnified privilege during the current global pandemic (Özkazanç-Pan and Pullen, 2020; Pereira, 2021; Plotnikof and Utoft, 2021). Indeed, mental health challenges (Jago, 2002), especially stress-induced conditions, and lack of work–family balance have all been recognized in academic and more general media publications as poisonous by-products of contemporary academic lives (Knights and Clarke, 2014). For example, in 2018 Marinetto denounced research targets as 'off the marks' in their contribution to *Times Higher Education*, and in 2019 *The Guardian* brought together a series of articles entitled 'Mental health: a university crisis'. Loss of academic identity (Clegg, 2008; Learmonth and Humphreys, 2011; Alvesson, 2013) has also been linked to decreased motivation and even unethical behaviour.

What's more, these masculine metrics negatively affect some groups of people in a disproportionate manner – for instance, those who do not identify as men, people racialized as non-white, early-career academics, 'older' academics whose earlier work did not comply with contemporary academic requirements, those with disabilities, and people with caring responsibilities. While these inequalities have been present for decades, the fetishized nature of metrics and measurable performance has been made even more visible under the COVID-19 global pandemic. Rather than simply generating new problems, the coronavirus outbreak and its related restrictions have shone a light on long-standing issues of discrimination and marginalization for certain groups of workers (for example, around flexible working, working from home, and metric-driven progression criteria). The metrics used to measure performance rely on variables that often go unquestioned or uncontested, such as quality of outputs, citation practices and research impact. One of the issues with contemporary neoliberal performance management is not just its approach, but also the indicators used themselves as instruments of knowing and judging: if these are intrinsically inadequate in terms of equity, and reinforcing systems of inequality and oppression, then the most likely outcome will be perpetuating inequality.

This global pandemic has also provided a glimpse of opportunities for change. Organizations, including higher education institutions, were forced to rethink their strategies, ways of working and communicating, work patterns, use of technology and processes. To some extent, this has had the positive side effect of increasing the visibility of how individual needs and challenges can be taken into account and embedded in work practices, thus normalizing circumstances and conditions that had previously been marked through alterity. When businesses worldwide were forced to reinvent themselves and consider alternative routes to feasibility or success, they faced a hard collision between the ideal worker and the ideal carer (as during the multiple pandemic lockdowns, many employees found themselves at home tending to work tasks and other caring responsibilities). The same applied to academia, where the image of the ideal scholar came obviously into collision with a variety of visible embodied ways of being an academic. The disembodied, rational, competitive and hyper-performative ideal worker (Acker, 1990) is also similar to the ideal academic (Sang et al, 2015; Strauß and Boncori, 2020) whose body is ignored, emotions dismissed, and non-work commitments considered inappropriate. Aspects of personal academic life which were normally hushed and hidden behind the mask of a professional persona became magnified through video-conferencing and meeting facilities, and we became accustomed to having children and other family members running in the background, seeing pets demanding the limelight, acknowledging different types of living conditions and access. Individuals in certain sociocultural contexts were able to adjust to these rapid and changing professional needs with different levels of success, depending on the professional and social norms guiding the academic environment *in loco*. For example, in a study on the Dutch academic environment, Bleijenbergh et al (2013) pose that the cultural construct of the ideal academic has fluidity, and it changes within different contexts. Many institutions, third-sector organizations and private businesses found themselves faced with the obvious clash between the masculine ideal of the perfect, reliable, professional worker and the reality of those who found themselves adjusting to the new situation while exposing personal and private aspects that would not have been considered 'appropriate' before. Toxic or *viral* masculinity – to borrow terminology discussed by Karen Ashcraft in her 2020 presentation – is of course not only detrimental to women but to many people regardless of their gender. Many universities recognized the fact that pre-pandemic conditions could not be sustained, and more flexible approaches had to be adopted to ensure some level of business continuity – for example, meetings were rescheduled due to caring responsibilities; people embraced a more casual attire; flexibility became more widespread in working hours and so on. All of a sudden, changes and adjustments that were deemed unthinkable before were implemented at scale. This showed us that challenges to the status quo are possible, systems can change, and new practices can be implemented. Changes that would have taken years to be implemented before in terms of personalized and flexible working arrangements were normalized and policies amended. Some teams have grown closer, and managers have learned more about their staff than they had ever cared to explore before. The need for a more caring type of relationality and compassion in the workplace became more visible. But will this blurring of what is acceptable remain, or are the normative goalposts simply been moved? Will the possibilities explored during the pandemic prompt a new impetus in change-making? Have the core masculine expectations and professional habitus actually changed, or has this been paused only for the time being, waiting to resurface as soon as the pandemic is over or under control? Will the recognition of the variety of needs and the related styles of work ignite a step change in inclusivity and flourishing for all? I remain hopeful yet doubtful.

Masculine structures and metrics

In this challenging professional panorama, over the past three decades, the ever-shifting performance goalposts of neoliberal academia have been creating pathological systemic failures that have deeply affected the way people experience work and their ability to maintain an acceptable level of well-being. Hyper-performativity and the impossibility of embodying 'excellence' in every required neoliberal criteria have fuelled loss of self-esteem and imposter syndrome (Wilkinson, 2020), especially among early-career academics (Archer, 2008; Kallio and Kallio, 2014; Bothello and Roulet, 2018). What has become important is not only the intrinsic content of one's research and teaching, but also the 'selling' of it, and the entrepreneurial spirit young academics are required to cultivate in order to survive and thrive in today's academia (Ylijoki and Henriksson, 2017). This type of environment actively encourages a climate of competition and comparison among individuals, premised on both individual and institutional dynamics of winners and losers. Some 'top ranking' journals in our field pride themselves of their high rejection rates – often well above 90 per cent – and for those who make it through the initial fissure of rejection, the revisions and publication processes can take years. The volume of work needed to ensure that some high-level contribution reaches the publication stage is increasingly demanding. Writing grant funding applications is also notoriously very time-consuming and very competitive.

While some years ago – and this may still be the case in some academic contexts – a high volume of published work was deemed to be a good enough indication of success, in the mid 2000s the name of the game was no longer 'how much' one published, but also 'where' and 'with whom'. Accumulating the 'right' type and number of academic outputs, funding and citations is crucial for today's academic (Bristow, 2012; Morrissey, 2015; Zawadzki, 2017) but often contingent on networks and collaborations with other scholars. These relationships take time to cultivate, and so early-career researchers or doctoral students (Zawadzki, 2017) who cannot count on their supervisors' support can be particularly marginalized and disproportionately affected in a negative manner. In particular, our previous research (Strauß and Boncori, 2020) has shown how women academics[2] often leave their country of origin in an elusive quest for academic meritocracy, to feel valued for their own abilities, to avoid hierarchical or masculine opportunism, to escape from authoritarian dependencies and other dynamics that reinforce inequalities within the academic professional context. However, it takes time to understand the politics and dynamics of different academic contexts, to develop genuine research collaborations and explore opportunities. Although the current academic context is likely to be challenging for many, early-career academics in particular find themselves lacking in the social and economic capital needed to compete in the imposed neoliberal game (Zawadzki and Jensen, 2020), and this is even more pronounced in the case of people who do not see their intersectional identities reflected in the academic environment they operate in.

Masculine dynamics and requirements still permeate the demarcations of membership in professional academic contexts, marking processes of inclusion or exclusion that have a direct impact on performance. As I mentioned in the Introduction, the masculine and the feminine are here considered as gendered practices rather than biological traits. Indeed, the feminist philosopher and gender theorist Judith Butler (1990;1993) has argued for this in stating that sex/gender is not localized at the genitalia, as people are not reducible to the presence of a member (or lack thereof). However, that biological difference is often used as a question of 'membership' to discriminate and marginalize (Höpfl, 2010). As such, the term 'masculine' indicates sociocultural approaches, values and perspectives that are ascribed to people identified as men and women. The key issue is that this categorization is not neutral, in the sense that it is entrenched within power dynamics and hierarchical positions. Thus, aspects that would traditionally be considered masculine (for example, rationality, logic, leadership, strength, independence, dominance, reliability and so on) are deemed better or more important than feminine traits (for example, collaborative, nurturing, emotional, intuitive, sensuous, sensitive and so on). As such, femininity is not made of qualities that belong to a woman, but rather denotes the performance of traits that a (Western) sociocultural context ascribes to or expects of women. Although very antiquated and generalizing stereotypes, these are still pervasive in most contemporary societies and professional contexts. Essentializing people by reducing them to a constraining typology based on their assigned gender at birth (see Harquail, 2020 on essentializing) is a form of power execution through a gendered control. When these traits are used to mark success and performance in academia, exclusionary systems and practices become ingrained in the texture of work. The more our professional and academic discourses centre around narratives that reject these limiting and myopic dichotomies, the more we can undermine the core sociocultural beliefs that shape our research and academic habitus. I believe that researching and writing differently can become a pivotal instrument of change in this quest.

Masculine structures are the extension of patriarchy – a system whereby the masculine dominates the feminine through a web of formal/informal, explicit/unspoken, overt/invisible norms, understandings and behaviour. In this system, the superior privileged masculine has created a justification for its status and it is organized to maintain it. As a structure of power and privilege – much like whiteness – patriarchy is based on dominance, identification and centredness (Johnson, 2005). This process takes men and masculinity as the benchmarking standard for defining what is 'normal' and optimal; therefore, anything other than masculine is simply not measuring up to this partial selection of standards, and ultimately not good enough. This view is embedded in sociocultural bias as well as Western relationship dynamics, and is widespread in everyday life. For example, there is an obvious and often taken-for-granted gendering of some professions (like the sociocultural image and the language used to define a fire*man* or a mid*wife)*; the parental leave allocation of most legal systems that reinforces unequal caring responsibilities; the way suits are considered the natural 'professional' form of clothing; work patterns for leadership positions that privilege presenteeism, overwork and lack of caring commitments. Those who enter the male-centred dynamics of a patriarchal system without conforming to masculine rules and metrics are forced to assimilate into this credo, or be relegated to the margins. The intersection of various foci of oppression creates what Acker (2006) calls 'inequality regimes'. These dynamics will continue *ad libitum* if interventions are not put in place to challenge, undermine and dismantle these hegemonic masculine structures of power.

Two decades ago, Heather Höpfl (2000) provided a powerful critique of the 'purposive rationality' of organizations, in line with Burrell and Morgan's critique of rules and control systems, technology as surveillance, the normative language of organizations and other aspects explored early in

'Anti-Organisation Theory' (1979). The currency of these concerns is still striking. Metrics are both powerful and dangerous measures, in that they can shift and mobilize focus 'from content to counting' (Bränström Öhman, 2012, 28). Often, and increasingly so over the past decade, in the higher education system we are asked to focus on a simplistic reduction of linear achievement to its numerically assessed parts for both staff and students. Masculine imperatives challenge us to become the embodiment of superior comparatives: we must work longer, produce faster, compete harder, win more, publish more.

However, counter-narratives to this approach to academic work and, in particular, research have already been developed. For example, in their book *The Slow Professor: Challenging the Culture of Speed in the Academy*, Maggie Berg and Barbara Seeber (2016) challenge this quest for speed, efficiency and excellence. Writing from the perspective of the Canadian academy, the authors' experience resonates with many other academic contexts. They advocate for a slowing down and savouring of the academic life. This need for slow, sensorial scholarship in reading and writing (Boulous Walker, 2016) may be utopic in several academic contexts. Given the systemic and institutional barriers to conducting this type of work, this approach, like the Writing Differently movement, has been labelled as stemming from the privilege of a tenured position, providing safety and allowing room for dissent (see Suzuki and Mayorga, 2014). It may be more challenging to espouse a contra- or undercurrent that goes against the mainstream contemporary way of being an academic; and in many academic contexts making that choice may still mean having to prioritize between a research-focused and a leadership/ education-focused academic post; a tenured and non-tenure track career; employment in one's country of origin or away from familiar connections; negotiations between work and family needs. Of course, not all positions in academia are privileged and afford choice, and not all in the same way or at the same level – many teaching and research staff are employed on short-term contracts, often not providing sufficient income and provision of pension and other benefits. For doctoral students and early-career academics, these power dynamics and hidden workings of academia are often invisible until one becomes faced with barriers and exclusion.

Given the heavy repercussions that defiance towards masculine structures and metrics can have on professional and personal lives, researching and Writing Differently[3] through and beyond masculine metrics is a political and ethical statement. Researching and writing understood in this manner are a quest for challenges and changes, for ruptures (Spry, 2011) and openings of future possibilities. This approach then can be seen as a political stance in its pursuit of an alternative to a system of knowledge creation, circulation and development, which inevitably marginalizes the vast majority to the advantage of a chosen few. In contrast to quantitative masculine metrics employed to justify and judge academic practice, researching and writing differently is a relational way of inhabiting academia that is mindful of others, thoughtful in its conception, aware in its dissemination. It questions our motives and unveils the power – individual, collective and systemic – behind the choice and imposition of masculinity in academic work. As an alternative non-numerical formula that draws from transformational power rather than coercive structures, researching and writing differently can motivate, inspire and connect singulars and pluralities. By espousing this approach, we are invited to slow down and engage with a different set of comparatives from the need to produce more, work faster and aim higher: listen closer, read better and speak louder about silenced issues. Through the lens of this perspective, the term 'value', then, is taken primarily in its meaning of principle, belief and morals, rather than in its quantification of worth, benefit and usefulness. Within the academic context, the development of knowledge should be linked to deep study, which is at the core of university, its educational process (Izak et al, 2017) and research. Deep, thoughtful, multifaceted and critically engaged study takes time, it fails, it experiments and it reflects. Education and research are about learning – learning about a phenomenon, learning as an individual, learning in relation to others. This perspective on the processes of learning is as important, if not more, than its outputs: it allows people to affect and be affected (both in terms of bearing the effects and changes, but also in terms of the affective and embodied character of learning). Through researching, learning and studying differently, we shape and are reshaped; change is folded into professional practices and unfolded into social or professional perceptions.

Challenging the status quo

Having set the scene of the contemporary neoliberal academic context and explained the possible consequences of masculine approaches for academic work, this last section of Chapter 1 considers ways of challenging this predominantly toxic status quo that breeds inequality. I argue that researching and writing differently can become a valid alternative to the current neoliberal academic model, both at the individual and collective levels. I am conscious of the fact that by using the term 'alternative' I am relegating this approach to researching and particularly the Writing Differently movement to a position of subalternity, otherness and abnormality. But here I use the term 'alternative' in a specific acception to refer to texts, experiences and subjectivities that are not subordinated, lower in status or importance, but instead 'alternative voices of organization, that is, voices other than those privileged by the organization itself' (Höpfl, 2000, 15). Although the Writing Differently movement is gaining momentum in management and organization studies – and an increasing number of these publications are made visible in top level journals and other channels – we are nowhere near a widespread 'mainstreamed' presence and appreciation. I hope this book will provide a small contribution to prompting change in this regard.

Critiques to the neoliberal academy have grown in number and resonance over the past decade, with recent calls from various geographical and academic contexts made to stand up or act up against the status quo of this professional context. There is clearly a tension behind the critique voiced by academics (me included) of the neoliberal academic system as people who are part of the system and benefit from it to a certain extent (for example, by getting paid a salary, by being able to take on positions or roles of prestige, by being awarded funding, by being published in internationally reputable journals and so on). In some ways, those of us who work as academics within established systems and structures, conforming to contractual obligations and promotion procedures, submitting work to research frameworks that crystallize a set notion of excellence that reinforces marginalization, are responsible and accountable for the perpetuation of such systems of oppression and inequality. Nonetheless, I still believe it important to challenge the status quo and reimagine different ways forward, even from the privileged position of the critical insider. In recent years, management scholars worldwide have come together in workshops, seminars and convivia to explore different ways of being, researching and writing in academia. These often resulted in academic collaborations or the creation of spaces to foster critique or enhance visibility for different approaches to researching. For example, in 2020 a special issue of the journal *Management Learning* on the 'Performative University' provided a range of perspectives and critiques on today's academia (see for instance Bowes-Catton et al, 2020; Butler and Spoelstra, 2020; Jones et al, 2020). These collaborations can be seen as a form of resistance or academic activism. Kate Grosser (2020) explores how academic activism can advance feminist social movement agendas by engaging in theory and praxis that is at the same time critical of and engaged in neoliberal contexts. The potential of change stemming from critical and feminist perspectives is also located in the political project of rethinking systems and proposing ways forward. For example, in 2020 Katie Beavan issued a strong and passionate plea towards scholars in the critical management field to interrupt the masculine hegemonic resurgence of patriarchy in a quest to break the 'masculine reckoning' and open up to more embodied, feminine and subjective ways of inhabiting and writing academia.

By embracing the researching and writing differently alternative, its counter-narrative and counter-practice, we can challenge the academic status quo. Drawing from Black feminist scholars and activities together with work by Antonio Gramsci and Judith Butler, Alessia Contu (2020, 72) highlights the importance of academic intellectual activism to challenge neoliberalism and promote 'equality, freedom and solidarity by embodying an academic praxis that is progressive, intersectional, critical and concretely engaged in the service of social, economic and epistemic justice'. Challenging the status quo also means surfacing, addressing and dismantling nodes of power and oppression, taken-for-granted inequality and embedded discrimination. Masculinity can as such be thought of also as a regime of power rather than just a mere issue of gender, normalizing dominance, privilege and subordination. This can be articulated, for example, in terms of whiteness in academia, which goes beyond biological essence to denote a system of deeply embedded racism (Essed, 1991; Deitch et al, 2003; Dar, 2018). Resisting inequality regimes can also manifest itself through shedding light on nodes of oppression and visible or invisible discrimination. For example, through an analysis of over a thousand posts on the social media platform Twitter signposted by #BlackWomenAtWork, Verónica Rabelo, Kathrina Robotham and Courtney McCluney (2020) show how academia is permeated by the 'white gaze', which frames all bodies through the lenses of whiteness, and marginalizes particular bodies in this professional context. The taken-for-granted 'right way' of understanding and being in a specific context (Bourdieu, 1977) then turns into conventional, normative and hegemonic forces of exclusion. By researching and writing differently, scholars can embody and promote more inclusive ways of inhabiting academia and relating to one another and the world. This is particularly important in some academic fields and loci of academic professional praxis that offer a fertile ground for inequality. For example, Sadhvi Dar, Helena Liu, Angela Martinez Dy and Deborah Brewis (Dar et al, 2020) have prompted scholars in management and organization studies to challenge the status quo. Their important paper, whose relevance extends beyond the realm of this field, stresses how today's business schools are built on capitalist approaches of racist foundations. The proliferation of this type of scholarship can foster and even enable a movement that provides anti-racist scholar-activism, calling scholars of colour to act up together in order to challenge and change the normalized white supremacist nature of systems of power articulated in innumerable ways and structures (Mills, 1997).

This perspective on researching and writing differently is still in many cases considered not 'proper' or 'rigorous enough' by the academic community. While the increasing presence of this type of publication in top-level international journals has offered novel opportunities to publish and collaborate, it can also be dangerous for academics to be visibly associated with this movement. This threat can manifest itself more prominently in terms of career stages (for example, for doctoral, postdoctoral and early-career scholars) but also for those academics of all seniority levels who engage in the important work of challenging the status quo, as activists and academics. The danger may lie in various aspects of our professional lives. First of all, on a practical level, if the value of writing differently is not appreciated, work may be rejected by journals and their reviewers; this would be costly within an academic performance management system which measures academic value as the sum of top-level research publications achieved within a certain time frame. Second, if writing differently is not valued by peers, publications will not be read and cited as much as they ought to be according to the key performance indicators in place in some countries. This may also result in the inability to be considered 'a good investment' as a member of staff or as a co-author, whereby this type of work may be discounted in probation or promotion applications, or in recruitment panels. Moreover, when hailed as feminists and members of the Writing Differently movement, it is easy to be seen as 'troublemakers', as someone the institution cannot trust, someone who wants to 'rock the boat' unnecessarily by pursuing their own research interests rather than those which may benefit the organization. This can, in turn, have extreme consequences of disciplinary action or job loss.

However, this is not a new problem, as those who do not conform with the norm are often relegated to the margins. The next chapter will locate the ignition of change through researching and writing differently in feminist perspectives. Feminism is a collective project that challenges inequality and supports the flourishing of all individuals. I believe that working together across different levels, career stages, roles, institutions and systems can help us challenge the status quo more effectively. This approach extends to more than research outputs and writing per se, as feminist ethics and care can illuminate alternative ways of being and working in academia. This can be done both at the abstract level through theorizing differently by extending the ways by which we interrogate, understand and take forward certain issues (such as inclusion, reflexivity, race, gender, sexuality) and on a more practical level. For example, an editor-in-chief can help shape more inclusive directions within a journal or in a book series; this will in turn offer opportunities to scholars of different levels of expertise to write differently and contribute to the growth of this movement through papers, workshops and conference presentations. As more papers are worked on, this type of research becomes more visible and further embedded in the texture of academic writing. This visibility may generate more teaching and training on the specific methods or processes needed to engage with such research, which enhances access and take-up by an increasing number of doctoral students and early-career researchers. This type of development has gained momentum over the past two decades, to some extent, with regards to qualitative methods and approaches in management and organization studies (for example, ethnography and arts-based methods). I believe the same can happen for researching and writing differently in terms of content, style, purpose, originality and methods. Academic choices on the type of research we conduct, and the type of scholar we want to be, carry considerations of an ethico-political nature 'because they call on us to make a stand on what kind of subjects we are, and what kind of world we want' (Contu, 2020, 739), the type of knowledge, relationship and agency we (co)construct or (re)produce. While accepting that 'it is not possible to ever fully understand, predict and control the consequences of one's co-participation, and what one is co-constituting and becoming' (Contu, 2020, 739), I believe that as academics we must reflexively engage in this embodied, emotional and intellectual dialogue with ourselves and others about how we can – and should – contribute to the shaping of our field(s). It should also be noted that this dialogue is likely to be iterative, developmental and incremental in its growth, since the levels of awareness, knowledge and experience we hold are continuously manipulated and (re)shaped by the relationship we have, the work we do, the mistakes we make, the people we encounter in our work and personal lives.

Researching and writing differently as a political and feminist project

The first chapter provided an overview of the neoliberal academy as a framing context for our argument highlighting the need to engage in researching and writing differently. I explored contemporary academic discourse, which is deeply rooted in neoliberal approaches and masculine ways of approaching academic work as a locus of inequality. This second chapter focuses on researching and writing differently as a political and feminist project and as a key to unlock positive change. In order to do so, I provide a brief overview of Feminism, which will be then linked specifically to management and organization studies, and articulated via examples of different currents of feminist thought and literature.

Feminism today

Feminism is beautifully complex in its various nuanced, interdisciplinary and intersectional interpretations and strands that have developed across different sociocultural contexts over the last century (see Tong and Fernandes Botts, 2017). Although Feminism per se is a movement that found its initial impetus in the 1960s, its (often hidden) roots stem from earlier initiatives around equality expressed via political rights, literary work and other fields. It is generally recognized that up to this point Feminism has witnessed three 'waves' of engagement, although some suggest a fourth one. Starting in the 1860s with a first wave focused on women's rights, with a particular focus on suffrage, Feminism became progressively more visible in the 1950s; the second wave (1960s–1980s) was characterized by investigations around gender equity and equal opportunities for women; while the current third wave focuses on egalitarian concerns and intersectionality (see Crenshaw, 2017). Other labels are often attached to the broader term Feminism – for instance Liberal Feminism, Radical Feminism, Marxist and Social Feminism, Black Feminism, Queer Feminism, Postcolonial and Transnational Feminism, to name but a few. It has been defined and described in many ways.

Building on bell hooks (2000), Harquail (2020, 15, emphasis in original) defines Feminism as 'a movement to *end* sexism, sexist exploitation, and all oppression; *establish* a political, social, and economic equality; and *create* a world where all people flourish'. These aims, with which I concur, are predicated on a foundational layer of assumptions. First of all, there needs to be a recognition that the world we live in is pervaded by a complex net of intersectional privilege and oppression. The power dynamics created through the establishment of this net, and reinforced through its development, create a state of inequality that rejects difference and prioritizes inclusion through assimilation. These dynamics of inequality are maintained through discrimination at the individual, collective, institutional and systemic level through structures and praxis that marginalize some to the advantage of others. Feminism illuminates these issues by interrogating, critiquing and challenging the status quo to reimagine a liberated alternative. Striving to dismantle the foundations of inequality, Feminism aims to achieve a social, political and economic space where all people can flourish. In Fannie Lou Hamer's words, delivered in her speech at the founding of the National Women's Political Caucus, Washington, DC, on 10 July 1971: "Nobody's free until everybody's free" (the audio file of some of her powerful testimonies is available on the Blavity website). In order to achieve this, Feminism emphasizes connectivity, community, ethics of care, diffused power, individual and collective accountability, autonomy and action. In agreement with bell hooks (1981) it is worth noting that Feminism is against sexism, not against men. Although women, or more generally people, are linguistically brought together into categories and labels, Feminism recognizes individuality among similarity – as each person is a unique intersectional encounter between religion, race, nationality, class, sexual orientation and so on. Audre Lorde highlights this plurality of issues and life experiences: 'There is no such thing as a single-issue struggle, because we do not live single-issue lives.' (2007, 138). Although Feminism can be thought of as a single collective movement, it incorporates a plurality of anti-oppression movements – at times in contrast with each other. Avishai, Gerber and Randles note that 'the historical development of feminism is, in large part, a story of feminists disrupting feminist conventional thinking and theories, or feminist orthodoxies.' (2013, 396). Also, different groups and individuals within those groups have different needs, wants and agendas that should not be blurred nor taken for granted (for example, that all women may want to achieve what men have; that disabled people aspire to the same professional standard as non-disabled people and so on).

In a recent publication (Boncori, 2020a, 680–681) I have outlined what Feminism means to me, in very simple terms:

> I have come to think of Feminism as inextricably linked with equality, diversity and inclusion — terms that are more widely understood and embraced but not necessarily less complex. Although stemming from women's rights, to me Feminism is really about offering all people equal opportunities, regardless of their sex, gender, age, race, ability, class, background and other factors that make up their identities. It's about

multi-vocal pluri-perspective conversations between individuals that challenge taken-for-granted structures and assumptions, which become collective projects linking the singular to the plural, the local to the systemic. To approach life with a feminist mind frame is to become (self)aware and (self)reflective about dynamics of power, privilege and discrimination at the individual, group and social level, with the aim to end oppression through equality for all. To think in a feminist way to me also means acknowledging and valuing difference; being mindful of intersectional issues; including voices, experiences and knowledge of women and others in every conversation and decision-making process, at every level. As a result of this, Feminism is also inherently political in its challenges to the status quo, in its advocacy for equality and its promotion of values rooted in fairness, agency, humanity and interdependence. I think I have always been a feminist, even before I knew what it meant. I am proud to call myself a feminist, and I strive to work every day on myself and with others to become a better one.

My approach to today's Feminism is about reflecting backwards and on the current position while looking ahead and moving forward. Although achieving equity and halting oppression are two key concepts within feminist perspectives, today's feminist goals also push these principles a little further in aiming for the establishment of an eudemonic world where all people (regardless of their locus of power, privilege and difference) can flourish (Cuomo, 1998; Nussbaum, 2011). Indeed, not being oppressed does not mean being liberated and flourishing. The tension between inclusivity and assimilation is often still ignored in contemporary notions of equality.

Unfortunately, there is still some prevailing uninformed bias considering feminists as a group of [rightfully] angry [people who identify as] women who protest [to obtain or maintain their equal rights] and hate [patriarchal structures and masculine norms traditionally reinforced and reproduced by] men. My interjections in the sentence above offer just one step up in the articulation of a superficial and trite view of who feminists are and what feminist aims have become over the past decades. Feminism should be a conversation had with everyone, not only in scholarly circles, perhaps informed and inspired by Ngozi Adichie's book *We Should All Be Feminists* (2014) or bell hooks' *Feminism Is for Everybody* (2000).

Feminism is theoretical in its propositions and values, but also deeply rooted in everyday life and practicalities. Its contributions and relevance are so entrenched in our present that they are often dismissed or taken for granted. As a young girl who had the privilege of being born in a fairly progressive family, I never thought of questioning my taken-for-granted rights. As I became older, I started understanding the incommensurable work done by feminist scholars and other feminist professionals that has allowed me, my sisters and my daughter to live in a better social context and have access to more rights. For example, the recent passing of Justice Ruth Bader Ginsburg has brought a powerful reminder of the changing legal landscape over the past century. I have always considered her approach to writing dissenting motions as a powerful example of writing differently. She not only tackled gendered legal knowledge and practice in a manner that was never done before, but she also did so in a beautiful narrative that rejected the masculine legal language accepted as the norm. This reminds me that although Feminism is not exclusively about women's rights, it is most definitely about women's rights. Through my research on gender and Feminism I realized the power of challenge and change stemming from feminist perspectives. For example, I was involved in a project called 'You Can't Beat a Woman', which stemmed from feminist values and perspectives. Funded by the National Lottery Heritage Fund, this initiative, led by June Freeman, collected oral history testimonies to trace back the 'herstories' of the women's refuges in the UK through the founding women's own words. In 2017, I had the honour of liaising with and interviewing some of these incredible women. Volunteering at the Colchester exhibition showcasing the history, value and contribution of the women's refuge, I was able to discuss the significance of this work with a number of people whose individual life experiences had been profoundly transformed by the support received through the Women's Refuge. The project covered eight women's refuges in East Anglia (opened between 1974 and 1981) and a refuge for Asian women in Newham, East London. One of my interviewees noted: "It started with a small group of women in a pub, wanting to make a change". As noted by Audre Lorde, 'Every woman has a well-stocked arsenal of anger potentially useful against those oppressions, personal and institutional, which brought that anger into being. Focused with precision it can become a powerful source of energy serving progress and change' (1984b, 127). By linking the personal to the collective, those women made a difference. This is why I see researching and Writing Differently as a prime example of Feminism in academia. The connection between Feminism and Writing Differently is perhaps best illustrated in the words of Nancy Harding: 'Each academic text "written differently" is a micro-revolution. Micro-revolutions add up, overturning dysfunctional, perhaps rotten, sometimes corrupt, practices that inhibit knowledge and understanding. Writing differently revolutionaries want to influence the world' (Pullen, Helin and Harding, 2020, 2). The value and potential of this type of understanding being espoused in academia lie in their ability to connect the personal and the local to the collective and to the systemic. Researching and writing differently can thus be understood as a feminist political project because it has to do with the challenging and changing of existing structures of power, inequality and oppression. Further, powerful feminist texts – for example, those created by Audre Lorde, bell hooks, Hélène Cixous, Julia Kristeva, Luce Irigaray and Sara Ahmed *inter alia* – can also be considered forms of writing differently *ante litteram*, both in content and style.

Black Feminism

Traditional feminist theories and definitions have been centred around white people. Critiques to this marginalization among feminist perspectives have rightfully led to more intersectional approaches to Feminism (see Yuval-Davis, 1998; 2006) and the development of discourses around specific categories of oppression – for instance, in Black Feminism and Queer Feminism. Critical race and decolonizing scholars have explored the historical formation and development of race and its relationship with white supremacy (see Moraga and Anzaldúa, 1983; Hall, 1997; Bhabha, 1994; Mohanty, 2003; DuBois, 2005; HoSang et al, 2012). Despite this rich intellectual history, management and organization studies remain broadly disengaged from these debates (Nkomo, 1992).

Looking in particular at the intersection between race and gender, Black feminist scholars have highlighted the considerably different oppression(s) that Black women and women of colour face every day, which are whitewashed, oversimplified or silenced by traditional Feminism (see Ifekwunigwe, 1998; Nkomo, 1988; hooks, 1989; Moreton-Robinson, 2000b; Lorde, 2017; Pow, 2018). Black feminists have highlighted the difference in struggle and the marginalization of their voices or experience. For example:

> Some problems we share as women, some we do not. You fear your children will grow up to join the patriarchy and testify against you, we fear our children will be dragged from a car and shot down in the street, and you will turn your backs upon the reasons they are dying. (Audre Lorde, 2007, 119, citing 1980 speech)

Patricia Hill Collins (1990) articulated the issue of different intersections of privilege and discrimination into a 'matrix of domination' to consider a more complex exploration of power, dominance and oppression, because the categories represented across different axes intersect and mix with one another to form a macro system of oppression. On the opposite side to oppression, she also identified 'unearned privilege', which, for instance, white people have inherently over others, and men receive through their gender assignment at birth. This unearned privilege must be acknowledged and challenged if all people are to flourish. In a powerful speech that has become iconic, Audre Lorde (1984a) states 'the master's tools will never dismantle the master's house'. Indeed, 'the rule of the master', also called kyriarchy (see Elisabeth Schüssler Fiorenza's work on this, 1993), needs to be dismantled in order for feminist systems and structures to replace – rather than just accompany – current systems of oppression.

As a white Italian-British woman and an interracial mother, I have often wondered whether it is appropriate of me to reflect and write about race and ethnicity. Do my voice and my writing take the space or displace another's? Can I use my privilege to be an ally? I do not want to speak for Black feminists or people of colour, or those racialized as a particular race. White feminists have often taken the space of Black feminists or spoken *for* them rather than *with* them, highlighting the need for a path to be forged that makes space for a Feminism that is not just exclusive to white middle-class women. Inspired by Collins (2000), I am moved to take advantage of my privilege as a white academic woman, to leverage my position to listen to, speak with, advocate and make space for those who are in less privileged positions. Sholock (2012) highlights that for effective collation and allyship white women must be aware and acknowledge their privilege(s) and recognize their lack of knowledge – both conceptually and in terms of experience regarding those who are racialized as Black or people of colour. While perhaps not best placed to provide a comprehensive outline of Black Feminism as a white woman, I feel that the exclusion of this important work from this book would be unacceptable, and that it is important as an ally to avoid being complicit in the silencing of those voices, studies and theories that are often overlooked (see for instance Erskine and Bilimoria, 2019 on white allyship, and Melaku and Beeman, 2020 on 'liberal white supremacy').

This section serves as a spotlight onto Black Feminism, as I highlight some of the work on Black Feminism and by scholars of colour that I have found particularly powerful and incisive throughout this book, especially in its dimension of advocacy towards equality and social change. This important body of work – which has personally inspired me as a writer – can be powerful in advancing Writing Differently as a movement in its own right. Also, this research is crucial in bringing in more voices that address racial inequalities, and showing how power intersects with other intersectional categories. Social justice is a collective responsibility that must be shared, and recent calls for anti-racist action (Bell et al, 2020; Dar et al, 2020; Meikle, 2020) and activism (Nkomo and Al Ariss, 2014; Holmes, 2019; Roberts, Mayo and Thomas, 2019) have highlighted the dire need that still exists for race equality and justice in academia, especially in business schools. It is important to recognize that the experiences of racialized activists, whether in academia or other contexts, can drastically differ, which implies that the ways in which activism is embodied and implemented are far from homogeneous. This is due to many intersecting factors including colourism, Islamophobia, anti-Blackness and contextual political environments that shape the nature of anti-racism activism (for example, the historical and sociopolitical context in the US is very different from the British one, or other European and Asian contexts). Like in Feminism more generally and in the case of different groups within the LGBT+ community in terms of Queer Feminism, it should be noted that there are differing power structures and hierarchical dynamics also within anti-racist spaces. These group generalizations are problematic also in terms of other groups of racialized activists, for example in 'the Global South' or 'African culture' or 'Asian countries', as these sweeping labels bring together radically different experiences and (sub)cultures within geographical areas of proximity.

In 2019, Nkomo and colleagues identified white supremacy and the Black Lives Matter movement as two key issues in the future of diversity scholarship. Aileen Moreton-Robinson (2006, 363, cited in Al Ariss et al, 2014) defines whiteness as 'an invisible norm against which other identities are measured and by which they are defined historically', and by which standards continue to be set and managed socially, economically and academically. Whiteness and white privilege in academia have been very pervasive, albeit with different connotations and political nuances in different national contexts. The notion of a 'post-race' academy remains an ideal, as our professional context – at least the academic environments I have experienced in Italy, China and the UK – is still pervaded by systemic racism and everyday discrimination. Work by Kalwant Bhopal and her colleagues in the higher education environment (see for instance Bhopal, 2016; Bhopal and Pitkin, 2020; Bhopal and Henderson, 2021) highlights how racism is deeply embedded within academia and how it hinders career progression, even more so than sexism. Further, Davis (1999), Jones (2003), Patton (2004) and Harris (2007), have all added visibility to how racism and sexism particularly affect Black women in the academy. White networks of privilege and support reinforce systemic racism (for instance, in recruitment panels, the provision of references for job applications and funding, and co-authoring). This issue is compounded by the fact that decision-makers and top-level managers, for example, in the British higher education context, are often exclusively white.

In order to affect change, intersectional barriers must be addressed at the individual, institutional and systemic level to meaningfully address the issues around race inequality (see Nash, 2019). This has been flagged in different fields of academic work, also considering obstacles to students and, in particular, regarding doctoral-level funding. For example, in 2019 Leading Routes reported that only 3 per cent of a total number of 15,560 first-year full-time United Kingdom students identify as Black (Higher Education Statistics Agency, 2019). Further, between 2016 and 2019, only 1.2 per cent (245) of the total 19,868 PhD funded studentships that were cumulatively awarded by United Kingdom Research and Innovation (UKRI) research councils were given to Black or Black Mixed students, with just 30 of those from Black Caribbean backgrounds. Rather than a 'leaky pipeline' on the academic career ladder, this seems to be a purposely blocked one. Therefore, the voices of Black scholars and, in particular, Black women who are feminist scholars are in a minority and bear the burden of representation (also in relation to an increasingly diverse student population in some countries) and activism (see Law, 2017). In the UK, statistical evidence is staggering: only 13 per cent of academics identify as people of colour throughout the sector (Advance HE, 2018). The patriarchal status quo to challenge here is both a gendered and a normative white one, as whiteness encompasses '(1) a location of structural advantage; (2) a standpoint from which white people look at themselves, others and society; and (3) a set of normalized cultural practices' (Liu, 2017, 458).

Key publications on Black Feminism span various decades, and although a review of this literature is beyond the scope of this book, I'd like to highlight some capstone works that have inspired my research and shaped my perspective. Patricia Hill Collins's (2000) book *Black Feminist Thought* is an extremely valuable source and an ideal starting point in an exploration of Black Feminism. Sara Ahmed's work and 'Feminist Killjoys' blog also celebrates a number of Black feminists and people of colour who are activists, researchers in various fields, and artists contributing to the tracing of 'paths to follow' for academics writing about racism and Feminism (see Ahmed, 2017; 2018). An important consideration in Black feminist work is the difference in experience, and the power relations and hierarchical order that have been imposed through whiteness, especially on Black women. In *Ain't I a Woman: Black Women and Feminism*, bell hooks (1981) surfaces the inequalities directed towards Black women from within the women's liberation and civil rights movements and provides a counter-narrative to include women who are not in the mainstream feminist discourse (that is, white, middle-class, privileged or formally educated). Also, Angela Davis's (1981) powerful book *Women, Race, and Class* denounced the manner in which Black women are silenced and often erased, marking their oppressors and their discrimination. A noteworthy contemporary text is *This Bridge Called My Back* by Cherríe Moraga and Gloria Anzaldúa (2015): originally published in 1981, it highlights the necessity to focus on intersectional approaches to race, class, sexuality and gender, and to problematize the notion of unity within different communities. This critical, holistic and intersectional approach is fundamental to understanding the nuances of human experience – Audre Lorde (2009) reminds us that 'If I do not bring all of who I am to whatever I do, then I bring nothing, or nothing of lasting worth, for I have withheld my essence' (2009, 182–3).

In the UK, some contemporary work is also worth noting that complements other feminist movements but is centred around the British sociopolitical landscape, such as *The Heart of the Race: Black Women's Lives in Britain* by Beverley Bryan, Stella Dadzie and Suzanne Scafe (2018). In *Feminism, Interrupted* Lola Olufemi (2020) challenges the neoliberal feminist promise of success premised on whiteness and acquiescence rather than challenges to hegemony. Olufemi highlights how by refusing a neoliberal approach and embracing instead critical feminist approaches, people can make 'a commitment to a world that has not yet been built' (2020, 5) beyond 'woman' or 'equality' where 'nobody is left behind, nobody's exploitation goes unseen' (2020, 5). This type of Feminism is central to rethinking a future through collective organizing as 'it asks us to practice radical compassion, to refuse to ignore the pain of others. It demands that we see how tackling seemingly unrelated phenomena like prison expansion, the rise of fascism, neocolonialism and climate crisis must also become our priorities' (2020, 5).

It should be clarified that there are many feminist groups of colour often associated with Black Feminism who have developed particular narratives and highlighted specific racialized experiences that differ from those of Black feminists. Although I am unable to discuss these in detail due to space constraints, there is a plethora of scholarly work, for example: Chicana feminists (see Alarcón, 1990); Indigenous feminists in Latin America and Canada (see Hernández Castillo, 2010; Suzack (2010); Indigenous and Aboriginal feminists in New Zealand (see Green, 2017; Moreton-Robinson, 2000b).

Queer Feminism

In line with the reflections and limitations guiding my approach to writing about race and ethnicity, here I outline some important issues developed within the umbrella term 'Queer Feminism'. Although this is explored separately here from Black Feminism, queer feminist approaches of course intersect across various groups, such as Afro-German activists who identify as lesbian, Chicana feminists and others. To mark these intersections, the term 'queering ethnicity' has often been used (see El-Tayeb, 2011, 66–8). Once again, in management and organization studies research on lesbian, gay, bisexual and transgender (LGBT) identities has lagged behind compared to other fields such as sociology, psychology and anthropology (see Parker, 2002; Ozturk and Rumens, 2014; Rumens, 2013); however, there is a growing volume of research 'queering' this field (see for instance Bowring and Brewis, 2009; Pullen and Thanem, 2010; Priola et al, 2014; Vitry, 2020).

Queer Theory to me is intimately linked to critical management perspectives and Feminism in its problematization around care, responsibility and accountability, recognition and representation, and the distribution of power and resources. Also, another point of contact among these three fields lies in their future orientation and propensity to (re)imagine possible alternatives. Stemming from work by lesbian and gay activist groups as well as sociological and philosophical explorations (see, for example, work by Derrida and Foucault), queer theory is intrinsically critical as it critiques hegemonic and normalizing ways of knowing and understanding gender, sexuality and related structures (Sullivan, 2003). As such, it is varied in approaches (Seidman, 1995), identifiable across a range of practices and positionalities, but often left undefined and unbounded as 'an ongoing and necessarily unfixed site of engagement and contestation' (Berry and Jagose, 1996, 11). It involves the rejection of equality as a form of assimilation, the refusal of static normative positions, and the problematization of binary notions of gender and sexuality.

The term 'queer' has been used in many different ways (see Sullivan, 2003), rejected and then reclaimed by the LGBT+ community.[1] It is often used to denote an umbrella of approaches to studies of sexual orientation and gender,[2] but it is also criticized in this role as a homogenizing force that veils differences within and across genders and sexualities (Anzaldúa, 1991). Some scholars also claim that we are now in a 'post-queer' phase. Further, the term 'queer' is not only used as an adjective to define identity or as a noun to indicate positionality, but also as a verb – to queer or queering. According to Halperin (1995, 62, emphasis in original): 'Queer is by definition *whatever is at odds with the normal, the legitimate, the dominant. There is nothing in particular to which it necessarily refers.* It is an identity without an essence. "Queer" then, demarcates not a positivity but a positionality vis-à-vis the normative.' The term has been used for people, theories and movements as well as for other aspects of scholarship. For example, Steyaert (2015, 163) brings together feminine writing with queer time, asking 'how it would be possible to break through heteronormative concepts of time and how to provide "other" concepts and practices that can infiltrate and interrupt?'

There are several key contemporary authors across academic fields who have contributed to the development of Queer Feminism. For example, Judith Butler's work, which has also been questioned as queer writing, especially in *Gender Trouble* (1990) and *Bodies That Matter* (1993), has explored the performative character of gender, highlighting the complex matrix of discourses, institutions and sociopolitical meanings behind notions of gender and sexuality. This also emphasizes the historical and cultural-specific character of gender and sexuality whereby dominant positions are open to challenge and change. Sara Ahmed (2017) is also often identified as a prime scholar in queer feminist studies who has been engaging with critiques of the academy, challenging bias and marginalization, and disrupting inequality at the systemic and institutional level. Queer Feminism challenges the heteronormative and cisgender normative structures in Western societies, which are also echoed in the workplace and in academia (Ahmed, 2016a).

The relevance of feminist theory and queer studies to the field of critical management studies (and its interdisciplinary nature) has been explored in a recent book edited by Alison Pullen, Nancy Harding and Mary Phillips (2017) entitled *Feminist and Queer Theorists debate the Future of Critical*

Management Studies. Reinforcing the intellectual, political and activist value of queer and feminist studies in the management field (Harding, Ford and Fotaki, 2013; Pullen and Thanem, 2010; Rumens, 2012), this volume brings together colleagues from different parts of the globe to offer ways of rethinking critical management studies through feminist and queer ways of organizing. Some of the contributions in this volume are also great illustrations of writing intersectionally (see for instance Swan, 2017; Liu, 2017), and writing differently (Sayers, 2017; Rippin, 2017). Ann Rippin's chapter, for example, takes inspiration from Eve Kosofsky Sedgwick's work and her unconventional methods to present some ways of queering a field through methods, theory and making; her work combines art, textiles and academic text to offer a different type of encounter with phenomena in organizations, and different ways to experience and perceive those.

Feminism in management and organization studies

Scholars in the 1980s and 1990s provided a significant impetus in the development of feminist examinations of organizational theory (see for instance Acker, 1992; Calás and Smircich, 1996 and 2006) whereby classic organizational theory was filtered through the lens of critical gendered perspectives. Unfortunately, although many scholars use feminist theory and a feminist approach, there is still limited feminist theorizing in management and organization studies due to the mainstream patriarchal context of this field. Gender, race and class are still the pillar of 'inequality regimes' (Acker, 2006) in organizations and organizing. As a feminist scholar myself, I have usually turned to the fields of sociology, philosophy and anthropology to learn about Feminism from an academic point of view and feminist theory. As I made my initial tentative and excited steps in the field of feminist literature and thinking, these scholars have been significant sources of inspiration and knowledge across different fields of study: Audre Lorde, Judith Butler, Donna Haraway, Sara Ahmed, Rosi Braidotti, Joan Acker and many more. In the field of management and organization theory, the work of a number of colleagues has definitely contributed to my development of a feminist sensitivity and a kinship towards writing differently: Heather Höpfl, Monika Kostera, Allison Pullen, Karen Lee Ashcraft, Nancy Hardin, Marianna Fotaki, Sara Gilmore to name a few. However, I agree with Celia Harquail who, in her accessible book *Feminism: A key idea for Business and Society* (2020), highlights the scarce formal engagement of management and organization studies with Feminism. In stressing the importance and relevance of Feminism for our field, Harquail (2020) also suggests the value of some of its aims, especially in terms of listening to women's voices, championing equality and implementing feminist values in everyday business practice.

The inherent jarring between Feminism and business is not only entrenched in the long-established patriarchal foundations of the field, but also in its purpose. Gender, in the words of Joan Scott (1986), is a pervasive symbol of power, which is intrinsic to organizing. Management and business principles are traditionally focused on 'competitive advantage' and the success of some over others; being successful in the business 'arena' is seen even metaphorically as a race, a war or a competition. Achievement in organizations is about leveraging power and influence to benefit a small group of people and generate a gain. On the other hand, Feminism is about ending oppression and establishing equality for all, allowing people to be represented and heard, with the aim to achieve a fair social (or professional) context where all can flourish. The gendering and power dynamics of management and organization studies are enacted both theoretically and in the processes and practices of everyday organizing. Within this framework, class, gender, sexual orientation, ability and other categories of privilege, power and oppression are inextricably intertwined and ubiquitous. While many of the manifestations of patriarchal systems are overt and embedded explicitly in organizational policies, practices and behaviours, the less explicit or obvious forms of gendering are located in what Joan Acker (1992, 423) calls the gendered substructures of organizations, which 'lie in the spatial and temporal arrangements of work, in the rules prescribing workplace behaviour, and in the relations linking workplaces to living places'. The mapping of these norms and arrangements against a taken-for-granted (male, white, middle-class, cisgender) masculine backdrop serve to perpetuate inequality, oppression and exclusion.

Clearly, the two systems are at odds. While it may not be common, a more attuned merging of the two spheres of theory and practice can be pursued. Feminist approaches should aim to infiltrate and disrupt old-fashioned business models and practices to provide alternative frameworks, models and structures whereby business aims and practices are no longer just for the benefit of the privileged few. Of course, those who are the natural heirs of privilege, financial gain and success in traditional models of business are not likely to support a shift in their power and advantage. This is the same in the case of academia, as universities can be considered just as a particular type of organization. In their caring for the majority at the expense of the few, 'business practices are extractive rather than generative' (Harquail, 2020, 6). As such, feminist-driven change in management and organization studies is likely to continue to encounter resistance from the gatekeepers of the status quo, who often also use a distorted and purposefully negative representation of Feminism itself to turn people against equality, posing that Feminism threatens people's rights and lifestyles to increase the ranks of its opponents. Looking around the social matrix in two internationally powerful countries during the initial writing stage of this book – Donald Trump's US and Boris

Johnson's UK – I am sad to note that these proponents of social inequality appear to be rather successful in leveraging fear, otherness and ignorance. There is a constant, powerful and systemic attempt at denying, belittling and frustrating feminist understandings and developments. However, alternative types of leadership are possible – for instance, in politics as shown by New Zealand's prime minister Jacinda Ardern and Sanna Marin in Finland, and in business. Now, more than ever, we need movements that counteract, challenge and resist xenophobia, misogyny and violence. Feminism is in action all over the globe through movements like #MeToo, groups advocating racial equality and climate sustainability, the end of female genital mutilation, activism for the abolition of child marriage and so on.

In the academic context, this systemic-level work also needs a rethink of what counts as 'proper' research (Höpfl, 2000; Phillips et al, 2014), including considerations of writing styles to disrupt objective and masculine structures (Prasad, 2016). This, I believe, can be embodied and successfully achieved through researching and writing differently, as I will explore later in this book. As indicated by Cixous (1976, 879), 'Writing is precisely the very possibility of change, the space that can serve as a springboard for subversive thought, the precursory movement of a transformation of social and cultural structures'. Writing, we are reminded by Katie Beavan, Benedikte Borgström, Jenny Helin and Carl Rhodes (2021, 1), is not neutral; the manner in which we write, and not only the topic and contents of our scholarship, 'is wrapped up in the possible meanings, affects, and effects that can result when our text intersects with a reader. In play is an ongoing deferral and displacement of meanings as texts fumble through time to be read, cited, debated or dismissed'. Therefore, researching and writing differently that draws from feminist approaches is embodied, personal, emotional, political and practical as well as theoretical.

In a great book of recent publication, Fotaki and Harding (2018) investigate Feminism as equality for all women and human beings, and discuss gender theory in management and organization studies by exploring a number of contributions, and considering developments for the future of research in this field. This insightful volume draws from different disciplines – arts, humanities, psychology, sociology and so on – to problematize existing knowledge and approaches, while pushing us to consider a way forward that is both theoretical and practical in nature. A number of scholars have taken a feminist approach to the investigation of organizational phenomena, thus asking for more critical approaches to the way we think of and work in organizations (see Gherardi 1994; Martin, 2006; Tyler, 2019), also considering processes on undoing of gender at work (Kelan, 2010; Thanem and Wallenberg, 2016). Joan Acker's early work (1990, 2006; and Sayce and Acker, 2012) highlights the dynamics of power that feed the substructural mesh of organizational dynamics of inequality, and influenced much of the subsequent research on gender in this field (see Calás and Smircich,1996; Ely and Meyerson, 2000). Harquail (2020) outlines six measures that have been adopted by organizations in order to address gender inequality: increasing the number of women overall and in leadership positions; help women understand and engage in 'the game', playing by masculine rules; value difference, which can be interpreted as capitalizing on what the organization perceived as women's strengths, for instance by allocating pastoral roles in the HE context; adjusting components of the system to provide a fairer environment; trying to achieve deep-rooted cultural change through projects or initiatives that provide some 'small wins' for the equality agenda; and a radical transformation of the system that promotes flourishing for everyone. Clearly, a key issue in some of the approaches indicated here is that rather than fixing the system in a holistic way, organizations may try to make the individual fit the existing patriarchal system, or suggest the implementation of small changes that have a lot of visibility but not much impact. This is equivalent to substituting one window in the patriarchal fort, which will not rock its foundations. Although 'small wins' can be the initial tentative steps on a longer more significant journey towards the appreciation of difference, equality and flourishing, these have to lead to a much more impactful and pervasive movement in order to make a significant impact in the life of an organization and society more broadly.

These mainstream and alternative perspectives, as well as the corresponding social movements, permeate people's conscious and unconscious behaviour, thus affecting decision-making and business practices. The challenge for Feminism today is not only to achieve equality, particularly in terms of women's rights, gender inclusion and racism – recognized as a moral imperative in organizations – but also to avoid the pigeonholing of these concerns and their encapsulation within tokenistic structures. Ridiculous as it may sound, there are equality rankings too that drive inclusivity agendas and the allocation of financial budgets in many organizations and institutions (including those in higher education). Of course, I acknowledge that initiatives like Athena Swan[3] and the Race Equality Charter[4] are important in raising awareness and instigating action. And yet, these are still at least partially based on masculine metric-driven competitive approaches that allow organizations to achieve a bronze/silver/gold status in relation to other institutions. Having been involved myself in the implementation of some of these frameworks, and in other initiatives such as the Stonewall Top 100 Employers ranking in the UK, I am aware that the criteria used are generally strict and also orientated not only towards immediate impactful action, but also more long-term change. However, I remain a little sceptical about the use of masculine metrics to assess performance, as there can be a blind over-reliance on benchmark data, which can help mask issues. For example, the fact that in 2020 a university is home to *one* of the 26 Black women who are professors out of a population of 19,000 individuals in the UK professoriate, is not good news. Equally, the department-level acknowledgement of some issues and actions put in place to mitigate against discrimination may still only benefit some groups of individuals over others.

While a number of organizations are truly engaging with the values and practices of feminist equality and care, which are evidenced but should not be limited to taking part in these rankings or charters, others actually use these as a smoke-and-mirrors tool, thus obfuscating systemic issues, shifting the focus onto individual action and responsibility rather than the rotten organizational structures. Within an instrumental masculine metric-driven organization, issues can be neatly compartmentalized and stored away, thus defusing the magnitude of the overall equality crisis. For example, the gender pay gap can be articulated as a simple matter of finance; recruitment bias can be limited to human resources policy; miscarriage and infertility can be merely considered as a matter for occupational health; gender affirmation surgery can be stigmatized as a medical problem; racism is swept under the carpet of staff training on unconscious bias, and so on. I see this type of organizational dislodging of the single factors and forms of inequality from the larger holistic collective and systemic issues as an active form of organizational resistance against equality. Like the quest for 'more data', 'more evidence' or 'more statistics' to legitimize and 'prove' appalling circumstances, this practice is a tool of the oppressor in the silencing and gaslighting process. Do we really still need to prove that racism exists in academia and its many articulations? Do we still need to provide data on gendered inequalities? We don't need more data to confirm for the gazillionth time that our structures are discriminating and our systems are marginalizing: we need to act now.

Feminism is a way to disrupt the status quo and move the equality agenda forward. In this context, researching and writing differently can become a feminist and political project within in the academic realm. As discussed before, Feminism has been classified within different waves, and different strands of feminist theory have rather distinct foci of inquiry (see Cavarero and Reistano, 2002). Although the French feminist tradition has often been the taken-for-granted point of reference for writing differently, it is also important to flag that other types of feminist theory are at play, such as the Italian feminist tradition, which includes a strong focus on embodiment (see, for instance, Pierazzini, Bertelli, and Raviola, 2021). It is also politically important to engage with various feminist perspectives that decentralize Anglocentric notions, problematize dominant schools of thought and experience within the feminist tradition, and develop alternatives to researching and writing in different languages and sociocultural contexts. This enhances the political potential of Writing Differently and the unsettling or questioning of normative understandings of both organizational research and academic writing.

Why researching and writing differently now

As I mentioned in the Introduction, inclusion should not mean assimilation, and it should not involve the minority being engulfed, minimized, belittled or erased by the majority. Based on the contextual and theoretical frameworks discussed thus far, here is where I locate researching and writing differently as a key part of a critical epistemology. Through researching and writing differently, we can articulate inclusion through the valuing and celebration of diversity, to amplify and heed a variety of voices. However, it should be noted that there is no universal capitalized 'We', as each of us can only speak from a specific context, informed by a particular intersection, cluster of privilege and life experiences. By engaging in researching and writing differently, we can speak for ourselves and not for/instead/over others, and contribute to the creation of a kaleidoscope of knowledge and experiences. Writing differently is a way of recentring and amplifying voices that have been pushed under the hegemonic normative discourses of gender, race, ability, sexuality and other categories of marginalization and silence. The more taken for granted neoliberal approaches to academia become, the more incisive critique and action are needed in order to combat violent assimilation and the stifling of scholarship. Stella Nkomo (1988, 1992) is one of many academics who have put forward powerful cases for the dismantling of white male dominance over knowledge production, which have sadly remained as a 'different' rather than a mainstream view (Jones et al, 2019). Indeed, thirty years after those contributions by Nkomo, academics are still subjugated by walls of privilege.

As discussed, researching and writing differently (in its various meanings) can be seen as a political feminist project in its aim to challenge the status quo, in its objective to transform the masculine approach to research, and in its quest to listen to different voices, inviting a larger articulation of interests, approaches, experiences and values. Through the lens of its feminist character and positioning, researching and writing differently is also inherently critical in its deep critique of the foundation of some fields of inquiry, the challenging of its hegemonic practices, the questioning of its defining values and priorities. Revisiting their work after ten years, in 2006 Calás and Smircich noted how, regardless of the meaningful and numerous contributions that feminist theorizing has made to organization studies, the reality of everyday organizations still warranted further feminist work: 'regardless of how many statistical contortions are made [...] or sociological, psychological and economic explanations are marshalled [...], to date no single indicator shows that the conditions of women in the world, as a whole, are at parity with the conditions of men' (Calás and Smircich, 2006, 284). After almost two decades, that is still the case. In the UK, a country that prides itself for being advanced, civilized and fair, the gender pay gap in 2019 was still 17.3%. Data on full-time employees shows a decline of the gender pay gap of only 0.6 percentage points since 2012 (ONS, 2020). In 2017, the European Commission reported that 'the gender pay gap in the EU stands at 16% and has only changed minimally over the last decade' (EC, 2018). We must act now – in theory, in practice, through reading and writing, through funding applications, through mentoring and collaborative relationships, in our editorial and review work, in the way we relate to ourselves, others and each other.

Through its approach and *forma mentis*, researching and writing differently can destabilize mainstream notions of power and inclusion, thus embracing the testimonies, theories and practices of all people to support collective flourishing. Researching and writing differently can be seen as a feminist project in its critique of the *values* we want to espouse and champion in our work. If academic careers are premised on competition and masculine metrics, how can organizations foster an environment of affective solidarity, collaboration, sharing and ethical choices? Where is the space for compassion, collaboration and empathy in the disembodied academic organization? In her beautiful book *Ordinary Affects* (2007), the anthropologist Kathleen Stewart reminds us of the affective dimensions of everyday interactions and the importance of ordinary encounters in shaping affective dynamics. As long as our systems, processes, rewards and career development are predicated on 'winners' and 'losers', we are likely to experience a vicious cycle of people who are better at playing 'the academic game', who are more likely to be promoted to powerful positions (editors, deans, professors, principal grant investigators and so on), and become smarter at reinforcing exclusionary strategies and academic praxis that has been beneficial to them. We know that women in academia continue to be given more precarious contracts, more supporting roles and more 'citizenship' activities, which make their career progression slower than their male counterparts (Guarino and Borden, 2017). There are some examples of different ways – more empathetic, more emotionally engaged, more equality-aware and less power-controlled – of being a leader in an academic context, or of researching and working through ethics of care, but these are still a minority.

A related issue revolves around a critique of what counts as *valuable* in today's academia, and particularly in the field of management and organization studies. An increasing number of academic systems worldwide have espoused a categorization of research outputs, such as the one adopted in the UK, which had been originally put in place (as the Research Assessment Exercise, REA) since the 1980s, but it started being used in a more policing way in the 2000s (it was later renamed the Research Excellence Framework, REF). The current iteration of the REA/REF professes to be 'the UK's system for assessing the quality of research in UK higher education institutions' (REF website, 2020), dividing research outputs into world leading (4★), internationally excellent (3★), recognized internationally (2★) and recognized nationally (1★), which are then benchmarked in academic journal listings. As the availability of government funding for research and education diminished over the past two decades, British universities have become even more reliant on the REF because these research rankings are used to allocate 'quality-weighted research funding' (QR funding) and to inform national and international rankings that are considered by fee-paying students while applying for their university degrees. So, once again, it is about the money rather than the intrinsic value of academic work. Of course, as an editor and a reviewer, I am aware that the processes involved with publishing work with top-level international journals or publishers helps ensure a high-quality academic output. However, I am also conscious of the inherently discriminating and political character of some of those systems and practices, and of the presence of very high-quality research in journals and book series that are not included or recognized in the highest bands of rankings and frameworks.

Other countries are increasingly adopting similar systems, with academic journals or publishers divided into bands or hierarchical structures that are used to assess academic performance and the quality of academic outputs. These metrics often snowball into decision-making processes for tenure procedures, probation, promotion and performance management regarding research. When professors and early-career scholars are forced to focus on masculine metrics to publish papers in top mainstream journals that reject innovation and examples of writing differently, their ability to create new breakthroughs in knowledge is stifled. Rather than being innovative and charting new directions in smaller journals, it is easier to conform to quality and researching that are considered standard and (re)produce research that conforms to established ways of investigating phenomena and organizations. If doctoral students and early-career scholars are taught that to be 'good enough' they have to conform to those masculine protocols of 'publish or perish' through processes that reinforce inequality in journals that reject experimentation and writing differently, how will they chart a different path? This set up will likely create an experience of internalized oppression (David, 2013).

Perhaps, in order to inhabit academia differently in a more inclusive way and to embrace difference in our researching, we have to keep asking these 'big questions'. What does it mean to be an academic? Who do we want to be as academics? It matters. Why are we writing organizations? What do we want to write about? What for? It can make a difference. Is the point of researching and writing really efficiency and the accumulation of outputs that foster financial growth, which can be quantified and measured? Is the current system appropriate for what we want to achieve? Of course, for some the achievement of goals may indeed be about financial advantage, career milestones, a long academic CV and so on. But for others who crave a different system, researching and writing differently can become a catalyst for agency, an opportunity to reframe and rephrase social/professional relationships, to rethink academic community-ship, and to 'invest' in ourselves rather than in outputs. Researching and writing differently can then be seen as an attempt to refract the homologizing male, white, ableist and classist gaze that permeates and dominates most areas in management and organization studies (and other fields of inquiry), even the critical ones. This movement is, like Feminism itself, an intellectual and sensorial crowbar to crack open a window of insights and experience through the closed doors of patriarchal academy. By choosing to challenge the status quo through researching and writing differently, scholars may find themselves navigating intersections of vulnerable fragility, powerful solidarity and marginalizing precarity. This is likely to result in delicate negotiations across identity boundaries, practical needs, ethical stances and professional values. This way of being and doing as an academic can be seen as an 'alternative' path aimed at reclaiming the value of academic work, reimagining knowledge creation and sharing through the dismantling or reframing of contemporary academic habitus.

The contextualization of today's academia within a neoliberal discourse, and the framing of researching and writing differently as a feminist tool of action and resistance to hegemonizing masculine structures, provide the starting point for the theorizing and rethinking of contemporary academia. I pose that researching and writing differently, articulated both at the individual and collective level, can become the vehicle to move from the current system of inequality to a more inclusive academic environment. In a recent paper (Strauß and Boncori, 2020), Anke Strauß and I contextualized today's academia within liquid modernity (Bauman, 2000) where social life has become precarious, unstable and 'interspersed with fundamental insecurity and radical individualism, both stemming from and supporting temporary forms of relations' (Strauß and Boncori, 2020, 1004). However, I have come to believe that contemporary academia – and researching and writing within this system – has reached a stage akin to what Zygmunt Bauman (2012), taking inspiration from recommendations made by Gramsci's work on the crisis of authority (Gramsci, 2011), calls the *interregnum*. The theorizing of the interregnum offers a poignant metaphor for today's academia. This is a liminal period of time characterized by in-betweenness – anchored but at the same time departing from an old system erected on structures based on taken-for-granted assumptions regarding what we do, how we must do it, and what rules must be followed. The old system is rotten, chronically ill – dying yet stubbornly resisting a slow death in its attempt to stay at the helm. It may be already dead, and yet it is still alive in the tentacular consequences it has engraved on people's ways of thinking and acting. But a new system is not here yet, we cannot even fully recognize it at the horizon. The interregnum is a tumultuous precursor to the [pre]regnum, which in my view does not necessarily need to lead to anomie (the absence of rules), but is characterized by discomfort, uncertainty, frustration, hope and ambition for the future. Bordoni (2016) states that in the interregnum things are suspended. While this is a time for positive change, it can also be a time of perilous 'negative capability' (French, 2001). And maybe this is where the current opportunity lies: we should not consider this state as 'a nerve-wracking wait' (Bordoni, 2016) but as a time of invisible ignition, a time for the seed of change to be implanted in our individual and collective agency to (re)imagine and (re)create a better system. The collective acknowledging of the moribund system is that seed. The emotions stirred by the inadequacy of the old system are that seed, whether consciously acknowledged or not. And so, although the new project may have yet to come into focus, this seed is the ignition that will allow us to imagine a different rhythm of researching, reading and writing, of being academics and creating or advancing knowledge. In my vision of the current academic interregnum, suspension is not characterized by immobility and the absence of rules; the in-betweenness is not lived as a vacuum, or a motionless and weightless state. Instead, it is a state of overlap between the old and the new, between the end and the start. This is made possible through the erosion of previous structures that become increasingly fragmented and transparent, allowing us to catch a glimpse of what lies in the foundations that was obfuscated by the structures of the old system. As those structures prove to be inefficient and inopportune, we can build onto the newly visible foundations to create a new system. Monika Kostera suggests:

> As institutions fall, they reveal what is beneath them. The foundation should be based on shared values, but all too often it was held in place by something entirely different: oppression, violence, raw power. In the flying dust and rubble of the collapse, the atrocious truth becomes visible and omnipresent. It is not possible to ignore it, as it literally flies into our faces and gets into our eyes and noses. In the chaos created by the debris it is, however, all too easy to ignore the values. (Kostera, 2020, 5)

The key here is in the careful development of the new system to avoid a masked mirroring of the old one. A trap often triggered through innovation is the over-reliance on the old system, its principles or practices, as a backdrop or referencing point for the creation of the new system. Rather than 'creating the new inside the shell of the old' (Vieta, 2014), the old shell needs to be recognized as irreparably broken before something truly new can grow out of it and thrive. In order to dismantle the old, while we should learn from it, we need to get to the values underneath and make *tabula rasa* of its faulty structures, rather than using those as the underpinning points to springboard from.

In the classic Latin understanding of the interregnum, this was a time where power was redistributed to the *patres* (plural rather than just a singular interim successor) in the absence of a ruler, to ensure continuity. We may want to rethink the notion of *patres* to avoid considering this just a plural form to indicate more than one *pater* (the 'father', the masculine leader/rule that shapes patriarchy) in favour of a more diffused understanding of the term, whereby *patres* are a seen as a collective of structures or individuals taking over a system. While in the classical notion this change of power is to maintain continuity, the *patres* also have the revolutionary apocalyptic power to dismantle the old. Monika Kostera's remarkable book *After the Apocalypse* (2020) invites us to think of apocalypse not only as destruction, but also as a revelation. As Kostera mentioned in an inspiring keynote speech at the In/Visible online conference (1 October 2020) 'if you resist the almost irresistible power of destruction telling you what is important, you find the revelation of what lies in the foundations of a system that was covered in structures that obfuscate opportunities'. I believe that under the heavy debris of patriarchy and its masculine structures, in the foundations of the academic system, brought to life like a sarcophagus through the eroding and corrosive workings of neoliberalism, we find feminist values. 'The speech of the interregnum is a lamentation, a constant cry for help, a repeated request, a formal declamation that is listened to but only superficially' (Bordoni, 2016, chapter 3) – a feminist expression. We can use our agency to illuminate those feminist values, take responsibility as *patres* within the interregnum, and use them well while dismantling a decomposing academic system of inequality (the patriarchal pre-regnum). I believe that we already have the seeds of change, and that researching and writing differently can be a pathway towards the creation of a new academic system (the post-regnum, or *regnum novum*).

The creation of a new system is, of course, complex. It is likely to take time and emotional labour. The good news is that we already have examples of what this may look like, glimpses of individual contributions and visions that are starting to become the collective movement of Writing Differently. In our field of management and organization studies, the attraction (either conscious or unconscious) of an alternative way of being and 'producing' as an academic which is underpinned in feminist values is already echoed in some conferences, journals and high-level publications. Writing Differently is gaining momentum as a movement, but (if it is maintained and keeps growing) we are still a long way from this becoming a replacing alternative, or mainstreamed system. This is why I advocate a broader perspective that encompasses researching and writing differently, to include not only ways of writing and publishing, but also different perspectives on being an academic and inhabiting this professional space.

In the next part of this book, I will provide an overview of researching and writing differently, by considering how we can write differently in terms of content, context and form, and by offering a selection of exemplars. Part 3 focuses on methodologies and methods that lend themselves to writing differently and on practical aspects related to researching and writing differently, including publishing and engaging in collaborative work.

PART II

Daring to research and write differently

While the first part of this book provided a framing background to advocate both the need for and the potential of researching and writing differently, this section will consider the many ways in which writing differently can be done with regards to the content, topics and sensibilities of academic writing. What does writing differently look like, and feel like – and how does it intertwine with all our senses? How can we – as academics who recognize the need for change – begin to recognize this as an alternative way to embody academic writing which fosters cooperation, equality and flourishing for all? How can we mould our writing and academic practice to shape new directions and lay strong enough foundations to allow new structures that are both flexible and supportive, dialogic and inclusive? Monika Kostera highlights the need for valid alternatives: 'We need alternatives more than ever, and not just any alternatives but ones which would give us resilient, sustainable and meaningful ways out of the interregnum and into a future worth living in' (Kostera, 2020, 7).

In this volume, I am not advocating for *all* research to be written differently, but for an appropriate space and place for such research to be presented, developed and published, so that these types of academic conversations are also given visibility, recognition and value. A recognized alternative system must be possible. In the next section of this book, I will explore practical approaches to researching differently, including methodology and methods.

3

Researching and writing differently

In this chapter, I now turn to writing differently in terms of the content of our researching and writing practice. Alison Pullen writes: 'I write to speak. Writing extends me, it reaches well beyond the confines of myself. At a very basic level, I would like my writing to speak from me, of me, when I am able to' (Pullen, 2018, 123). Indeed, writing extends us and helps us to reach beyond ourselves and the current status quo. This chapter explores key aspects of this by discussing some examples of Writing Differently and writing differently – as a movement and as an academic project. This is not intended as a review of the literature on writing differently, and as such the inclusion of materials is limited, subjective and by no means exhaustive. It is not aimed at defining the contours and boundaries of what writing differently means, but rather to provide a collection that hopes to inspire. I will first discuss some common aspects of writing differently, and then focus on a few themes that have been particularly relevant across research that is written differently. It should be noted that while the writing differently community, albeit growing, can still be considered as occupying a niche space, many scholars in the social sciences and humanities have provided great examples of theorizing and Writing Differently *ante litteram* and beyond labels, or work that is empathetic to the ethos and approaches to writing differently.

What is writing differently?

As I mentioned in the Introduction, writing differently has become increasingly popular over the last decade, and the phrase has been used to refer to a process, a perspective, an ethos, a methodology, a type of scholarship and a scholarly movement (in this latter acception the term has been capitalized here). The term 'differently' implies a comparison with something, and in this book is used to highlight ways of being, thinking, reading, writing and researching in academia that go against or in parallel to more mainstream and traditional ways of inhabiting research and academic work. My perspective stems from management and organization studies, but it can apply or be articulated across a variety of fields of inquiry where there is a dominant notion of what academic work and writing should look like that marginalizes different or dissenting voices.

As such, researching and writing differently can be 'done' in many ways and can be actualized through different practices and outputs. One of the key points to bear in mind from a feminist perspective is that all ways of interpreting writing differently from an inclusive standpoint and a care-oriented approach are valid. While some examples of writing differently may be more known or shared, all voices and experiences are equally valued regardless of hierarchy, location and resonance.

> Writing. Writing against. Writing for.
> Together, in part, with difference.
> Collaborative. Desire for change.
> Disrupting mainstream ideologies and practices.
> Resistance. Activism. Against neoliberalism.
> Feminism in its multiplicity.
> Fragmented. Moving forward. Rupture.
> Writing for social change. Writing for life.
> (Amrouche et al, 2019, 881)

This text above is the entire abstract of an article written in 2019 by 'Charlotte Amrouche, Jhilmil Breckenridge, Deborah N. Brewis, Olimpia Burchiellaro, Malte Breiding Hansen, Christina Hee Pedersen, Mie Plotnikof, Alison Pullen plus each of the other participants of the writing group' (2019, 881). The abstract itself, its content and the description of the authorial team are to me a perfect illustration of what it means to write differently in management and organization studies. This example of writing differently is provided – and provides a strong statement – even before the start of the main text of the article.

It is important to take some time to consider this 'before' aspect of writing differently, as well as other research processes that may be considered ancillary albeit necessary in the writing process, without focusing exclusively on the written output. This can be done in terms of reflecting on how we go about relating to other authors, the resources we use, the materials we read and the aspects we decide not to focus on. In a paper that is a great example of writing differently, Jenny Helin, Nina Kivinen and Alison Pullen (2021) advocate the use of patient writing:

> Reflecting on how knowledge is produced and written, being patient enables relational work [...] based on trust and care between us, and with the community in mind. This is writing, which is often written repeatedly, not to get 'right' for the reader, but to ensure that the writers are connected to the text. Writing patiently encourages reflection with words, intimacy, and care beyond transactional economies. The potential of writing beyond rigid hierarchies that divide. Being patient prevents impulsive relationships, quick judgements, and the inevitable violence that pursues whether through collectively writing with others

or through the review and editorial processes. Critical engaged dialogue in *ephemera* offers a space for patient reading and writing, and as Lena Olaison reminded us in her editorial letter *ephemera* helps 'shape a "world in-between"' the theory and politics of organization studies, where writing can evade norms between classification, hierarchy and conformity to standards.

Writing patiently, or indeed learning to write with patience, prevents the epistemic violence between the knower and the known, the rational and emotional, the disembodied and embodied. In this way, patience ruptures systems that lack patience, it teaches us to breathe, and it teaches us of the importance of writing which breaths. Waiting to write, and when the time comes writing with patience in mind, embodies a care ethics that is relational, contextualized, embodied, and realized through practices. Such care ethics is political and destabilises intersecting hierarchies of power and privilege.

Before writing differently, it is important that we *think* differently about our research, *read* differently, slowly, listening differently, from the body (Cixous, 1993), in dialogic exchange with the text(s), with emotions, as a sensuous and aesthetic process (Bolous Walker, 2017). Bernadette Loacker (2021) highlights how thinking differently is entangled with writing, organizing and producing differently. Situated within the journal *ephemera*, her reflections show the importance of spaces that are critical, challenging of assumptions regarding knowledge, practice and the status quo. Being open to explorations that go beyond the familiar, these spaces include but do not contain, thus welcoming multi-perspectivity and interdisciplinarity. To me, writing differently opens up conversations where learning is seen as a dialogic conversation engaged with artistic, creative and embodied knowledge; in contrast, traditional academic writing in my field seems like a conversation punctuated by assertions (for example: I found a gap. I contribute. I know the literature. I have enough data. I found some interesting points. I am expanding the theoretical framework. And so on).

Writing differently is often premised on some key features in terms of content that pivot around the exploration of neglected topics; the active listening to silenced voices (inner as well external ones) and the body; and the production of scholarship that is illuminating the margins and giving centre stage to different approaches, methods, epistemologies, groups and texts. While this has been espoused by some niche or smaller journals and publishers, there still seems to be reticence or outright rejection in top-level mainstream journals in management and organization studies. Some exceptions exist (for example *Gender, Work and Organization*; *Management Learning*; *Organization*; *ephemera;* and *Culture and Organization*), which are also a good first point of call for finding and reading work written differently. I recognize that writing differently can be considered as a risk, in its 'amalgamate[d] knowledge with non-knowing within the semantic horizon of probability' (Beck, 2007 cited in Bauman, 2012). However, the increasing frequency of papers that are written differently also offers novel spaces and opportunities for engaging in this type of researching and writing.

Writing differently in terms of content and form that stems away from the traditional norms has thus far been articulated politically, epistemologically and ethically in a number of ways, some of which are discussed here in more detail. For instance, it has been explored as dirty writing (Pullen and Rhodes, 2008), feminine writing (Sayers and Jones, 2015), writing as labiaplasty (Pullen, 2018), and writing as love (Vachhani, 2015; Kiriakos and Tienari, 2018). Writing differently often illuminates affective ruptures, eliciting involvement from the reader through words exuding experience, embodiment, emotion, resistance. Words pushing through the gates of normative academic writing. The abstract for this article is powerful, it is eight words long, and it is written differently: 'Woman. Active. Passive. Erased, in writing and thought'(Pullen, 2018). In her article 'Writing with the bitches', published by the journal *Organization*, Astrid Huopalainen (2020) offers an example of writing differently and reflects on its disruptive power in her chapter:

Beginning with bitches

Bitch [/bɪtʃ/]
[a female dog, wolf, fox, or otter]
[A spiteful or unpleasant woman]
Bitch, a common means of misogyny, humiliation, and denigration,
no desired subject position in organisational life.
Female forms across species, genders, races
typically stereotyped, written out, or locked into structures
    of othering.
Complaint. Critique. *Disruption.*
Who is the subject?
Whose bodies or writings are currently heard?
Power and politics, intersecting.
Experimental writing? Boundary-crossing?
Moving away from the hu-*man author*-ity
to sense, feel, and seek to express
the nuances of the *more-than-human* world
differently.
Paying close attention to the animal other,
learning how to respectfully meet – on more equal terms.
How can I change from our meeting?

Writing and thinking *with* nonhuman animals
for inclusion and multiplicity,
critique and transformation.
Writing *humanimal* relatedness into organisational scholarship.
(Huopalainen, 2020, 2, emphasis in original)

Positioning her feminist dog-writing as a form of *écriture féminine* (see, for instance, work by Cixous, 1976; Dallery, 1989; Vachhani, 2019), embedded with political, performative and material aims, she continues on to ask:

As a daily and almost taken-for-granted practice, our academic writing continuously deserves to be 'explored, investigated, and questioned' (Cloutier, 2016: 69). Could we, organisational researchers, then, write to critique and disrupt the seemingly rigid norms around 'standard' hu-*man*-centred academic writing – the kind of disembodied, distant, sterile and cleaned-up writing that conforms to a patriarchal discourse (Ahonen et al, 2020; Höpfl, 2000), upholds binaries, and firmly supports human superiority over other living beings in the world (for a critique, see Benozzo et al, 2013; Fotaki and Harding, 2018; McMurray and Pullen, 2020)? (Huopalainen, 2020, 2, emphasis in original)

Another fundamental issue related to this type of inquiry is to understand writing differently not just as a mode of writing or expression, but as an epistemological stance and a community of belonging (see more on this in Part III of this book) where academics can come together to discuss, research and share their scholarly work. For instance, a writing workshop held in 2018 at Copenhagen Business School generated the text mentioned by Amrouche and colleagues (2019). Further, writing differently enables scholars to share worries, lives, emotions, inequalities, joys and hopes through academic text. In their beautifully edited book on Writing Differently, Alison Pullen, Jenny Helin, and Nancy Harding (2020) speak of Writing Differently as a 'movement'. Ericsson and Kostera (2020) identify it as a 'wave'. Over the past few years, I have been able to perceive its growth almost sensorially through the increasing number of voices and affective interactions of scholars joining this community from all over the world. The exposure to others through our work and collegiate interactions has made a significant difference in how I situate myself and understand myself in my professional context. In a chapter on writing autoethnographically (Boncori, 2020b) I discuss how, when writing text stemming from the self, some of the vulnerability comes from the exposure of our personal narratives, but also from the fact that, once published, we no longer own the text. Writing differently can bring strong critique and challenges from mainstream researchers, but the growing community of scholars whose work is part of or in tune with writing differently can provide a supportive and formative environment for academic growth, fostering experimentation and pushing the limits of academic praxis. Taken more broadly, this point can be considered as a positive key feature of writing differently in its relational and dialogic nature.

All academic writing is relational, as writers connect themselves not only to co-authors and readers, but also to those whose work they build on, the resources they engage with, the reviewers and editors who help the development of a manuscript. This highlights the importance of thinking not only of *writing* differently, but of *researching* differently to stress the need to reflexively engage with the various taken-for-granted aspects of academic work. These processes involve choices, ethical stances and value-driven decision-making. Indeed, like Cixous (1993), I would argue that we never 'own' academic text – we may own the creation of the sequencing of the words we write, and the copyright to its reproduction, but the text is never solely of the authors. This is because when we write we enter in dialogue with the other sources, texts, theories and researchers that we construct our work around. We choose whom to enter in dialogue with in our bibliographies, and how we inscribe them in the body of our text; how much relevance and visibility we give to their persona or work. We also write for a particular journal, and so craft our manuscript for a specific audience, including the editors and reviewers who influence and often shape the way our text is (re)produced. We may have co-authors and colleagues who give us feedback on an early draft; we then share our work with those who read it and interpret it after publication. As such, all academic writing – and particularly examples of writing differently that make some or all of those steps consciously open, dialogic and relational – can be approached through a lens of shared ownership, which also questions the established commercialization of authorial teams, rules and conveniences. This fluidity and the relational character of research make it vulnerable to (mis)understandings, (mis)interpretation, (mis)use, and (mis)appropriation. In some countries, researchers get paid a bonus to publish single-authored papers rather than co-authored one – what is the intrinsic academic value of this? Why is collaborative work not valued more than, or at least equal to, individual work? Is it all down to rankings, funding, citation indexes and remuneration? Is this still hooked on the ideal figure of the lone academic who is the source of knowledge and genius? This type of approach has given rise to a number of power struggles, nepotism and hierarchies around authorship: for example, disagreements around the order of authors in a paper, as the first one in line is more visible and more important; and the formation of authorial 'teams' that involve the inclusion of people who had nothing to do with the paper as a returned favour for the same treatment on another paper. These practices are all serving the gods of neoliberal academic metrics that privilege the fast production of publication, the accumulation of outputs, the commercialization of research, and the marketing of researchers' profiles rather than the meaningful development of scholarship, genuine collaborations and ethical authorial processes.

However, albeit slowly, processes and ways to work with each other have to some extent changed over the past years. Researching and writing differently have influenced the way scholars work together and relate to one another. Twenty years ago, publishing an article in a top journal in the field of management and organization studies with more than ten authors would have been very rare. Even less so if that authorial team was to include doctoral students and early-career researchers. Today, the space for such research is still rather limited, but possible in journals like *Gender, Work and Organization* (see, for instance, the following two papers: Pasi Ahonen, Annika Blomberg, Katherine Doerr, Katja Einola, Anna Elkina, Grace Gao, Jennifer Hambleton, Jenny Helin, Astrid Huopalainen, Bjørn Friis Johannsen, Janet Johansson, Pauliina Jääskeläinen, Anna-Liisa Kaasila-Pakanen, Nina Kivinen, Emmanouela Mandalaki, Susan Meriläinen, Alison Pullen, Tarja Salmela, Suvi Satama, Janne Tienari, Alice Wickström, and Ling Eleanor Zhang, 2020; Mie Plotnikof, Pia Bramming, Layla Branicki, Lærke Højgaard Christiansen, Kelly Henley, Nina Kivinen, João Paulo Resende de Lima, Monika Kostera, Emmanouela Mandalaki, Saoirse O'Shea, Banu Özkazanç-Pan, Alison Pullen, Jim Stewart, Sierk Ybema, and Noortje van Amsterdam, 2020). Practices around authorial teams and the way these are cited are political in nature. We are so used to the silencing of writers through formatting elisions and textual conventions, that even the two examples included in this text with a full list of the authors' names seem disruptive and distracting. However, reading and writing can be reframed in a way that does not favour the interest of one author to the disadvantage of others. Writing differently and collaboratively can be designed and planned in a different way that is respectful, mindful and embracing of the interconnectedness of our work with others and their work. This is in itself a form of resistance (see for instance Ahonen et al, 2020; Abdellatif et al, 2021).

The rhythm of reading and writing is also another overlooked aspect to consider when writing differently. Devi Vijay, Shalini Gupta and Pavni Kaushiva (2020) show how, by committing to a deep reading of literary text, readers can access hidden and taken-for-granted practices of engagement. By slowing down (both literally and metaphorically), we can look, really focus our gaze and senses, and listen to what is usually perceived as noise at the margins of the mainstream fanfare of stellar publications, limelight and mainstream thought. The beginning of the path in writing differently is in reading, critical engagement and academic dialogue that focus on 'listening' to work presented or written differently. Reading differently also means curating one's ability to perceive otherness and value difference. Boulous Walker's (2017) book *Slow Philosophy: Reading against the Institution* considers different reading practices, stressing how reading 'can help to establish an ethical relation of openness with the otherness, ambiguity and strangeness of the text, and how this openness to intensity and intimacy can be transformative' and this way of reading 'allows the world (and the book) to return to us differently' (2017, xv–xvi). Therefore, reading differently is also a way to link the individual perception and affect to social ones, transporting meanings through various academic and non-academic media. Writing and reading slowly in order to pursue meaningful knowledge and processes of collaborative development has become, bizarrely, a form of resistance against the widespread 'smart ways of playing the academic game' instead of being the norm. Writing that is innovative, experiential, experimental, risky and off the beaten track can take time. Or it may take very little time to write, but a long while to share. In a profession where the aim is supposed to be the advancement of knowledge, the creation of new theories or the furthering of our understandings through experience and evidence, the time dedicated to the numerous processes happening before, alongside and after writing seems to occupy increasingly less space. Therefore, researching and writing differently can also mean rethinking the way an authorial team works together, thus rejecting the speed and utilitarian aspects of the neoliberal academic context, by focusing on the journey of writing as much as the task and outcomes.

One way of slowing down and (re)focussing our work is to create safe or at least caring spaces and places to foster reflection and engagement with writing differently. These spaces can be created through personal relationships and collaborations, but also more visibly through different ways of inhabiting positions of leadership in journals and publishing houses. In August 2020, a special issue of *Gender, Work and Organization* was published under the newly created 'Feminist Frontiers' section. This special issue was initially focused on the experience of working and living through a pandemic outbreak from a feminist perspective. The two editors, Banu Ozkazanc-Pan and Alison Pullen, opened up a space for conversations that would give visibility to scholars (in a top international journal) who wanted to tell their stories of struggle, alienation and difference. My article, entitled 'The Neverending Shift' (Boncori, 2020a) – written in the first few weeks of the first COVID-19 lockdown in the UK (March 2020) – became the first publication in response to this call. The open-ended nature of the call for papers and the flexibility in the style and tone of the articles is a great example of how journals and editors can facilitate writing differently, not only because of the specific topics investigated and the type of writing it generated, but also because of conscious editorial choices. These choices were articulated across many levels in this particular case. For example, the call is open-ended, so writers do not have the pressure of having to meet a deadline, as we know that during lockdown women researchers' productivity was particularly affected in comparison to their male counterparts due to competing responsibilities of care and home. Further, the flexibility in terms of style, tone and type of writing allowed the sharing of experiences that would not normally fit into an academic article, to reach others across the globe who may have been experiencing something similar in those unprecedented times of a global pandemic outbreak. An avalanche of submissions was received in the first few months, providing an archive of a kaleidoscope of national contexts, private environments, sociocultural habits and stories. This gave visibility to the invisible or silenced work done by women, joined together through a community of writing and belonging. This work matters: it challenges patriarchal norms, critiquing dynamics of power, exposing inequalities and violence; it provides opportunities for scholars (and in particular early-career scholars) in casting a non-restrictive net of connections to illuminate experiences and advocate social change; it allows experimentation through form and method, empirically and theoretically; it builds embodied and affective relationships between readers and writers, as well as reviewers. Numerous exemplars of academic text written differently can also be found, for example, in the journal *ephemera*, an independent open-access journal centred around theory and politics in organization. In particular, two special issues – one focused on 'Feminism, activism, writing!' edited by Sine Nørholm Just, Sara Louise Muhr and Annette Risberg (2018) and one dedicated to its twentieth anniversary by the *ephemera* collective (2021) – host various articles that can provide an illustration of different ways of researching and writing.

The feminist perspectives and values behind researching differently in its broader articulation can help us illuminate more spaces and experiences, from both theoretical and empirical perspectives. As a member of the Humanistic Management Network, I believe in the importance of managing and organizing through feminist values of empowerment, sharing, and care inter alia. Placing the human at the centre of organizational, managerial and leadership practices entails the valuing of people above organizational and financial outputs, with a focus on valuing the whole humanness. This means that people are appreciated for the entirety of their being, without one aspect (see rationality, productivity and masculine ways of being) being considered as more valuable or deserving of others (see emotions, embodiment and feminine ways of being). As such, it is important that all aspects of experience are investigated in research, respected, and equally regarded in both our personal and professional lives. Writing differently then can also be seen as a way of translating humanistic management principles and feminist values into research practice, by inscribing experience onto theory, breathing emotions across our scripts, and making space for our bodies to collapse on paper within our words. Writing differently stems from the human body, mind and emotions in their many articulations; it can unfold creases of content that are joyous as much as tragic; it can focus on the mundane or the extraordinary; it flies high or explores 'the lowest and the deepest' ('[t]he writers I love are *descenders*, explorers of the lowest and the deepest' (Cixous, 1993, 5, emphasis in original).

Intersectional approaches

Intersectional starting points are intrinsic to writing differently, and so carving out a specific section on this topic seems redundant and a bit of a pointless tautology, but I hope it is useful for those who have not encountered this concept and framework before. Intersectionality is a key concept for feminist knowledge production rooted in critical race theory and sociopolitical activism. It is political as it is concerned with how interlocking systems and structures of power and oppression are conceived and implemented. In her blog, launched in 2020, Helena Liu provides an accessible, thorough and stimulating exploration of intersectionality and its link to Feminism, highlighting how the term can be used to refer to different things: 'A scholarly theory; An advanced level of wokeness; Black women; Anyone who is "multiply marginalized"; A critique of white feminists and white feminism'. Indeed, this collection of foci related to intersectionality highlights its complexity. It should be noted that, although intersectionality is often considered at the individual identity level, it is also an analytic framework which allows a multifaceted investigation of the intersections of political, sociocultural and economic structures that impact both individual and collective experiences. The connection between writing differently, intersectionality and Feminism is also explored in the edited collection by Nina Lykke (2014). Highlighting intersectionality as a critical methodology, the book offers different perspectives exploring writing that investigates spaces between 'monolithic identity markers' like gender, race, class, nationality, sexual orientation and so on.

Being a multifaceted concept, intersectionality can be considered in different contexts and from different perspectives. The roots and sentiment behind feminist intersectionality go back to the 1800s, although the term had yet to be coined. Anna Julia Cooper was one of the first authors to write an in-depth analysis of the specific situation and circumstances of Black women in the United States. Her book *A Voice from the South by a Black Woman of the South* published in 1892 – three decades after the 1865 13th Amendment to the US constitution focused on the abolition of slavery – is a collection of essays and speeches recognized as a seminal contribution to Black feminist thought highlighting the racialization and sexualization of gender, considering the interlocking oppression across systems of race, gender and class. And so intersectional Feminism is about acknowledging, identifying and challenging individual, collective and systemic nodes of privilege and oppression. This can be done intellectually and as a form of activism in academia as well as more broadly in society. Early definitions of intersectionality and scholarly work in the legal field by Kimberlé Crenshaw (1989, 1991) have been adopted and adapted across disciplines. Here, intersectionality can be treated as a critical framework to understand the human experience through the lens of power and inequality, looking at how different identities are articulated and treated in different contexts for all social actors. It is also a way to understand oppression and privilege, and ways in which resistance to inequality can be activated through scholarship that understands and celebrates difference. As highlighted by Sara Ahmed (2006b, 2012), intersectionality helps to expose the loci of inequality and the spaces within dominant frames which obscure institutional violence. Alison Jaggar (2015) offers an overview of feminist interdisciplinary approaches, considering not only concepts and theory, but also methodological reflections and methods.

Gender and race, intertwined with class, have been prime aspects of inquiry in intersectional research. In her 1991 essay, 'Mapping the margins' (Crenshaw, 1991), Crenshaw considers political intersectionality in terms of both oppression and resistance, describing the many ways Black women resist their experience of systemic marginalization in civic and political spheres. Further, she critiques the narrowness of single-axis Feminism and civil-rights activism:

> among the most troubling political consequences of the failure of antiracist and feminist discourses to address the intersections of race and gender is the fact that, to the extent they can forward the interest of 'people of color' and 'women,' respectively, one analysis often implicitly denies the validity of the other'. (Crenshaw, 1991, 1252)

As such, resistance to multiple dimensions of marginalization and inequality can be seen as a feminist project in its discursive and collective practice. Collins (1990) provided an early conceptualization of 'the matrix of domination' (also referred to as 'interlocking systems of oppression' by the Combahee River Collective) as a multidimensional space in which intersectional oppressions are organized. Here, people at different intersections can experience varying degrees of privilege and oppression. Recognition of these dynamics can also produce intersectional coalitions (Cole, 2008; Cole and Luna, 2010) which develop and sustain solidarity through social movements that address individual needs and structural processes. These become an intersectional feminist strategy by creating sociopolitical allegiances across differences that do not require sameness (see, for instance, the reproductive rights movement against reproductive oppression).

In recent years, scholars in management and organization studies have published a number of studies stemming from an intersectional approach. We can consider this as linked to writing differently in its purpose to expose complexities in inequality that avoid masking or homologizing experiences within strict and unrelated categories. The examples included here are by no means exhaustive. It is important to acknowledge that intersectionality is not merely additive, and so it is not just about the adding up of different identities that make fewer intersections less oppressive and more numerous ones more marginalizing. Rather, a key feminist step is developed through relating back intersections of oppression to wider interlocking systems (or matrices) of power, and questioning them at the individual and collective level. There is a growing volume of scholarship in management and organization studies which stems from intersectional approaches. For example, work by Martyna Śliwa and Marjana Johansson (2014, 2015) looking at gender and foreignness, and also by Kate Sang and colleagues on migration (see Sang, Al-Dajani, and Özbilgin, 2013). Together with Anke Strauß, in 2019 I wrote a paper on the experience of academics at the intersection of gender and foreignness. We interviewed 23 women academics at different career stages and found that this particular intersection created what we termed the positionality of the *double-stranger* as someone who is both included and excluded from the workplace, a person who belongs and does not belong at the same time to the system, the professional context and the institution. We considered issues around academic mobility, performance and inclusion in different geographical contexts. Drawing from the notion of the double-stranger within an intersectional framework, we found that not all categories of difference are the same in terms of impact on the individual and in their treatment in the workplace. Indeed, different dynamics and temporary hierarchies emerged between different categories of disadvantage (here gender and foreignness), which are not simply additive and may develop over time. In this very specific case, estrangement on the basis of gender remained a rather constant category of marginalization over women's careers, while the impact of foreignness changed over time and seemed to diminish after an initial adjustment period to a new sociocultural context. Marginalization is not just added layer upon layer, but it is marked by different intensity and also different temporalities. So, in the case of our participants, being a woman in the academic context proved to be a continuous source of discrimination, which seemed to intensify at different times of the work/life continuum – for example, when having children or other caring responsibilities; when requesting flexible working; when applying for promotion and so on. However, foreignness, understood in terms of being new to a cultural and professional environment, was more intense at the start of one's academic career or at the start of new jobs in different countries and institutions, but then tended to decrease. As such 'the position of the double-stranger is reinforced through the varying rhythms through which categories of difference are articulated. This creates a permanent, yet oscillating, state of the double-stranger encapsulated within cycles of belonging and non-belonging' (Stauß and Boncori, 2020, 13).

Understanding the dynamics behind intersectional identities and experiences which are the target of inequality and oppression is key to the development of a critical approach in the crafting of academic theory, as well as in terms of the practical implications of research. Taking this a step further, intersectionality can also be seen as an approach to methods of inquiry, and as posed by Rosenthal (2016) in the case of psychology, which can become an opportunity to promote social justice and equity. As such, I see intersectional perspectives as inherently feminist in nature, and at the heart of writing differently.

However, criticisms have been raised that the increased popularity of this concept or framework has created a dilution of its sociopolitical potential, a concern long advanced by Black feminists and scholars of colour who have highlighted the appropriation and white-washing of intersectionality across disciplines (see for instance Dhamoon, 2011; Alexander-Floyd, 2012). Salskov (2020) provides an interesting critique of intersectionality, encouraging scholars to reflect on the possible reinforcement of whiteness (and privilege more generally, I would suggest) through the use of this framework. Indeed, Collins (2000) highlights how interdisciplinary literature is the foundation of interdisciplinarity as a form of critical social theory, which was developed by Black feminist and women of colour scholar-activists. Beyond the logic of structural equation models or cluster analyses, Collins's matrix formation imagines social worlds and arenas that are radically contextual and dynamic even as social forces also retain consistency across space and time. The 'adaptability' of this theory and approach to research (Davis, 2008) has become the reason why, in its popularity, intersectionality has been eroding and erasing its critical race and activist roots. Hancock (2015) and Grzanka (2019) have traced the history, uses and abuses of intersectionality, which has also been labelled as being an empty academic trend or a 'buzzword' (Grzanka, 2020).

However, I would argue that the way intersectionality is used, theorized and analysed can be valuable and meaningful in understanding individual, collective and systemic dynamics. This, done through the use of content, forms and methods of writing differently, can become a powerful source of knowledge and understanding. For instance, in the field of psychology, Dill and Kohlman (2012) highlighted how intersectionality can be investigated in depth and as a transformative approach by considering individual issues in connection with systems-level analysis and social advocacy, or in a 'weak' manner by simply looking at multiple and additive categories of difference or multiple identities. Grzanka (2019) stresses the potential of this approach and adds: 'intersectionality's transformative potentials are a license to experiment with new approaches to psychotherapy training and practice that take a radical approach to human cultural diversity that rejects the easy buzzwords of "diversity," "inclusion," and "intersecting identities" and embraces the challenging discourse of power, inequality, and justice' (Grzanka, 2020, 245).

In the context of Writing Differently, scholars often write to transform words into agency and action (Lorde, 1984b) and an intersectional approach can help acknowledge multiple layers of social difference and power. Caroline Rodrigues Silva (2021, 1) eloquently speaks of 'Escrevivência', described in her article abstract as follows:

> I transpose the act of writing in order to survive (… and breathe). A piece of writing, writing that is laden with love, pain, daily experiences and experiments. "Escrevivência" as writing from the experience of a Black Brazilian woman – sensibilities happen with/in my body in the encounter with the structures of the world. Subversive, insubordinate, and disobedient to the injustices of the world. This work believes that academia and research are potent in contributing to this struggle together with a subversive praxis and the strength of everyday micro-practices. Take a breath we keep surviving.

She explains that due to the privileged space usually occupied by elites through writing, writing itself is for a Black woman an act of insubordination, which as such can disrupt imperialist academic praxis, and contest patriarchal, racist and disembodied understanding of academia (Bell et al, 2019). Writing differently and intersectionally is also about resisting 'the cut' of the body in and of the text (Pullen, 2018), and about acknowledging and including difference across race, ethnicity, class, ability and other categories of difference. As Silva puts it (2021, 7), these stories echo around the world, in specific contexts that still reverberate and resonate with others in a kind of déjà vu, 'because oppression and insubordination have certain equivalences around the world'.

Interdisciplinary approaches

Writing against the mainstream tide then can be espoused per se as a political act that disrupts conventions. As Sarah Richardson suggests (1995), writing research is a 'dynamic creative process' that should not be 'homogenized in the voice of "science"' (Richardson, 1995, 517). Although 'writing differently is scary' (Boncori and Smith, 2019), because it exposes feminine traits and perspectives that tend to be rejected by dominant masculine discrimination at the individual and systemic level, it can be a powerful way of conducting and communicating research. Every piece of work written differently, including this book, contributes to the challenging of traditional ways of writing and publishing which are 'haunted by the spectre of scientific discourse shoehorned into dry genres and bullied by audit regimes that try to wring out the passion and romance of thought' (Rhodes, 2015, 290). Each contribution fosters an even stronger momentum, greater reach, and higher visibility for writing differently. Like intersectionality, interdisciplinarity (for example, reading, writing and researching across fields of study that have been formally divided into different subject areas to draw from different theories and methods that can enrich our work) also allows us to come into dialogue with difference, and better capture the different perspectives that contribute to the experience of people. Interestingly, the demarcation between disciplines is also rather fluid as different countries and academic traditions combine or associate academic fields in different ways.

I am a firm believer that *organizing* (see Law, 1994) – rather than *organizations* – is the meso-level link between society and the systemic on the one hand, and the individual experience on the other. This can be investigated from many different schools of thought and disciplinary perspectives, thus enriching the theorizing and the understanding of our field. Organizing is rooted in values that shape a shared sense of direction, and is dependent on meaning-making and communication at the individual and group level. The investigation and understanding of this meso level is deeply influenced and can benefit from interdisciplinarity. So, for instance, the work of Foucault (philosopher, historian, social theorist, and literary critic) on power (1980) as knowledge enacted in the everyday techniques and instruments of the workplace is an important source in the analysis of dynamics and regimes of oppressions in organizations. Foucauldian perspectives are particularly interesting in considering power 'at its extremities, in its ultimate destinations, with those points where it becomes capillary [...] in its more regional and local forms and institutions' (Foucault, 1980, 96), and as a tool employed in organizing people's time, tasks and performance. While this type of link between philosophy and management and organization studies is well explored and has been espoused in many types of qualitative and quantitative studies, other less masculine approaches (for example, some stemming from arts-based methods) are still considered experimental.

Some subjects of inquiry may be well established in some social sciences and humanities, but still lagging behind in specific fields. For example, while studying issues around sexual orientation, gender and the experience of transgender and gender non-conforming people (Boncori, 2017a; Lawley and Boncori, 2017; Boncori, Sicca and Bizjak, 2019), it became apparent that research in management and organization studies was very underdeveloped compared to other disciplines such as sociology, psychology and anthropology (with notable exceptions like Thanem's transgender work and O'Shea's work on transgender and gender non-conforming people). By espousing an interdisciplinary approach to research, scholars can enrich mainstream understandings in their field of inquiry. For example, the work of Judith Butler (1990, 1993, 2004) is instrumental in exploring the performativity of gender, and investigating how the heteronormative binary conceptualization of gender and sexuality espoused by most Western societies has placed the burden of non-conformity on individuals. These sociological perspectives can support the development of work on identity negotiations, the development of gender roles and belonging, which are also often analysed in dialogue with psychological literatures. Psychology and psychoanalytic studies deal with the individual and the conscious or unconscious mental processes that guide our behaviour. These also consider the importance of emotions and dreaming, and how people's individual experiences are affected by their inner worlds. Emotions – explored below in more detail – are a fundamental part of understanding and supporting people in the workplace. These nuanced and open approaches to academic investigation are central to a critical perspective in researching and writing differently which aims at pushing the boundaries of what is considered 'normal' or 'good' research in a field. Due to the relative scarcity of this work in mainstream management and organization studies, scholarship focused on the relevant individual and collective experiences that is informed by a plurality of disciplines can be considered an example of writing differently about marginalized perspectives in the workplace.

In addition to theory, methodology (which I will discuss in the next Part) can often become another bridge across disciplines. For example, Sandra L. Faulkner combines autoethnography, poetry and the use of images to argue for the use of poetic inquiry as a feminist methodology in women's, gender and sexuality studies (2018). Her work, a great example of writing differently, highlights the cross-contamination and blurring across fields of inquiry:

> I *write* poetry because I am a bad (BAD!) social scientist. [...] I study personal relationships; I am most interested in what relationships feel like and sound like and smell like more than how they function as some kind of analytic variable to be deconstructed. I believe in poetic truth(s) more than social science Truth punctuated with a capital T. [...] What I understand is that one can write poetry as social science. What I believe in is the value of poetry *as* relationship research. (Faulkner 2017: 148)

> Poetry can help us see our relationships bleeding out, hemorrhaging from the invisible inside, spilling outside the neat axioms of theory. Poetry is theory. Poetry can have us experience the social structures and ruptures in situ as we read, as we listen, as we hold our breath

waiting for the next line. Poetry is bandage and salve. Poetry lets me goodwill my secure cloak of citations, argue in verse that there is space for critical work and personal experience in the study of close relationships. (Faulkner 2017, 149)

Narrative inquiry and arts-based methods lend themselves to researching differently and allow scholars to explore some of the themes outlined in this book that are often part of texts written differently.

Exploring key themes in writing differently

Time and movement

Another aspect of writing differently that can be reflected on before, during and after the creation of an output, rather than in the content of research itself, is the dynamic between time and movement. Inextricably bound with emotions and embodiment, time and movement can be useful to reflect on when writing differently. Time in relation to publication is often thought of in terms of how long it takes to get a paper published from the time of submission, or within each round of reviews. However, we can open up the time considerations to delve deeper into our approach to writing. Jenny Helin (2020) insightfully encourages us to 'write vertically' and reflect on the time of our writing. Writing differently is linked to movement and temporality. The latter stems from the fact that 'to write is to move and being moved in time' (Helin, 2020, 2). This can be considered horizontally – linear storytelling, chronological order of events, a flow moving from past to present – but also in more fluid ways; for example, through memory, thought and recognition.

Time is also linked to growth and development in research, so I have been considering the reinterrogation of data used in previous studies and the questioning of my 'old' analysis – would the academic I am today interpret the data in a similar way, or would the knowledge and experience I have accumulated since that study allow me to generate new insights and shed new light onto previous studies? Based on today's focus on producing 'on-trend' scholarship, collecting and analysing up to date data and the production of new research contributions, I am not sure if this practice would be widely accepted for publication in management and organization studies. And yet, when we review literature and cite studies in our writing, we tend to jump through time in non-linear ways – both in terms of years captured next to in-text citations, decades identified with certain research strands or developments, but also possibly in terms of stages of intellectual development of the authors. So it is useful to consider the cycles and juxtapositions of times within our research and publications, not only in terms of the currency of data or the research life cycle, but also the more hidden dynamics of time within those research practices.

There is also an unspoken rhythm and time within a research contribution. Those who are versed in acting and performative methods know how important timing is during the delivery of a monologue, a line or a silence. In terms of the written text, punctuation and spacing can become a metronome, a way of accenting particular words in the reader's mind, deepen the pauses, let the text expand and breathe to leave room for affective responses. Within writing differently texts, this is particularly visible in poetry or autoethnographic narratives. The interdisciplinary journal *Qualitative Inquiry* (QI) provides a variety of articles that hold a specific cadence and rhythm. For example, Esther Ohito and Tiffany Nyachae (2019) use poetry to understand the experience of Black girls and women from a critical feminist perspective. Here is an extract of their paper (2019, 846) which exemplifies the time and space of their narrative:

Be a Bad Black Girl

Be (un)desirable
Be single
    or married
    to him
    or her
    or them
Be sexual
    with her
    with her or him
    with her and him
    with them
Be free
Eat what you want
Exercise—or don't
Take a break
    free
    from expectations
Accept who you are.

The concepts of time and movement are also poignant in terms of academic writing if we consider the timeliness of the written word, time boundaries for the production of written words, the lack of time to write across all the different types of tasks in today's academic work, and the pace of publication that has become an increasingly stringent focus on outputs in the academic world. In today's neoliberal academia, one has to produce outputs, fulfil key performance indicators (KPI), achieve results, increase scores and finalize publications, which is what academic value is judged against. Time and 'progress' are conceptualized in a Western manner as consequential and linear. We need the outputs to justify the time we have invested in the process, even though outputs cannot exist without the processes that create them, while processes exist even without outputs. Writing Differently is as much (if not more) about the process of researching as it is about its outputs. In this context, writing differently can be considered as an epistemological breakage. Rather than focusing on single points of arrival in the charted map of one's career and daily professional activities, through writing differently we can also explore, understand and delve into the processes that are connecting the dots – questioning their development, surfacing issues, exploring how one led to the other and the dynamics behind the fluidities of time and movement. As such, our learning is no longer limited to the 'unending succession of new beginnings moved more by a swift forgetting of the previously acquired knowledge than by an acquisition of new knowledge' (Bauman 2005, 313) that characterizes the educational sector in liquid modernity, but a more holistic connected process of learning and becoming. In the mad rush to get the outputs out, produce more and publish faster – often with less time and fewer resources – we run the risk of emptying our writing out of its meaning, and forgetting the importance of a thoughtful and meaningful process of thinking and writing. This contemporary academic context increases the risk that research and writing become 'a cognitive process [that] leads to harmonizing instead of problematizing, neutralizing instead of contextualizing, and generalizing instead of specifying' (Bränström Öhman, 2012, 34).

The disruption of a linear way of thinking about time, doing research and writing, can also be seen as a feminist project in its problematizing power. First of all, it questions the Western-centric approach to time and timekeeping, so different approaches that are open to cultural difference and to *not knowing* would be more in line with feminist approaches. Secondly, Freeman's work (2010) together with other studies on temporality and 'queer time' by Jack Halberstam (2011), Heather Love (2007), and José Esteban Muñoz (2009), contributes meaningfully to this discussion by exploring how interrogating activities and scenes in non-linear ways is a form of resistance against oppression that questions dominant accounts of time and history. This can be done by 'unstitching narratives' to consider 'nonsequential forms of time' (2010, xi). Writing differently is thus also linked to 'undoing', with memory work, the preservation of unwritten stories and experiences that have a feminist potential. When stories are not published due to inequality, the unwritten stories of our past deserve to be interwoven with our present.

Memory also has a special place in writing differently through time and movement. This is generating a growing body of literature on memory in management and organization studies (see, for instance, Johansson and

Jones, 2020). Heather Höpfl (2000) highlights how management strives for orderliness and control, and thus predilects a linear conception of time in an attempt to gain control over disorder and frayed experiences, which I believe can also be applied to the writing and researching in management and organization studies. Frequently hailed in negative terms as fallible, biased and something to control within masculine structures of rigour and accountability, the creative and affective potential of memory is often neglected. This is especially the case for embodied memory that is connected to the senses, igniting a narrative through a visual sequence or words, touch and so on. Masculine ideals of management promote order, linearity and tidiness, and 'looking good/professional' ways to approach organizations and the writing thereof. In contrast, Writing Differently is about embracing the creative chaos, the leaky embodiment and the emotional swirls in organizing. Writing differently is about movement: rejecting the linear, digging deep, unravelling the sensuous, understanding through imagination and metaphoric knowing. It embraces difference in movement: physical, bodily, imaginative, and virtual movement. It can also be about moving forward, moving across positionalities, and moving across different mobilities. It is movement in and out of the self, through different layers of consciousness and experience, transported by transformational fluidity; it is movement that advances emotional motions, movement of the limbs, and movement of affect. The engagement with this iterative movement of discovery, feeling and knowing fosters experimentation and knowledge creation that spills out of the traditional masculine management and organization studies box into new ways of researching, knowing and theorizing.

The idea of embodiment and movement of the body has been considered by numerous researchers in management and organization studies (see for example Biehl and Volkmann, 2019). We can also consider the notion of movement in relation to Writing Differently in terms of spaces, and as per Goffman's (1959) theatrical metaphors. If we think of academia as a theatre, we can see how the professional world can be considered a stage inhabited by academic actors who perform a script as part of their daily lives, like actors on stage. Some spaces encourage improvisation that builds on the actor's personality, talent, body and instincts; they use different lighting, costumes, scenes, and update the language. Other types of theatre remain more loyal to the classics, rigid in their interpretation of the original script or the norms dictating how it needs to be enacted. Some academic actors move in and out of different types of spaces, others choose space that feels more in line with their way of knowing and being in academia. Goffman (1959) proposes the contrasting images of the 'front stage' and the 'back stage' in various lived contexts, whereby the former is a public space of conformity in following a script, while the back stage is a private space sheltered from the public eye that allows more freedom and involves fewer normative requirements.

Where systems do not recognize and value difference, some actors – in this case, academics – have relegated the production of writing differently to the back stage, as the impact of a failed performance can be much more serious in one's social and professional life as compared to theatrical performances (Höpfl and Linstead, 1997). Writing differently within an academic context that values its contribution at all levels would allow a convergence of seemingly dichotomous aspects: a fluidity of movement between the back stage and the front stage, the private and the professional, the creative and the normative, knowledge and emotion.

More literally, we can also inscribe movement within the content and the format of a paper. For example, in their article entitled 'It takes two to tango: Theorizing inter-corporeality through nakedness and eros in researching and writing organizations', Emmanouela Mandalaki and Mar Pérezts (2020) set the 'writing differently' content and tone from the abstract, which reads:

> Dance with us, on the dance-floor and with words, as we reenact our individual and shared tango autoethnographic experiences to develop an understanding of field inter-corporeality as a phenomenological experience of nakedness empowered by the transformational potential of eros. We write as we dance to discuss how eroticizing through the other's presence our embodied nakedness, beyond sexual stereotypes, pushes us to meta-reflect on ourselves as organizational ethnographers and writers to reinvent our field and writing interactions as inter-corporeally relational and intersubjective. We problematize the sexual gaze that traditionally associates nakedness with shame and objectified vulnerability to stress the capacity of eroticizing our academic nakedness to enable free, embodied knowledge stripped of the traits of the dominant masculine academic order. In so doing, we join burgeoning autoethnographic and broader debates in the field of organization studies calling for the need to further unveil the embodied, erotic, and feminine aspects of organizational research and writing. Shall we dance?

The paper then also offers an autoethnographic account written by the two authors (see Chang, Ngunjiri and Hernandez, 2012, on collaborative or duo-autoethnography) that is formatted as if the text was pirouetting across the page, and interspersed with theorizing:

> Without names, phone numbers or obligations. All the poetry
> of the world contained in our abrazo. Violins bring our breath
> closer together. Then silence separates us. The dance floor
> reclaims its cathedral-like emptiness, waiting for us to come and
> re-inhabit it once the music starts again. I feel myself existing

not only for you but also with you. I don't know who you
are, or if we'll meet or dance again. But in that brief eternity,
we were one. What does this mean, for me, for us, for those
who danced with us that night? Then rationality kicks in: I
remember that I'm doing fieldwork.

Oh yes, academic rationality giving more importance to thinking
than to becoming. I felt perplexed: how was my body able to star in
this playful interplay between these vulnerable other selves searching
redemption in the fluidity of dancing?

I remember the feeling of being inhabited by a host, keeping so
much of my fieldwork data trapped within my skin, in the pit
of my stomach, in the fatigue of my legs, growing inside my
womb and not knowing whether the birth of this—thing,
ance, text?—would get the better of me.

The data lived in our bodies...
(Mandalaki and Pérezts, 2020, 4)

Embodiment

One of the ways in which writing differently is distancing itself from
patriarchal and disembodied ways of understanding organizations and
academic writing of organizations is through a focus on embodiment.
Anzaldúa (2015) highlights this close relationship between body, thought
and writing:

For me, writing is a gesture of the body, a gesture of creativity, a working
from the inside out. My feminism is grounded not on incorporeal
abstraction but on corporeal realities. The material body is center, and
central. The body is the ground of thought. (Anzaldúa, 2015)

Embodiment involves reflection both on experience and as experience,
through, with and despite the body. Writing is about movement, and
the body; how it moves literally and how it connects with the inner and
outer environment. As such, Writing Differently, against the grain of more
traditional ways of publishing and writing academic texts in one's field, can
feel like breathing through a challenging yoga stretch, bringing the somewhat
surprising pleasure of engaging with a meaningful and thoughtful practice
while cutting through a painful stage or inhospitable environment. To me,
writing differently also means writing through, with and despite our bodies,
using the body as a lens, mirror or text engaging the individual to consider

the social, political or cultural world. This creates a dialogue between the exterior and the interior, the singular and the plural, the physical and the conceptual.

Embodiment refers to how we understand, experience and make sense of the world through bodies (Merleau-Ponty, 1962). Perry and Medina (2015) provide an overview of different theories of embodiment, divided into naturalistic, semiotic, phenomenological, poststructuralist and affect theory, social theory and Feminism, posthumanist and Foucauldian theory. Two insightful books that explore the subject of embodiment in research are *Embodiment in Qualitative Research* by Laura Ellingson (2017) and *Embodied Research Methods* by Torkild Thanem and David Knights (2019). Ellingson's book is similar to this one in approach as it brings together the theory and practice of embodiment, and as such it can be particularly valuable to students and early-career researchers, or those who want to begin their conscious embodied research journey. Tracing the philosophical roots that created a divide between reason and feeling, rationality and embodiment, both volumes provide a range of examples of scholarship that focuses on embodiment and the body. Embodiment can be investigated both conceptually and in practice as it is at the same time protective and fragile, flexible, coloured, porous and sensorial. Bodies are relational in conception, loci of instinctual and sensorial knowledge. Bodies are gendered, racialized, interpreted, contested and discriminated against. Real bodies in organizations are set against a backdrop of the ideal worker, and the ideal academic, which is still white, male, able and cisgender (see Acker, 1990; Carrim and Nkomo, 2016; McCluney and Rabelo, 2019a, 2019b; O'Shea, 2019). Irigaray (1985, 46) positions the body as a field inscribed with intersecting forces which are material/concrete, as well as symbolic/non-physical forces (race, gender, sex, age and so on). This field of the body becomes the contested site of inequality, interacting and relating to the outside world through individuals, institutions and systems. This book argues for more embodied and affective writing, which I will explore methodologically in the next section.

Writing embodiment is also linked to what Rosalyn Diprose (2002) calls corporeal generosity:

> [Corporeal generosity] is, in a sense, writing in blood and love of that. Corporeal generosity is writing passionately in blood, writing in matter that defies the culturally informed habits of perception and judgement that would perpetuate injustice by shoring up body integrity, singular identity, and their distinction between inside and outside, culture and nature, self and other. (Diprose, 2002, 190)

This does not mean loving 'what is written *on* blood, or *about* blood, but *in* blood' (Diprose, 2002, 190, emphasis in original), being engaged with a type of scholarship that moves beyond the text and disembodied research, as 'generosity is a kind of life force, a passionate defiance of corporeal borders in response to being cut, touched, or wounded, and overflowing that is neither simply active or passive'(Diprose, 2002, 190).

Over the past two decades, researchers in management and organization studies have turned their scholarly lens towards the more 'felt' aspects of organizations and organizing (see Styhre, 2013; Küpers, 2014; Pérezts et al 2015; Fotaki et al, 2017; Jørgensen and Holt, 2019). Therefore, an increasing number of researchers in this field have been progressively advocating the use of the body and the senses – writing with and through the body – to explore methodologically and epistemologically forms of sensorial knowing in organizations (Kostera, 2007; Strati, 2007c; Warren, 2008; Bell and King, 2010; Pink, 2009; Gherardi, 2019a; Thanem and Knights, 2019). There are numerous theoretical pieces and empirical ones focusing on embodied experiences in organizing and organizations – for instance, in terms of breastfeeding, menstruation, miscarriage, menopause experiences in the workplace (see, for example, van Amsterdam, 2015; Porschitz and Siler, 2017; Boncori and Smith, 2019; Steffan, 2020). And yet, in the practice of organizations and academia, work and professionalism are still encoded through masculine disembodied and non-affective criteria.

It is therefore important to foster spaces to illuminate embodied approaches for academics, students and professionals, where these experiences are discussed, appreciated and valued. This creates an acknowledgement and awareness of embodiment for doctoral students and early-career scholars, but also for those who will leave academia to enter other professional contexts. This rejection towards the body happens in many fields of inquiry, and is even more marked in the case of queer, disabled, non-white and marginalized bodies (Simmonds, 1999; Brown and Boardman, 2010; Ellingson, 2017). In my own professional practice, I have tried to create opportunities to shed light on embodiment by working with different audiences. For example, various aspects of embodiment were also discussed in interdisciplinary contributions within an inclusivity-focused book series, drawing from research and personal experiences written by staff, students and alumni at the University of Essex across three edited volumes centred around LGBT+ perspectives (Boncori, 2017a), race and ethnicity (Boncori, 2018), and health and well-being (Boncori and Loughran, 2020). In 2019, this led my colleague Deborah Brewis and me to organize a seminar series funded by the Wellcome Trust called 'The Body of Work', where we invited academics and third-sector professionals to discuss a range of related silenced topics in organizations.[1] We had the pleasure of hosting academic colleagues who engage in conversations that are both theoretical and practical around embodied experiences, like Lara Owen on menstruation (Owen, 2020). These academic perspectives were often linked to writing differently and embodiment. For example, important contributions shared during the seminar series included Saoirse Caitlin O'Shea's work exploring issues pertaining to transgender bodies and embodied experiences such as gender affirmation surgery (O'Shea 2018b; 2019; 2020), and Astrid Huopalainen and Suvi Satama's work on birthing, of which I provide extracts:

> Memories circle me like wolves, attempting to corral and herd me towards a horizon that I can only glimpse. At times they recede but there is only a brief respite before their return. Always there when I feel most vulnerable they reveal my vulnerability; they make me vulnerable. I cannot escape my memories, they help make me what I am.
>
> A wolf breaks the circle, takes Shylock's price between its jaws and leaves me exsanguinated...
>
> ...My mum tells me a story of a family day out and my subsequent allergy to penicillin. I don't remember that day. I don't remember paddling in the water wearing one of my sister's bathing costumes. I don't remember my father's unexpected appearance. I don't remember being told to remain hidden to escape a wrath that would surely follow if he saw me. I don't remember the aftermath of being rushed to A&E: the fever, pneumonia, the oxygen tent, the intubation, or the penicillin ... I have been told these things so many times but I don't remember anything of a day that apparently started so well...
>
> ...I remember what followed a few months later. I remember my sister screaming. I remember my mum running in to the kitchen. I remember realizing I had done something wrong even though I was trying to do something right. I thought that my father might stop raging if I was more like my sister. Alone in the kitchen I took a knife and tried to remove what marked my difference from my sister.
>
> The knife was not particularly sharp and I was too young to do much damage. 18,000 days later what I regret is that I failed. I do not need a scar to remind me – the memory surfeit. 18,000 days later there is no end to these memories. (O'Shea, 2018b, 6)

> In 3 weeks, I will attend a conference in the UK alone and be away from my 4-month-old baby for three nights. It feels both liberating and scary at the same time. Whereas I am quite confident that our son will be perfectly fine with his father, I wonder how I'll handle the separation myself. At least my unruly maternal body will constantly remind me of being absent from my baby: instead of rushing to breastfeed my son during conference breaks, I must rush to the bathroom to pump. (Anna) (Huopalainen and Satama, 2019, 109)

When everything I knew had suddenly changed and my scars of birth were still sore and healing, it was comforting to have something 'old' to hold onto back home. Different to the unknowns of new maternity, a mix of intense happiness, joy, gratefulness, confusion, physical pain, animal hunger and thirst, tears, blood and sore breasts that initially hurt like hell, my thesis was a 'safe', less confusing project that I felt fairly in control of. (Anna) (Huopalainen and Satama, 2019, 111)

I remember taking my baby to one informal research workshop in which I felt a totally different kind of atmosphere when my baby was present. Maybe this was only my feeling, but nevertheless, my son's presence affected the ways in which other academics interacted in the classroom. (Rose) (Huopalainen and Satama, 2019, 113)

Bodies unscripted and deciphered through writing differently are often out of place for their colour, gender, size or ability (Hurston, 2000; Puwar, 2004). Judith Butler (1993), a prominent feminist sociologist voice in today's feminist studies, argues that the skin's surface is a porous and politicized boundary where people's internal image of self is projected, while also being interpreted through and compared with social gender norms. In 2019, I co-edited a special issue for the journal *Culture and Organization*, stemming from the 2017 Standing Conference on Organizational Symbolism (SCOS) (Boncori, Brewis, Sicca and Smith, 2019). The theme of the conference and the related special issue focused on embodiment and the body – '*Carne* – flesh and organization'. It sought to bring together contributions not only about bodies but also about the flesh. Juxtaposed to writing *as* skin, writing differently can also be about writing *without* skin – without that layer of protection that hides our vulnerabilities (Brewis and Williams, 2019). So our skin can be a vehicle of writing differently, a source of our writing, but also a site of collision and conflict (O'Shea, 2018a).

There are numerous other examples of spaces that embrace and spotlight embodiment, both informal ones and those created through journal publications that ignite academic discussion and inspire further scholarship. In 2018, the journal *Organization* published an article written by Alison Pullen entitled 'Writing as labiaplasty', which has become for many scholars, like myself, a key piece in writing differently and a prime example of this type of research. This is one of those papers that I feel like quoting almost in its entirety, but I offer a small extract here from the start of the text:

I write to speak. Writing extends me, it reaches well beyond the confines of myself. At a very basic level, I would like my writing to speak from me, of me, when I am able to. Spaces have been created for embodied writing, leaky writing, dirty writing, feminine writing ...

yet I am asking whether this is a place that is assigned to women and what are the terms of being in the organization studies community? Do we need to be more subversive, transgressive? Are we at risk of losing this space unless writing becomes activism, until we change the regulatory systems that assign this place for us and hold us accountable for our writing? This activism starts by speaking of writing, and women's place within it. This activism arises from relations between us – it is not something we do in isolation except that I am writing this text alone, but I am constantly imagining you in front of me. I am working through how what I write will be received, and whether I should edit myself. I am also mindful that much confidence stems from writing this text by myself. Speaking these words, speaking me, breathes, lives, connects. Writing exposes, and with this exposure, we get cast in a sea of risk, insecurity and vulnerability. There is a need for radical engagement with women's bodies and their relationship with writing. Given the power of women's writing, what can we do to challenge and change the systems that govern us? Women's bodies as sites of radical transgression through writing differently. For writing to touch, we need to establish the affective sociality between writers and readers – it touches by promoting an ethico-political relationship between us. (Pullen, 2018, 123)

I asked Alison for permission to tell the story behind this article, because to me it is a perfect illustration of what I am hoping this book will inspire others to engage with. Writing differently is not easy for a variety of reasons (for example, it can take us out of our comfort zone, as it's scary and exposing; often we have not been 'trained' on how to do this; we don't see enough of it being respected and valued in top-level publications; and it is belittled in traditional academic performance management processes), but it can bring enormous personal and professional satisfaction. I know that this specific publication has been very meaningful and inspiring for many academics, and especially many women who have felt the academic embrace of being part of a different but equally important conversation. Alison wrote the paper in one sitting after it had lived in her for a long time; she told me, 'I needed to write as I was feeling, so that someone could read it but not to pre-empt that reading'. At the moment, Alison works in Australia, where the academic system of performance assessment is different from the UK-based framework (journal rankings are based on the Australian Business Deans Council (ABDC) list, but this list is not acknowledged by the main funding body, the Australian Research Council), but it is nonetheless based on metrics, rankings and funding. Within that system, each publication is remunerated according to its level and the number of authors. Some time after its publication, Alison realized that this article had not been included in her list of publications counted in the university system. After some investigation, trying to find out why and how this paper had not been included, she was referred from individual to committee to office/r. It was finally clarified that according to the Research Committee Panel of her academic institution, this single-authored paper published in a top international journal (A rated), which had been cited 12 times already before publication, had been downgraded and classified as a research note or letter (C rated). A supporting letter from the journal editor was required to evidence that the article had gone through a process of peer review, and to confirm the value and the contribution of this piece. This type of belittling is not unknown to papers written differently, regardless of their impact or innovative character, as academic work in many cases continues to be judged against mainstream masculine notions of academic quality. This paper had not been initially intended for publication, but went on to become one of the top cited articles in the journal, evidence of its contribution to the field and how it had stretched knowledge creation. Papers like 'Writing as labiaplasty' go against the grain of the most established classification regimes and traditional assessment frameworks. As such, they pose a challenge to mainstream structures as they simply do not fit in the rigid box and metrics of the field. In offering a counter-narrative to patriarchal understandings of quality, this paper rejects the system itself. It is unlikely that the gatekeepers and managers of this system will accept and welcome these threats to the way they understand and pursue research. In the case of this specific article, for example, its academic quality was also initially assessed within the institution quantitatively by its total number of pages, which apparently was not 'enough' to be a full article, and as such undeserving of being considered a 'proper' article. This is where research guardianship, censorship and silencing are enacted, reinforcing patriarchal orders formally and in invisible ways – behind the systems, the databases, the quality frameworks, the committees and the filtering of what is to be considered acceptable. During our video conversation (27 November 2020), Alison highlighted how such examples of writing differently, of embodying research and collaborations through papers like her 'Writing as labiaplasty', can never be neutrally assessed, as they require a personal judgement that either advocates or rejects the threat to established standards of research.

Writing differently can be risky and can come at a high personal and professional cost. Often, this alternative way of writing is considered as straying too far from the narrow beaten academic path that can be excused, tolerated or simply considered laughable. That is, until they become powerful forms of resistance which threaten the success of the people who manage the system, in which case the authors may be silenced or marginalized. These institutionalized forms of violation of research and academic voices are tools that prop up unequal structures of dominance, power and oppression. As I will discuss later on in this volume, this type of writing requires changes in various processes linked to researching differently, together with understanding and support by gatekeepers, such as editors, reviewers and conference organizers, to ensure that the aftermath of these challenges to patriarchy is not exclusion and silencing.

Alison's paper reminded me of writing by Heather Höpfl, for its embodied dramatic flair but also for the use of 'shocking' terminology that goes against the grain of mainstream academic register. For instance, in 'A question of membership' (2010) and 'Becoming a (virile) member' (2003), Heather highlights the phallocentric nature of organizations entrenched in masculine values and practice.

> In this way, conventional representations of the organization reduce *organization* to abstract relationships, rational actions and purposive behaviour. This can be seen in the numerous check-lists which infest institutions at the present time. Organization, it seems, is subject to obsessive 'alpha male' behaviour, frenetic male posturing, and a compulsive desire to see who has the biggest member. In order to make the contest appear rational and abstract, organization becomes synonymous with regulation and control via metrics. In this way, metrics preserve the pecking order and retain an apparent justification for hierarchy and status. This is achieved primarily by the imposition of definition and measurement. Under such circumstances, organization comes to function in a very specific sense to establish a notion of *membership* and it is quite clear that the definition at work here is a male one. Men do not realize the extent to which women live as strangers in their world. What is normal and taken for granted is a world which is defined, constructed and maintained by male notions of order where membership is determined by male notions of what constitutes *the club*, by what determines the pecking order and, by who is able to exercise power. (Höpfl, 2010, 40, emphasis in original)

> To become a 'member' a woman must render herself homomorphic. To be rendered first androgynous is, hence, to be set apart from, or in other words, abjected from, the capacity for bodily reproduction as a condition for male membership. The reward of membership is given for being more fully conformed to the symbolic order, for homologation. This is a bizarre transgression by which the appropriation is by what is conferred rather than by what is taken. She is given a metaphorical member in order to become a member. By rendering real women, physical bodies into mere representations the disruptive power of the female body is neutralized and made safe. [...] If the feminine

threatens to subvert male order, then the move to confer the honorary penis, the metaphorical phallus, marks the reversal of the potential for transgression. The feminine is, thus, incorporated, and given membership by being made to conform with the phallogocentric order. It is ironic that the acquisition of the phallus as conferred in this way is represented as a triumph of Feminism. Clearly, it is entirely the opposite of that. (Höpfl, 2003, 26)

We are not used to terms like 'labiaplasty' and 'phallocentric' in management and organization studies, and much of this type of work constitutes an unlabelled example of writing differently.

Emotions

Embodiment, emotions and vulnerabilities are deeply connected through sensory experiences. Fuchs and Koch (2014, 9) explore this connection: 'Emotions result from the body's own feedback and the circular interaction between affective affordances in the environment and the subject's bodily resonance, be it in the form of sensations, postures, expressive movements, or movement tendencies. Through its resonance, the body functions as a medium of emotional perception.' Through the senses and our emotional reactions we can tap into another layer of knowing that is holistic and connected. Jenny Helin and Marie-Jose Avenier (2016) speak of 'arresting moments' felt by authors – and readers – which provide an in-depth engagement with the text, a lasting impression, an emotional imprint. I have previously argued for the centrality of emotions in (auto) ethnography (Boncori, 2017b) as a bridge connecting the scholar and the reader. Writing differently, whether through autoethnographic narratives or other methods, is a way of establishing and maintaining this emotional connection between the self, our scholarship, participants and readers. In line with this approach, I believe that emotions, and more broadly affect, are fundamental traits in writing differently. In agreement with what is described by Kiriakos and Tienari (2018) in the article 'Academic writing as love', I believe that writing differently is a form of love, a way of thinking and researching (Richardson, 2000), a mind frame, an embodied and emotionally nuanced practice. Due to its political and social connotations, this still carries risks in today's management and organization studies (Antoniou and Moriarty, 2008; Bell and Sinclair, 2014; Pullen and Rhodes, 2015). Kiriakos and Tienari write:

Academic writing is not (only) about putting ideas on paper and getting them published. Material circumstances matter for writing and so do the physical body and its state. Writing is embodied and sensuous.

Writers move ideas around as pieces of text and *feel* them. We cut and paste, we try out different things on paper, we scribble and erase, we revise our writing before we arrive at a structure and form that seems to work. We utter ideas aloud for ourselves and *hear* them. We sample how they *taste* in our mouth before we write them down. We *look* at our ideas on paper or the screen. But writing is more than that. It is an inherent part of who we are. For us, writing is something that forms our identities, not only as scholars but also as human beings. (Kiriakos and Tienari, 2018, 269, emphasis in original)

By getting in touch with our hidden vulnerable self, and sustaining that relationship of exposure and vulnerability, we can unlock emotional treasures to inform our scholarship: 'when we are not holding our breath, and locking our vulnerabilities in, they can become our strongest source of power allowing us to climb all the way up or dig ourselves deep down along the slope of that which touches us deeply' (Helin, 2020, 3). However, vulnerability can become a double-edged sword in its relation with exposure as it involves 'interdependency; risk of harm and loss *and* connection, through our relations to others; emotional expressions; power; and recognition' (Corlett et al, 2019, 560, emphasis in original).

Knowing the criticism that emotions and vulnerability carry in today's hyper-performative academia, daring to be different (Cunliffe and Bell, 2016, 113) becomes a challenge – especially for PhD students, early-career academics and those who need to secure job safety (if that is even at all possible in today's academia). This stems from the fact that the consideration of emotions in early scholarship and embodiment are often discouraged by supervisors and mentors to avoid rejections and failure to meet masculine metrics. As I mentioned earlier, careful consideration of the 'before' and concomitant aspects (or those considered the by-products) of writing is also very important – this is true for our emotional engagement and reflexivity as well. The rejection of vulnerability, self-doubt and failure has been addressed in management research in a recent article by Sandra Corlett, Meadbh Ruane and Sharon Mavin (2021), who highlight the positive aspect of vulnerability, also articulated as a way of learning to be different. They pose that vulnerability understood this way can be a way to counteract sociocultural norms dictating what managers and leaders are expected to be like in organizations. They consider how dominant masculine norms shape discourses and practices of leadership and management, which I think is paralleled in research and writing discourses in our field. The adoption of 'a mask of invulnerability to protect themselves' (Corlett et al, 2019, 557) is a way to conform with taken-for-granted masculine assumptions of the 'right way' of being a manager and a leader, or a writer, to avoid being 'different' and 'vulnerable'. In Writing Differently, the embracing of difference is encouraged together with its counter-narrative enacted at the singular and plural level. The fear of publication, deadline-fuelled anxiety, worry towards a family member who is unwell, joy, love and a myriad of other emotions are inevitably inscribed in the subtext of our academic writing, as much as grammar, lexicon choices, and word count. Townley (1994, 25) highlights the problematic nature of this lack of emotional engagement: 'the purpose, the reasons, the anger, the context, the location of the academic historically and contextually is removed [from the text] by academic convention'.

Academic workshops, seminars and conferences are very valuable opportunities to investigate alternative approaches to researching where discourses can be shared and co-created. These spaces can provide enabling environments to explore embodied and emotional aspects of writing, while forging connections and collaborations with other academics. These encounters are embedded in some conferences that are particularly attuned to writing differently work, such as the Art of Management conference or the Standing Conference on Organizational Symbolism. However, more recently other traditional academic spaces have also started developing strands and initiatives that speak to the writing differently community. For example, in 2021 Maria Daskalaki, Tania Jain, Marjana Johansson, Sara Persson, Ruth Slater, Julia Storberg-Walker and Kristin Williams organized a paper development workshop at the Academy of Management on the theme '"Just About Managing": Collaborative Explorations of Our Times through Autoethnographic Writing'. This workshop brought together a diverse group of scholars and was developed to explore vulnerabilities and collaboration that embraced emotions and embodiment. This practice echoed work by Corlett and colleagues (2021, 1) recognizing the relational potential of writing in an emotionally open manner (relational vulnerability), implemented through 'co-created trusted and safe spaces with others which facilitate openness to learning (not) to be different' (Corlett et al, 2021, 1). In another example from 2021, the Critical Management Studies network organized an online series of events called 'CMS InTouch', bringing together scholars from different geographic locations to discuss topical issues. The availability of this online session was one of the few benefits brought by the COVID-19 pandemic, which restricted our ability to travel, attend conferences and collaborate face to face but enhanced the availability of virtual encounters. On 18 February 2021, the event 'Embodying Methods in Management and Organization: before, during and after COVID-19' included presentations from Rafael Alcadipani, Alia Weston and Louise Wallenberg, who shared some personal experiences of using embodied methodologies, conducting fieldwork anchored in the senses, and encountering visceral responses to qualitative research.[2] There was an interesting discussion around failure, and whether to be considered 'professional' a researcher needs to remain seemingly distant and untouched by emotion. I am so used to researching with, through and on emotion, that I had not considered the possibility of using embodied research methods while trying to remain (or at least appear) emotionless. One of the presenters saw the surrendering to emotion – for example, during an interview that included a visceral response to a gendered narrative of discrimination – as a failure. They considered whether the emotional dynamic is different in fieldwork and data collection conducted with other researchers, and whether the emotional component of researching is also depending on individual ways of being 'without skin' (meaning more exposed, more prone to be 'touched' and less able to filter the outside world). Rafael Alcadipani noted that some sociocultural backgrounds are more tuned in with public displays of emotion, and made a point I wholeheartedly support – engaging in embodied qualitative studies means embracing emotions, vulnerability, and allowing oneself to be 'hijacked by research as you become entrenched in the field'.

Given that this type of vulnerability and exposure can be challenging to navigate, this level of emotional openness in and through writing is often first explored with established co-authors or familiar collaborators. For example, I was able to engage in my early writing differently work with Charlie Smith because we are friends. Having attended a doctoral programme around the same time, knowing each other and having shared some very personal experiences, I knew I could trust her not only with my text, but also with my vulnerability, with my professional uncertainty about this new way of approaching academic work, and with the emotional labour that I knew the publication process would entail. Reassured by that first experience of publishing work that was written differently, and supported by the extremely positive feedback received from editors and reviewers, we were both able to pursue further opportunities to write differently from a personal perspective.

During the pandemic I had the privilege to start working with a small group of colleagues on a project rooted in emotion and writing differently, even though I had never written with any of them before and we barely knew one another. I knew the research they had written differently, which had led to the establishment of a basic level of trust that allowed us to explore a vulnerable collaborative space. Here, I am not discussing the mechanistic process of writing, or how to sustain a good rhythm of writing within an authorial team, or how to become more productive or efficient in the crafting of one's text, but rather the emotional landscape related to writing differently. In my experience, this emotional and embodied sphere of academic writing, together with the perils and potential of its dynamics, is not routinely taught or even discussed with doctoral students, which makes it an exception to standard practice, a journey of self-discovery later in one's career, and possibly a component of writing which can go completely ignored.

Emotions, whether negative or positive, mark the essential and primordial character of some topics and can become propellers of change in academic inquiry. Women fighting for social justice, feminists and Black feminists in particular (Doharty, 2020) have often been accused of being angry. Anger is important and a crucial propeller of change, igniting agency and action. Lingis (2000, 188) notes, '[a]nger marks what is inadmissible, intolerable. Anger marks a refusal, a resistance beyond what resistance itself can reasonably accomplish'. And so emotions are important and to be acknowledged, not only while we write and as a legitimate topic for what we investigate, but also as an important aspect in guiding our research choices and motivation. I espouse, like Audre Lorde and Sara Ahmed, the idea of writing with anger as a feminist approach that reclaims the 'angry feminist' stereotype as a valuable point of departure for inequality-focused scholarship. Why are others *not* angry about inequality and marginalization? As a critical management scholar, I feel that the ignition of anger, indignation and offence to challenge and problematize the status quo is a productive space to pursue research interests that challenge inequality.

Recognizing the emotional component of research, and particularly in writing differently, is important not only for the author but also for the reader. When crafting a piece of writing in a holistic manner which incorporates, reflects on and acknowledges the emotional journey of the writer, the dialogue thus instigated is activated not only at the cognitive and sensorial level, but also at the emotional one. Very often, in order to facilitate my writing differently, I need to 'get in the mood' through embodied processes, like listening to a specific type of music, or going to a place that has 'good vibes', or writing at a specific time of the day when I am better able to get in touch with my unfiltered emotional life. This affective landscape within researching and writing can then connect the author to the topic and the reader at a different level. Meier and Wegener (2017, 195) note how 'when academic writing resonates, it has affective potential to move us', thus propelling movement at different levels. Rather than being relegated to a subordinate space of non-acceptance and superimposed academic ghetto, that emotional resonant space of writing differently that percolates or inundates the reader's sense is to me extremely empowering. Through this type of involvement, the negative perception of vulnerability is turned into positive agency and power. As I explore in a chapter on autoethnographic accounts (Boncori, 2021), emotions in our writing help establish bonds and strong connections with the audience of our work. Emotional resonance in research is as important as cognitive resonance, as writing that moves can have a stronger impact on scholars and generate further waves of resonance. As such, emotion is a key component in critical feminist inquiry: it motivates action and ethical decisions, it fosters learning (Höpfl and Linstead, 1997) and propels change. Emotion also holds the foundation of another key feminist tenet: solidarity (see Etzioni, 1988). Further, it fosters a specific type of relationship called *affective* solidarity (Hemmings, 2012), which can be experienced at the macro-societal level (Goodwin, Jasper and Poletta, 2001; Flam and King, 2005) as well as at the micro-individual level. Rosemary Hennessy (2009) highlights the centrality of affective relations in collective agency, which is echoed by Sara Ahmed (2004) who explores how emotions can be considered as a form of cultural politics that unite or separate people. The sharing of emotions in research and writing creates particular relationships, links and ligaments, or trust, commonality, hope, mutuality and vulnerability which promote community-building and maintain commitments to each other (Dar et al, 2020).

The challenging of masculine discourses around emotions, and the championing of the counter-narratives of passion and care, has become an increasingly visible theme in management and organization studies. For example, Rebecca Lund and Janne Tienari (2018) build on Emma Bell and Amanda Sinclair's (2014) notion of eros as one uniting heart, mind and the body in the neoliberal academic context. Eros here (2018, 99) is investigated as 'longing for learning and making sense of the world, becoming a whole human being, and engaging with others in this pursuit and as actions that interrupt ruling orders'. Audre Lorde also writes beautifully on the potentials of the erotic in the essay '*The uses of the erotic: The erotic as power*', initially presented as a paper in 1978, where she explores how 'The erotic is a resource within each of us that lies in a deeply female and spiritual plane, firmly rooted in the power of our unexpressed or unrecognized feeling' (Lorde, 1984b, 87). This is linked to writing differently because it counteracts the masculine norm that has relegated emotions, embodiment and eros to a place of marginalization.

> As women, we have come to distrust that power which rises from our deepest and non-rational knowledge. We have been warned against it all our lives by the male world, which values this depth of feeling enough to keep women around in order to exercise it in the service of men, but which fears this same depth too much to examine the possibility of it within themselves. So women are maintained at a distant/inferior position to be psychically milked, much the same way ants maintain colonies of aphids to provide a life-giving substance for their masters. (Lorde, 1984b, 88)

On the contrary, writing differently asks us to connect with that as a powerful source. In its rupturing and dismantling character, together with its unifying and joyful traits, eros has the power of feminist action to ignite social justice – it offers alternatives to masculine and normative understandings, it refuses homogenizing praxis and gendered orders. Eros, and other emotions experienced and explored in combination or isolation, ignited by or alongside embodied experiences, can become forms of resistance towards the gendered neoliberal university (Lund and Tienari, 2018).

Therefore, writing differently also provides new sources, or recognizes the value of marginalized sources within people, for the germination of knowledge that has value beyond rationality and quantified generalizations. These points of departure are particularly useful to give visibility to silenced experiences of inequality. Writing inequality in Writing Differently can be seen as writing at the macro-systemic level of inequality, in particular professional and organizational contexts, or writing of specific articulations of marginalization and discrimination at the group and individual level. These particular *standpoints* are in line with feminist inquiry (Haraway, 1988; Harding, 1993, 2007). In the recently published edited volume on Writing Differently, Alison Pullen writes: 'Writing Differently needs to be constantly undone from the spaces in which we inhabit, providing rich localized knowledge through the way in which we write, what we write, the collaborations and friendships and violence we do to each other along the way' (Pullen, Helin and Harding, 2020, 10). There is no doubt that academia is a context of white, mostly middle-class, heterosexual cisgender privilege. Writing Differently to me is a political feminist project, but it is also an act of hope. Hope here is intended in agreement with Zygmunt Bauman and Monika Kostera (Kostera, 2020) who pose that it is not a manifestation of optimism but 'a radical act, because it is immortal, has its roots in the future and needs no proof, which is rooted in the past. It makes like worth living'.

One of my favourite books of all time is *The Master's Tools Will Never Dismantle the Master's House* (2018), written by one of the most inspiring authors I have encountered in my academic life, the Black feminist Audre Lorde. This book is to me also a prime example of writing differently. Most of her essays published in this Penguin collection were given as conference papers in the US between 1978 and 1982, and it is striking how relevant these words still are today, after four decades. I keep going back to those essays, a pinnacle of feminist writing, where powerful words are beautifully crafted to envelop pain, inequality, beauty and emotionally dense testimonies. Her work I feel is a masterpiece in bringing together intersectional perspectives of the mind, the body and the affective realm. It is a prime feminist example in its urgent demands for equal rights and human flourishing; it is a striking illustration on how individual perspectives become collective, social and political through shared experiences that are shaped by large systemic influences and barriers.

In the next chapter, I further discuss some key issues related to writing differently in terms of vulnerability, exposure and failure. These are often perceived as negative by-products of writing, something to be swept under the carped to simply be mentioned in passing regarding a qualitative piece of research. Here, instead, these aspects of writing are espoused as crucial to the practice and ethos of writing differently.

Vulnerability, risk and exposure in researching and writing differently

As I mentioned earlier in this book, emotion and vulnerability are two key aspects of writing differently that embrace both an affective and embodied dimension of the self as an author and a researcher. Alison Pullen (2018, 123) reminds us that 'writing exposes, and with this exposure, we get cast in a sea of risk, insecurity and vulnerability'. Although vulnerability has been generally understood as a space of danger, and often perceived in a negative manner, it is an invaluable resource while writing differently. Jenny Helin (2020, 1) poses that 'when we use our scholarly voice to write from within our vulnerabilities, it becomes possible to climb all the way up or dig ourselves deep down'. Writing differently embraces vulnerability in its counteracting the need to be (or at least appear) 'successful' within the hypercompetitive higher education system (Lund and Tiernari, 2018), and in problematizing mottos such as 'leaning in' and 'fake it till you make it', aimed at winning (or coping) while playing the academic game according to masculine rules.

Honesty is a key enabling factor within vulnerable writing practices that require openness and provide genuine access to the story and the verticality of the writing (see Helin, 2020). In writing differently, stories are not considered historical accounts and so the exactness and factual accuracy is often not the prime concern of the writer. Stories are not dissected for truthfulness and precision of factual reporting but rather absorbed for their embodied and idealized nature, being perhaps considered as 'poetic elaborations of actual events, as wish-fulfilling fantasies built on everyday experience and as expressions of deeper organizational and personal realities' (Gabriel and Griffiths, 2004, 124). Some texts have the ability to touch the reader with a long-lasting impression, reaching a deeper layer of recognition and sense-making, and remain engraved in the mnemonic repertoire of the community. Others, however, dissipate while still remaining an important textural component of the collective storytelling. Indeed, numerous research contributions have stayed with me long after the first reading, and I have sought to pinpoint why – is it the crafting of the argument, the elegance of the language, the particular topic or something else? The two reasons I was able to trace as key in this process were my ability to identify with the content of the story, and (or) the 'raw honesty' and emotional dynamics of the writing, which I would find moving and compelling even though I had no personal shared experience reflected in the text. A prime example of the latter is Saoirse Caitlin O'Shea's essay entitled '*Cutting my dick off*' (2019), which provides a powerful and touching account centred around experiences of self-harm, tattooing, self-mutilation and auto-castration, showing the violent normalization of bodies imposed by society and medical practices.

Writing differently can be experienced as 'pre-reflective, open and vulnerable texts, and they offer the voices of our bodies, entanglements of mind and body, murmured voices spoken and unspoken elements sitting on the page' (Valtonen and Pullen, 2020, 1). Writing differently asks for energy, effort and openness: '[g]iving oneself to writing means being in a position to do this work of digging, of unburying, and this entails a long period of apprenticeship, since it obviously means going to school' (Cixous, 1993, 6–7). This is usually related to the author of the text, but it can also be case for the reader. Writing Differently, both as a movement and as an academic project, allows us the vulnerability to encounter ourselves, as people, as academics, and as academic people. It requires dedication, self-discovery, reflexivity and self-awareness. And in order to enter into that encounter truly and honestly, sometimes we need to embrace vulnerability, tear up the academic masks we bear and the impersonal bandage we put on our scars. However, vulnerability is a relational process which is not limited to exposing the self to others in an inward-outwards movement; it is also about the relationship with other people, and even with non-human subjects. Vulnerability then, rather than a negative aspect of one's academic persona, can be pursued as an enabling aspect of agential research, or a lens through which scholars can pursue feminist or activist objectives. Karen Barad and other feminist scholars write about our entanglements with inhuman beings and objects (see Barad, 2012), as writing differently can also mean allowing ourselves to be vulnerable by letting ourselves being exposed by the interactions with non-human bodies around us and how they can affect our writing through our bodies and emotions (see Huopalainen, 2020; Valtonen and Pullen, 2020). Understood often as a form of posthumanist multispecies ethnography (see for instance Hamilton and Mitchell, 2017; Hamilton and Taylor, 2017), this type of writing aims to consider dignity and other emotions or experiences as something that goes beyond human species and includes animals.

To borrow language from the journal *Management Learning*, I see writing differently also as a 'provocation to debate', especially when considered from a feminist perspective. Willmott's (1994) framing of the provocation essays in this journal, and the more recent editorial by Deborah Brewis and Emma Bell (2020), identified some key points that I think are also relevant to writing differently. First of all, there is a crucial aspect of writing and critical engagement leading to change that has to do with disruption: we need writing, ideas and research that rub against the grain of taken-for-granted knowledge and practice, going against the aerodynamics of conventional academic writing. The second point focuses on the value of bringing together theorizing and 'cognitive insights' with experimentation (Willmott, 1994, 106), which I articulate in this book both in terms of content and methods of writing differently. Provocation goes hand in hand with uncertainty (Willmott, 1994), and as such with vulnerability. This vulnerability is also about the conscious decision to step out of the mainstream and experiment (see, for example, Mandalaki, 2020), regardless of, or notwithstanding, the risks. Although it is certainly important, and a welcome feature of some journals, to have dedicated sections for more 'polemic' or 'activist' writing, I would argue that this type of writing should be included in the main articles and not enclosed within separate sections of the journal, as this segmentation itself gives visibility but also creates difference.

This type of researching and writing requires a rewiring or at least a reorientation of what are traditionally considered unwanted feelings and unintended consequences in relation to academic practices. Writing differently demands 'a very different orientation to feelings of ignorance, uncertainty, confusion, ambiguity and even chaos' (Willmott, 1994, 122). The discomfort generated by vulnerability, emotion and difference can actually be productive (Brewis and Bell, 2020), especially in the case of researching and writing differently. In discussing his experience as an academic, David Knights (2006, 700) reveals how feedback received from colleagues pushed him to dare to put himself in the text, also illustrated in Amanda Sinclair's suggestion, that 'finding a different way of writing seems to me to be part of continuing to subvert authoritative renditions in the discipline.' However, while discomfort can be generative, it can also be destructive (hooks, 2003).

Researching and writing differently through honesty and vulnerability can also involve higher risk, in the surfacing of tensions between the familiar and the Other, the individual and the collective level of experience. It can mean reliving trauma through life experiences – personal or belonging to others (Eddo-Lodge, 2018; Lorde, 1984b) –, suffering the burden of representation and action, or the closing of career opportunities and other practical consequences. Vulnerability here is thought of not only in terms of exposure, but also in terms of a shared existential condition stemming from social and systemic violence that makes people vulnerable to oppression and marginalization. This includes feminist impositions over certain groups – as explored for instance by Saba Mahmood (2011), who problematizes the approach of secular liberal feminists in their critique of religious movements (in this case, Islam) being considered both patriarchal and oppressive. Kakali Bhattacharya (2016) uses a personal narrative to argue that vulnerability can be a way to reconceptualize and rethink possibilities for addressing social inequities in academia. In promoting vulnerable writing, Tiffany Page (2017, 13) focuses on 'explicating and recognizing vulnerability in writing' as a feminist approach to research, engaging with postcolonial and queer theoretical approaches to understand experience. In particular, she develops an ethical argument about writing that describes the lives and experiences of others, especially those communicating trauma and suffering, considering how vulnerability can help reflexive engagement and in bringing into focus forms of knowing and unknowing. Page explains (2017, 15): 'what is at the heart of vulnerable methods and writing are ongoing questions about what unsettles and relations to the unfamiliar and strange, and how this might start to be addressed through the slow examination of the varying and multi-layered modalities of vulnerability involved in research practices'.

Exposure and risk connected with Writing Differently are articulated and negotiated on an ongoing basis at different levels. In researching and writing differently, the first risk and form of exposure is within oneself and the people involved with autoethnographic or personal narratives – how much do we want to reveal, who else is affected by this, do we need an ethical approval for sharing our own stories, how is our professional identity impacted now and in the future (See Prasad, 2014)? Also, exposure and risk are related to research participants – will they disclose material that is useful to the study, how do we protect them, how do we sustain trust and professional credibility throughout longer longitudinal research, how do we manage their expectations of the study and of the scholar herself, how are embodiment and emotions managed in the field? Another aspect connected to exposure and risk that is linked to vulnerability is related to the context in which the study is conducted – is it an overt or covert operation, are there social or environmental dangers for the researcher (COVID-19 added another risk to fieldwork), is it a familiar or strange context? While this can be applicable to traditional qualitative and quantitative research, the political character of writing differently makes the exposure even greater. For example, Rafael Alcadipani, during his talk at the CMS InTouch event (18 February 2021) discussed issues around risk, drawing from his fieldwork experience with the Brazilian police. He did not focus merely on the actual risk to be harmed in the middle of a police operation, but considered the iterative ways in which risk is negotiated in qualitative ethnographic research. What is the risk of writing differently in a normative masculine system that rejects the fundamental nature of who we are as scholars who want to research differently and promote a different way of inhabiting academia? These are all fulcra of risk and exposure that need to be considered even before the writing differently is materialized through paper or a digital screen. That is not to say that mainstream studies are devoid of these traits, but that these are particularly evident and often consciously deployed in writing differently. Feminist approaches to texts and stories that are written differently are born from the individual experience juxtaposed against a collective sociocultural and professional backdrop.

Having discussed key traits of writing differently in this section of the book, and reflected on different aspects of the meaning and importance of this type of writing from an individual and collective perspective, Part III will focus on how we can go about writing differently. I will therefore outline some of the methods that better lend themselves to writing differently, and explore some practical implications of engaging in this type of research.

PART III

Researching and writing differently: methods and processes

Following from a discussion on the contemporary neoliberal academic context and the framing of writing differently as a feminist political project in Part I, Part II provided an overview of some key aspects and themes in writing differently. The previous section also offered a selection of exemplars of researching and writing differently. Part III will now consider epistemological approaches that can inform researching and writing differently, and outline some of the methods which lend themselves to the pursuit of a Writing Differently agenda. Reflections and choices around methodologies and methods are important in guiding our research – as noted by Harding (1991, 40) 'whoever gets to define what counts as […] scientific […] also gets a powerful role in shaping the picture of the world that results from scientific research'. As such, writing differently and, through its critiques, the establishment of positionalities around methods and what counts as 'scientific' or rigorous academic research, are political and linked with power. The last chapter in Part III will discuss some practical aspects and processes connected to researching and writing differently, before drawing to a conclusion.

Qualitative inquiry

The underpinning intellectual rationale of this book, which was outlined in the previous chapters, is linked to different ways of thinking and researching not only in terms of theory and content, but also through specific research methods and alternative ways of presenting and publishing academic work. I believe that this is how we can challenge the status quo in terms of style, format and content of our research; how we can form critical perspectives on the ways we relate to each other and other lifeworlds; and how we can become activists and catalysts for change, in the manner we recognize and inhabit spaces, to expose marginalized experiences in and of organizations. Indeed, Rhodes (2019, 34) reflects on 'scriptologies' as political acts. Through a human-focused mind frame, relevant epistemologies and methods, we can embody and transfer on paper emancipatory impulses, communicate experiences that are politically engaged and stress emotional upheaval. This allows us to question, challenge and change the traditional, patriarchal, 'objective' and desensitized way of writing in and of organizations (Boncori and Smith, 2019). In terms of research paradigms, critical or interpretive approaches are the most suitable to investigations that favour subjective, qualitative studies of sense-making for individuals, communities and cultures (for more information see Bell and Thorpe, 2013; Bryman, Bell and Harley, 2019).

Qualitative approaches

Edward Sapir argued that the 'true locus of culture is in the interactions of specific individuals, and, on the subjective side, in the world of meanings which each one of these individuals may unconsciously abstract for himself from his participation in these interactions' (Sapir, 1961, 151). Researching and writing differently often revolves around these personal interactions and experiences that bring together the affective, embodied and cognitive aspects of life. This points us firmly towards specific ontological and epistemological positions. By ontology I mean the approach taken to the understanding of being and becoming, and how things or people relate to each other; while epistemology is about the nature of knowledge and how we go about knowing and making sense of phenomena. These positions or stances taken by researchers in terms of ontology and epistemology are quite fundamental and underpin everything else in their inquiries, cascading down to inform the choice of methodology and methods in one's research. Therefore, if one believes that there is a true reality out there that can be discovered, understood objectively and tested, then results are sought which can be measured, generalized and reproduced (in line with a positivist paradigm and quantitative methods). Consequently, the methods chosen to investigate a phenomenon would speak to this ontological and epistemological perspective in trying to be 'scientific', quantifiable and objective. On the other hand, towards the other end of the continuum, where research is underpinned by the belief that there is no singular truth to be found, and the common experience of thousands of people is not considered more reliable or valuable than a singular one, testing, statistical significance and vast sampling are not considered fundamental. Denzin and Lincoln (2011, 3) explain that 'qualitative researchers study things in their natural settings, attempting to make sense of, or interpret, phenomena in terms of the meanings people bring to them'.

Given the way I understand the world – as socially constructed, constantly negotiated and based on subjective experiences and sense-making – I simply could not be a positivist quantitative researcher. This is not to say that positivist or quantitative research is less valid or valuable: it is simply informed by a different mind frame and research objectives from the one I espouse. I firmly believe that one's way of being, thinking and understanding the world and those who inhabit it dictates the ontological stance taken in research. I use the word 'stance' here on purpose, rather than 'choice' because I truly believe that from my *forma mentis* a different stance is impossible, as it simply would not make sense. When thinking of this paradigm conundrum, often experienced by doctoral students at the start of their research journey, a beautiful Sicilian saying always came to my mind: "*Cu nasci tunnu un pò moriri quatratu*", meaning that those who are born round cannot die square, which perhaps sounds unnecessarily strict and rigid (it can be roughly translated as "square peg in a round hole" too), but denotes a way of thinking and understanding that just does not quite fit and cannot be forced into becoming something else to match a pre-existing shape.

In the social sciences, there are varying degrees of comfort and familiarity with the different 'paradigms' as well as ontological, epistemological and methodological traditions. Some fields have developed to blur those boundaries – for example, critical accounting and behavioural finance – often by branching out to borrow theories from different fields (accounting + philosophy or sociological theory; finance + psychological theory). This cross-pollination of approaches, mixed methods and knowledge creation has allowed our research to develop into new areas, aim for new horizons, wear different tinted lenses, and collaborate with scholars across disciplines. I remember attending a wonderful research event a few years ago presenting research on work–family balance. This event brought together American quantitative researchers and critical qualitative scholars from the UK, both offering different but excellent approaches to this topic. As a qualitative researcher, the vast and rigorously obtained quantitative data set (over 5,000 people answered the questionnaire) left me wanting more nuanced understandings and people's sense-making narratives. I craved to know more and get different types of data. I wanted to know the 'why' behind possible correlation and causation, to talk to people. I always knew I was going to be a qualitative researcher, and even when engaging in surveys I cannot resist the urge to have some open-ended questions. I want to hear people's stories, I want to let them explain more than what is included in a pre-populated box, to understand the nuances of their experience, and how they felt about it in their bodies and emotions. However, from a quantitative perspective, I could see some discomfort with regards to the presentation of qualitative data at that event, stemming from longitudinal diaries kept by 15 people, and interviews with 10 new mothers, as that pool of participants to a quantitative researcher is not representative or statistically significant and does not allow generalizations. Where quantitative studies focus on investigating phenomena by observing and measuring them, qualitative research focuses on understanding the meaning that these experiences hold for individuals. Therefore, as a qualitative researcher, I am not trying to find 'the Answer', or the *correct* answer, or 'the Truth'. These approaches all are equally valid, but they are used to investigate different aspects of research, and so they differ.

Research approaches, methods and ways to analyse data can change and develop over time. Over the past two decades, qualitative inquiry in my field has widened its boundaries and amplified its reach. When I started my journey into the wonderful world of (auto)ethnographic methods, about 15 years ago, I saw a lot of raised eyebrows among academics in business schools. Colleagues would at times say "Oh that's *interesting*" or "That's a *brave* methodological choice" and "Surely you will not just try to publish *that*? You will integrate it with some *proper* methods and *real data*". The not-so-veiled innuendos were not lost on me, a young academic who had been in a teaching-focused lecturing post for just over five years, and had decided to venture into the mysterious world of academic research. As I have explored before in other texts (Boncori and Smith, 2019; Boncori, 2022) ethnography came to me completely by accident, although my supervisor had gently suggested this may be a way forward. At the end of my first year as a PhD student, I had signed up to attend the Social Sciences Summer School at the University of Essex on research methods, but unfortunately the course on qualitative interviewing I wanted to attend was oversubscribed, so I registered for the one on ethnography instead. It changed my life, especially when it got to autoethnography. I did not even know that this type of research was possible, let alone publishable. The work of Carolyn Ellis, especially the wonderfully written book *The Ethnographic I* (Ellis, 2004), unlocked a whole new chamber of knowledge and possibilities echoing inside my mind, opening the gates to potential research and interesting narratives written in a way that I had not quite encountered yet in my field. It was at that point that I realized why my supervisor had encouraged me to look at other disciplines, like sociology, anthropology, cultural studies and other fields that were far ahead in the use of ethnography. At the time, these methods were often snubbed by scholars in management and organization studies as lacking rigour and substance. She invited me to read novels and watch movies for my doctoral studies on expatriate adjustment, and in that very nascent state of my awareness as a researcher, I really did not understand what the point would be of doing that. But then I discovered this different way of reading and understanding research, which could be applied to organizing and organizations through an interpretive or critical lens.

Luckily, our field has since moved on, and ethnographic studies are now increasingly popular and visible in top journals. For example, Lisa Jane Callagher, Ziad El Sahn, Paul Hibbert, Stefan Korber and Frank Siedlok (2021) wrote a multivocal autoethnographic account of early-career researchers' experiences of discrimination that constitute identity threats. Their personal texts highlight experiences of discrimination regarding race, gender and foreignness that are both spoken and non-verbal:

'The three of us, me, Claire and Craig – the industrial partner who organized the gig – were standing in front of some fifteen managers from local companies. Being informal, as usual, Craig went on about our contributions to the day, weaving some news and politics into his comments. When attempting to make a point about me, a foreigner being involved in research on some local co-operatives, he looked at me and asked: "what boat did you get off?" The room went dead silent...' (Viktor) (Callagher et al, 2021, 8)

We were invited to a half-day of strategic events that started with an Annual General Meeting and then a strategic session. There were about 50 people and were told in advance that people would be interested to know who we are and would be welcoming. Before the first session, between the sessions, and after the second session, there was a lot of networking, and as we were told to expect, a number of people came up to introduce themselves and find out who we were. While talking, it was suggested we talk to an older man who was well-known in the area. When the older man passed us, the person I was talking to waved him to join us and introduced me as a researcher. The older gentleman replied that he was known as 'the godfather' of the industry, that he was happy to see a new lady in the district, and had a son looking for a wife if I was interested. My sharp reply saying if only I wasn't married played to his gendering of my identity. (Claire) (Callagher et al, 2021, 8–9)

However, in the management and organizational studies field there is still a remnant of a mainstream positivistic quantitative bedrock, which in some top journals is still hailed as a pinnacle of research quality. When trying to publish studies that are solely reliant on qualitative data, authors can still encounter reviewers stemming from quantitative and measuring approaches who expect something different: in order to appear 'rigorous' one seems to be required to show years of participant observations, a lifetime of recordings, millions of words sifted through from across transcripts in order to show that one has done 'enough', that the quantity and volume of work justifies the apparent frivolity of this research choice. Of course, I am exaggerating here, but these ridiculous quantifications of qualitative research are not a rarity – a few years ago I was told that to publish a qualitative study in a top-level journal one needs at least 41 interviews, or it's just not going to make the cut. While these bizarrely artificial thresholds and unwritten rules may be in place in some publications, this is definitely not the case for every journal, which is why it is important to carefully consider where research should be published. I will discuss journals and publication choices later in this book.

As qualitative researchers, we espouse a particular stance not only with regards to our data or the phenomena we want to study, but also in terms of the researcher's positionality and voice. For example, this involves considerations of whether research can ever be objective (Boncori, 2022b). Harquail (2020, 30) articulates this in a powerful way: 'the notion that there is an "objective" point of view is instead a falsehood imposed by the group in power. Not only is this "objective" viewpoint not neutral, but also it specifically privileges and serves the interests of the group in power themselves'. In contrast to the quest for objectivity in research based on Western scientific ways of approaching knowledge production, feminist critiques highlight how scholarly activity, research and academic studies (see Donna Haraway's work, in particular 1988; Collins, 1990) are influenced by the positionality of the investigator in their own particular personal 'standpoint' (Harding, 2004). This specific position is also then shaped by different standpoints or positionalities coming from other people or non-human actors within research, such as participants, and interpreted by the reader/audience with their own particular views and bias. Current masculine metrics and patriarchal approaches to research are hegemonic, and as such claim to be *the* way, the *correct* way, the 'objectively' *best* way of researching and writing academic work. Therefore, all other perspectives are belittled, silenced, ignored or cast away as second-class and less valuable. Epistemologically, alternative views from the classic positivist paradigm put forward the case of different interpretations of phenomena and socially constructed knowledge. This implies that there is no totemic monolithic knowledge to be discovered 'out there', but that the creation and understanding of knowledge is an iterative, relational and negotiated process. Barnes (1996) critiques the idea itself of an independent objective researcher, suggesting that academics side either with the oppressed or the oppressor. In this context, qualitative feminist approaches to research embrace the first-person voice, the singular and collective 'I' in the text that illuminates experience without aiming for it to be generalized. Singular pluralities and difference lie in the crannies of human experience, in the cracks behind professional masks, the untold stories, the taken-for-granted workplace habitus and power dynamics. These aspects of organizational life cannot be uncovered from the top of a mountain of statistical data, and are instead found in narratives, artistic expressions and in the folds of rich and nuanced qualitative data. Theory and critique can stem from individual experiences, with a powerful political direction, as noted by bell hooks (1991, 11) 'I am grateful to the many women and men who dare to create theory from the location of pain and struggle, who courageously expose wounds to give us their experience to teach and guide, as a means to charting new theoretical journeys. Their work is liberatory'. Ethnography is a methodology and a family of methods which allows the researcher, participants and field of study to become entangled through in-depth interaction and access to different layers of meaning and experience.

Ethnography

Quantitative positivist research is concerned with size, replicability, generalization and volume of data. At the other end of the research spectrum, we have (auto)ethnography and arts-based methods, interested in the detail, the minutiae and kaleidoscopic facets of peoples' lives, emotions and thinking. In some cases, ethnography, as a methodology and family of methods, has been marked by the scarlet letter of academic narcissism and indulgence, and so more analytic ways of approaching (auto)ethnography have been suggested that place it closer to canonical masculine ways of understanding research (Anderson, 2006; Boncori, 2021). However, in the second decade of this century, these issues have developed into more in-depth conversations, and 'concerns about ethnographic objectivity have been replaced by a recognition of the ethnographer's responsibility to interrogate social locations and power differences' (McQueeney, 2013, 451). As articulated by bell hooks in the quote above, these personal experiences are also valuable sources of theorizing and academic activism.

Understood as a deep immersion in a community within a specific sociocultural context, ethnography can also be considered more broadly as a study of culture and, by extension, society, history and the economy, that involves the self. In contrast with its origins, criticized for a colonial approach and masculine gaze towards the 'exotic' Other, ethnography has today developed into an embodied and emotional process of learning and knowing about the self and others (Kleinman and Copp, 1993). Here the researcher's body moves across the field, connecting epistemological and methodological positions to the practice of engaging with everyday research. As a prime channel for embodied understanding and sense-making, ethnography enters into conversation not only with participants and bystanders, but also with non-human subjects and the environment around us. This methodology can help explore social issues, surfacing contextual circumstances, acknowledging power dynamics and highlighting potential for change. For example, Yvonne Black (2020) created a study based on a collaborative performance ethnography (Denzin, 2003) to explore the role of community gardens in igniting social and environmental change for well-being. She suggests (Black, 2020) that the creative approach employed through this ethnographic work not only provided new perspectives on data collection and analysis, but also expanded her thinking in working towards radical reflexivity. Other ethnographies have focused explicitly on the silenced (see Cruz, 2008; Kidron, 2009) to bring groups, phenomena and problems from the margins to the centre. In their excellent edited book on organizational ethnography, Monika Kostera and Nancy Harding (2021) provide numerous examples of how this approach can support the development of richer and more in-depth organizational scholarship to explore everyday experiential minutiae and sense-making in organizing.

Ethnography can veer in the direction of many foci. One to mention here, given the sensorial aspect of researching and writing differently, is 'sensory ethnography' (Pink, 2009), also called 'multisensory ethnography' (Dicks, 2014), which draws from phenomenological anthropology and epistemologies of the flesh (Merleau-Ponty, 1989; see also Ingold, 2008). Included in a range of 'sensory methodologies' (Warren, 2008; 2012), this type of ethnography channels knowledge through the senses, amplifying sensorial-emotional awareness and interpretations to explore and make sense of the phenomena under study. Somewhat overlapping with this is affective ethnography, which highlights the internal resonance through emotions rather than focus on the sense. These physical and emotional experiences, individual but also influenced by sociocultural contexts (Sunderland et al, 2012), are often captured through reflexive field notes that pay particular attention to the sensorial experience of the researcher.

Another type of ethnography that is often linked to writing differently is autoethnography, with which I started experimenting during my PhD alongside more traditional qualitative methods (Boncori, 2013). It has been defined by many scholars in relation to its social component as a self-narrative 'that places the self within a social context. It is both a method and a text' (Reed-Danahay (1997, 6), and one 'that critiques the situatedness of self and others in social context' (Spry, 2001, 710). The political nature of this approach is made more explicit by Neumann (1996, 189) who sees this method as a way of democratizing 'the representational sphere of culture by locating the particular experiences of individuals in tension with dominant expressions of discursive power'. Autoethnography can be envisaged along a continuum from analytic autoethnography (Anderson, 2006), which highlights rigour in analysis and coding, to interpretive (Denzin, 2014) or evocative autoethnography (Bochner and Ellis, 2016), which highlights the power of narratives akin to poetry. Autoethnography can also be seen through the lens of power and resistance, especially in terms of critical autoethnography (Liu, 2020).

Initially focused on the narratives and text as a method of data collection, my use of autoethnography later matured into an understanding of it also as a methodology (see Holman Jones, Adams and Ellis, 2013). In subsequent work, I explored the use and value of ethnography both empirically and theoretically (Boncori, 2017b, 2020a; Boncori and Smith, 2019, 2020). In agreement with Ettorre (2017), I consider autoethnography a feminist method that can meaningfully allow access to a plurality of experiences and to different sociocultural perspectives. This helps the researcher and the reader achieve an understanding of personal lived circumstances that go beyond specific contexts or contingent shifting dynamics of power and (in)equality at the singular level.

Drawing from the power of narratives and storytelling, using autoethnography can help the researchers inscribe themselves into collective action and speech. As such the theorizing of autoethnography is political (Holman Jones, 2008), and can be transformative for both authors and readers. Effective autoethnography is complex and multilayered, and echoes Liz Stanley's (1994, 133) view that 'feminist conceptualizing of the self, within as well as across conventional discipline boundaries, needs to be correspondingly complex'. It requires reflexivity on one's positionality and also the surfacing of fallibility from the researcher (Cunliffe, 2003), alongside an exposure of weaknesses and bias. Reflexivity here can thus be understood as 'recognition that all knowledge is affected by the social conditions under which it is produced and that it is grounded in both the social location and the social biography of the observer and the observed' (Mann and Kelley, 1997, 392).

There are numerous examples of autoethnography in researching and writing differently, some of which were explored in Part II of this book. The article I co-authored with Charlie Smith (Boncori and Smith, 2019, 77–78), which offers my autoethnographic account of baby loss, is also an example of this method:

Something could be wrong, and I am here alone in a University dorm with the carpet of a colour designed to hide stains. Or maybe what I am experiencing is normal, just the implantation stage I read about on the train. Everything will be fine. I'll text him now and go back to sleep, and when I wake up it will all be fine. And I'll go hang out with my friends at the conference and listen to motivating presentations, and it will all be fine.

A practice fire alarm rudely awakes my cramping limbs. I don't remember where I am. My body is leaking. He is not next to me in bed. I stumble without glasses into the unfamiliar bathroom with its annoyingly cold yellow led lights. My baby is gone. I have never experienced this before but I know with absolute and unmistakable certainty that I have lost my baby today. I feel... despair. And shock. Shock at my despair. Why do I feel like this? It's not even a baby yet – my stupid phone app says it's the size of a cute poppy seed. I had only known for sure for two days, after weeks of speculation. My academic logic mind comes to rescue me as my emotions echo against the squalid thin walls, and my pain flows through my body. Useless body. Failing body. Old body. Empty body.

I can't stay in this room alone. I can't stay alone with my broken flesh. I get dressed, decide to go to the conference to listen to other stories, other lives. Work, it's good to focus on work now. I'll get those articles done by Christmas; and my books. Books don't die.

Stories and first-person narrative accounts of experiences in the workplace can be very powerful in exposing exclusion and inequality, as writing autoethnography entails the espousing of authenticity and reflexivity, which creates a relationship of 'emotional resonance' with potential readers (Ellis, Adams and Bochner, 2011). Ellis poses that autoethnographers are both ethnographers and storytellers, positioned at the intersection of the personal and the cultural (2004). Denzin (2014) further explores how qualitative methods, and particularly interpretive autoethnographies, are ideal for stories that include epiphanies, perform an act of resistance, and those that 'demand telling' (2014, 3), including 'decolonizing autoethnography' that is inscribed through performative writing. The power of writing is multidirectional, as it can be felt (through cognitive, embodied and affective dynamics) by the researcher as well as the reader. Halley (2012) highlights the cathartic aspect of writing, reflecting on how trauma and violence can be lived through, out of the past into the future (2012, 12). Although not all autoethnographies need or aim to be cathartic, these can be instrumental in giving voice to political projects. Stories of the self are located into personal experiences of race, gender, disability, class, sexuality, race and so on, which are nailed into a backdrop of social praxis and (sub)cultural understandings. As such, these experiences are shaped by politics of representation, rendering them contested and political.

Autoethnography can be articulated across disciplines and into many intersectional strands of social life and personal identities (see for instance Griffin, 2012; Boylorn, 2013 on Black experiences, and Adams and Holman Jones, 2011 on queer experiences) to gain better understanding of complex phenomena. This is particularly important in the case of groups that have been marginalized or relegated to minority status by dynamics of power and privilege. For example, Calafell and Moreman (2009, 124) state that 'feminists of color have long argued for the importance of listening to the experiences of women of color and attending to the politics that underlie these voices', which can be achieved through autoethnographic accounts. In the communications field, Davis (1998, 83) asks 'where is the critical voice which speaks to Black women's identity constituted in the experience of slavery, exile, pilgrimage, and struggle?' – this is where autoethnography can help fill the vacuum of emancipatory scholarship and critical narratives on the experience of people as it lends itself well to intersectional narratives that write the 'self-reflexive-self' (Reed-Danahay, 1997) within sociocultural matrixes ingrained through various levels of consciousness and revelation that link the personal to the cultural (Ellis and Bochner, 2000).

Personal experience and individual knowledge are informed and at the same time fed into one's social positioning, inequalities and culture. There are numerous examples of feminist autoethnography (see Averett, 2009; Avishai, Gerber and Randles, 2013), which allow women to engage in strategic 'talking back' (hooks, 1989) and to stress common struggles without the necessary erasure of the diversity among different people and groups:

> moving from silence into speech is for the oppressed, the colonized, the exploited, and those who stand and struggle side by side a gesture of defiance that heals, that makes new life and new growth possible. It is that act of speech, of 'talking back' that is no mere gesture of empty words, that is the expression of our movement from object to subject— the liberated voice. (hooks, 1989, 9)

The commonality or contrasts with experiences of Others in ethnography can be further articulated. The practice of writing and how one engages with this academic process can become a reason for othering and marginalization, a political stand and a way of 'talking back', as explained by Ann Cunliffe (2018): 'Doing research that is "different" is about alterity [...] — being constituted as "the Other" and as the Other there are practical consequences in terms of getting published, gaining tenure, building a career and being seen as a credible scholar.'

These differences in approach and narrative can be physically juxtaposed through the method of bricolage (Handforth and Taylor, 2016), but also considered from a theoretical point of view and from an ethical standpoint of togetherness in difference. Heather Höpfl (2000) understands writing that is inclusive (that is, not confined to masculine norms which render it 'motherless', arid and disembodied) as stemming from a position of love and embracing of difference. This is echoed in an article by Daniel Ericsson and Monika Kostera (2020) who, with a focus of organizational ethnography, explore writing for the sake of love and the self in relation to 'the radical imperative to encounter and understand the Other' in terms of alterethnography. Alterethnography is thus defined as:

> ethnography with a focus on otherness, to emphasize that it is not just a matter of research interest but a commitment to transgressing the boundaries of the ego as much as possible within the research endeavour and strive for a mode of writing invoking the presence of the setting de-egoized, as Hugo Letiche (2020) advocates: stripped of the authorial 'I' of science. It is an epistemological approach inextricably linked with a writing style communicating otherness and difference, everything that cannot be patriarchally ordered, including non-hegemonic gender and nationality.

Through this process, otherness becomes togetherness, which is linked to the idea of writing together, collaboratively and through community agency as a key step in change-making. Echoing Ericsson and Kostera (2020), here I understand ethnography as a key methodological approach and method in researching and writing differently that makes a difference.

Organizational aesthetics and arts-based methods

Art, to me, is the most diverse and inclusive mode of expression as it allows storytelling through different media and tools, formats and channels. However, it should be noted that art (especially in terms of access and what is considered 'artful' or 'proper art') can also be exclusionary and a site of privilege. As such, art is worthy and valuable in itself as a form of cultural enrichment and expression, but also as a research method. The arts are also ideally placed to tell stories that connect the mind with emotion, providing wordless narratives that capture the imagination and leverage instinctual and sensuous knowing. This is true for visual forms of what in the European tradition is considered 'fine art' (art developed for aesthetic and beauty rather than just for decorative purposes, such as painting, sculpture, drawing), but also for the more embodied art forms such as dance, music and theatre.

The pursuit of understanding, inquiry and expression through arts-based methods in research does not necessarily require excellence or mastery in the arts. I consider art as a democratizing method of inquiry as it goes beyond the textual coding of academic research and allows a direct channel to people who may not have access to or experience of academic research. In this book, I have chosen to separate the discussion of more textual-based art forms (narratives, poetry and so on) from the more visual, movement- and performative-related arts, although this segregation is purely one of convenience.

Organizational aesthetics knowledge draws from the fundamental belief that knowledge in the context of organizational studies can be developed through sensorial, emotional and embodied experiences and aesthetic judgments (Strati, 1992, 1999, 2000) from both researchers and participants. This is described by Witkin (2009) as 'cultivating an intelligence of feeling' and is linked to writing differently in and of organizations as it poses that work itself 'includes an essential aesthetic element; [...] aesthetics pervades the everyday life of organizations' (Ottensmeyer, 1996, 192–193); which represents a 'shift from almost exclusively objectivist approaches towards a sensuality that is the rich tapestry of organizational life' (Carr and Hancock, 2003, 1). Consequently, this theoretical stance – linked to materiality and corporeality – is in line with the belief underpinning this book, which espouses an embodied and affective approach to how we experience and write about organizations. Indeed, aesthetic ways of knowing bring together sensible and sensorial knowledge with passionate knowing (Gherardi, Nicolini and Strati, 2007, 316) and organizational practice (Strati, 2007b) as 'individuals and groups act in organizations by heeding their feelings, desires, tastes, talents, and passions' (Strati, 2010, 880). Aesthetic experience then can be considered an important way of contrasting or complementing traditional approaches of organizational understandings and learning that draw from experiential and action-based approaches (Welsch, Dehler, and Murray, 2007). Antonio Strati, one of the key scholars in the development of the field of organizational aesthetics, has identified a variety of methodologies and methods that are linked to this type of organizational inquiry, grouped into four macro areas: the archaeological, the empathetic-logical, the aesthetic, and the artistic approach (Strati, 2009, 2010). These approaches represent an 'epistemological polemic' against mainstream research in the management and organization studies field (Mack, 2013), and as such can be used and interpreted as feminist tools of resistance against hegemonic patriarchal ways of understanding and representing research in this field. These methods have been used in organizational scholarship and practice, and also in supporting students' learning of management and organizations (see Wicks and Rippin, 2010; Mack, 2013). Further, these approaches can be used not only to produce findings, but also as a tool to support the data creation and development stage. For instance, Bramming et al (2012) employed 'snaplogs' (snapshots and logbooks) created by research participants to facilitate focus group discussions.

In the following sections, I will focus on various arts-based methods – which I believe include the empathetic-logical (emotional) and the aesthetic-artistic approaches highlighted by Strati – to explore how the sensible and sensorial lens, through which we can theorize organizational experience, can support researching and writing differently. I consider aesthetics (drawing from sensory and affective experiences) and arts-based methods political tools and a powerful feminist instruments in their relational, dialogic and multilevel ability to link the individual to the plural. These approaches to research, whether individual or collaborative, open up possibilities of *knowing differently* (Liamputtong and Rumbold, 2008).

Leavy (2018, 9) provides a review of the main strengths of arts-based research. Among the numerous benefits identified, the following seem particularly relevant in the design of studies drawing on feminist principles: the provision of new insights and learning through the jarring potential of seeing and thinking differently; the ability to capture processes that mirror 'the unfolding nature of social like' (2018, 9) and to establish micro–macro connections not only between people but also across disciplines; their evocative and provocative nature that moves thanks to its immediacy; and the power to raise awareness, critique the status quo and awake critical consciousness – for instance, by unsettling and questioning stereotypes, challenging power structures, inequalities and dominant ideologies which marginalize voices and perspectives.

Arts-based research (ABR) is an umbrella term (Leavy, 2018) used to describe an approach to research based on the principle that arts and the humanities are valuable sources of knowing to foster and enhance knowledge creation. McNiff (2014, 259) defines arts-based research as 'a process of inquiry whereby the researcher, alone or with others, engages in the making of art as a primary mode of inquiry', whereby 'Art' and 'art' become universal and transdisciplinary ways of knowing (Allen, 1995), understanding and communicating. It combines tenets of the creative arts within research contexts and processes (Leavy, 2015; McNiff, 1998, 2011), and can be understood as a methodological tool to be used across the various stages of research, as a methodological field within the qualitative approach, or as a paradigm in itself (Rolling, 2010, 2013; Gerber et al, 2012; Leavy, 2018). Coined by Eisner in the 1990s, the term 'arts-based research' and the development of the related field of inquiry found fertile ground of application in psychology and therapy, education and learning (see Barone, 2000; Eisner, 2008). Patricia Leavy's edited handbook (2018) on the subject is an ideal starting point for anyone who wishes to embark on a journey into arts-based methods. Leavy takes an inclusive approach to the notion of 'arts', and includes in this field literary genres together with performative, visual and audiovisual arts. This edited volume is not exclusively aimed at scholars in the field of management and organization studies, or even in the social sciences, as arts-based methods are ideally placed to foster interdisciplinary and intersectional research. Jenna Ward and Harriet Shortt (2020) curated another accessible, interdisciplinary and insightful volume on the use of arts-based research methods for creative research in business, organization studies and the humanities.

The thought of engaging with art as a method or approach to academic inquiry may seem far-fetched to scholars in the field of management and organization studies and other social sciences. However, arts-based methods can be considered not only as a data collection point, but also as a coherent approach in dialogue with research that is committed to thinking conceptually, symbolically, aesthetically and metaphorically with openness. Two decades ago, Bochner and Ellis (2003) proposed the idea of art as inquiry, which has been highlighted as particularly useful approach in developing connections with emotional experiences that can be accessed and communicated in a liminal space (Page, Grisoni and Turner, 2014). The value of this type of research has been recognized now across dimensions – between the aesthetic dimensions of art, and the more performative organizational functions that it can be related to. Unfortunately, the use of arts-based methods and knowing in management and organization studies can still result in criticism related to lack of rigour (see, for instance, Najda-Janoszka and Daba-Buzoianu, 2018), which can, however, be addressed through transparency in research design, analytic approach and theoretical contribution (Ashworth et al, 2019). Adler (2006) highlighted how leadership and other aspects of life in organizations have grown increasingly closer to arts to explore complex and global issues. Similarly, artists have also created or further explored links with business (Meisiek and Hatch, 2008) to support the ignition of different ways of thinking and problem-solving. Consequently, artistic fields have developed ties in management, education, theory and practice (see for example Phillips, 1995, Linstead and Höpfl, 2000; Taylor and Carboni, 2008; Taylor and Ladkin, 2009).

Although there are numerous artist-scholars or artist-scientists (Janesick, 2001) who are talented artists, arts-based methods can be pursued by researchers who have an understanding of the method and practical engagement with the tools, without needing refined artistic skills. Barry (2008, 33) highlights how art infuses creative potential *ex nihilo* – both in researchers and participants. However, arts-based methods require a certain openness to experimentation and lack of control, exposure and vulnerability as 'a fundamental premise of artistic inquiry is that the end cannot be known at the beginning' (McNiff, 2017, 32) and can take a myriad of different unpredictable directions. Researchers, therefore, need to be open to persuasion and surprise, exposure and vulnerability. The indeterminate potential of aesthetic knowing in organizations (Taylor and Ladkin, 2009) fosters engagement with the unknown in terms of results and findings (Barry and Meisiek, 2010). This is linked to the concept of 'aesthetic risk' (Strati, 2007a; Baldacchino, 2009; Mack, 2013) in pursuing aesthetic knowing given the traditional dominance of mainstream ways of understanding knowledge in this field. Nonetheless, an aesthetic approach to understanding work and organizational life experiences has received increasing interest in management and organization studies over the past two decades (Minahan and Wolfram-Cox, 2007) with students and more established scholars experimenting with artistic, arts-based or aesthetic forms (see Taylor and Hansen, 2005). Minahan and Wolfram-Cox (2007) also referred to this growing body of work as 'The Aesthetic Turn in Management'.

The inclusion of arts-based methods and sensibilities in research and teaching that is considered 'useful' or 'high value' can therefore also be seen as a political statement in response to the commercialization of education and the imposition of neoliberal marketized metrics onto fields of knowledge. Arts-based inquiry (Taylor et al, 2002; Taylor, 2003; Darsø, 2004; Taylor and Ladkin, 2009; Elm and Taylor, 2010) has also been used to ignite new life into organizational praxis, to illuminate what is not in focus or centred in organizations, and to inhabit the space between the public and the private (Grisoni, 2012). There are many examples to show the value of this approach to research in our field. Margaret Page, Louise Grisoni and Arthur Turner (2014) show how poetry, visual inquiry and social dreaming can contribute to bring to light and enliven tacit knowledge (Tsoukas, 2005) regarding equality and diversity in organizations. Therefore, choices in terms of research and writing are important to establish which bodies we speak from and to, which networks we inhabit, who we chose to work with, and what we consider 'valuable'. The methods we use to investigate, disseminate, perform or represent academic work are also crucial to find different vocabularies and tune into other rhythms as these help us fight the erasure of marginalized experiences, stories and bodies. Marina Fotaki (2013), and Mary Phillips, Alison Pullen and Carl Rhodes (2014) highlight how writing in organization studies is a gendered practice, which is hierarchically positioned (Acker, 1990) as women and men are bound to the masculine order. And so our response to artistic, embodied, female, feminist and different types of researching and writing is also something to be mindful of in the mobilizing of connecting voices and affective solidarity. The feminist academic community (Vachhani and Pullen, 2019) can be a powerful force to counteract sexism, metric-driven notions of value and masculine normativity. This can also be attempted through the use and championing of arts-based methods, ethnographic approaches and writing styles that demand acknowledgement, require a response (not necessarily always positive, but that is one of the risks of writing differently) and inhabit a space that avoids containment.

This research journey is about embracing and engaging in not-knowing as much as it is about knowing, and a commitment to 'rupture the epistemic containment that continually oppresses' (Pullen, 2018, 126). By using methods and tools that are unexpected, or that push the boundary within a specific field of inquiry, researchers can also disrupt the taken-for-granted sense-making processes and narratives that participants (and scholars themselves) are accustomed to. These *arresting moments* can provoke *affective moments* that ignite understanding and knowing. To develop new insights and consider alternative perspectives, researchers need to approach phenomena differently (Hesse-Biber and Leavy, 2006, 2008). Reflexivity, sympathy and empathy can be fostered (Dunlop, 2001) through the artistic medium and the art of writing or 'doing' inquiry differently, promoting care and compassion (McIntyre, 2004).

Given the personal connection established through arts-based methods, the impact of such research can be stronger, jargon-free and more accessible, to minimize academic gatekeeping. Here participants can be treated as equal collaborators (Finley, 2008) engaged in non-hierarchical relationships that allow the opening up of multiplicity in meaning-making and the decentralization of academic researchers as authorities or the only valid sources of knowledge. Moreover, by looking at different spheres and modes of knowing from different perspectives, aesthetic reflexivity (DeNora, 2000; Sutherland, 2013) becomes a way to foster critical engagement with workplace experiences that are complex and plural. The narratives – whether textual or through other media – become multinarrative perspectives that offer kaleidoscopic representations of experiences that are both unique and universal (Estrella and Forinash, 2007). Several scholars across disciplines (see, for instance, Strati, 1999; Dewey, 2005; Whitfield, 2005; Gerber et al, 2012; Chilton and Leavy, 2014) have suggested that the arts are critical in achieving self–other knowledge based on multiple ways of knowing that are not only intellectual, but also emotional, sensory, kinaesthetic and imaginary. This can also be applied to the experience of organizations (Warren, 2002), as arts have a particularly relational quality in the production and interpretation of knowledge, in how sense is made through bodies, minds and nature (Conrad and Beck, 2015).

Researching and writing differently in management and organization studies can benefit from interdisciplinary approaches from the arts and humanities as imagination and creativity are particularly fostered through arts-based methods. Sutherland (2013) highlights a 'growing cry' for different approaches to management and leadership development, identifying a three-stage theoretical model of experiential learning processes of arts-based methodologies. These are not only useful to understand people's experiences in organizations, but also for management and leadership education, which otherwise is premised on decontextualized, disembodied and abstract notions of organizing that are not mirrored in the everyday life of organizations (Cunliffe, 2002). When using arts-based methods – whether visual, narrative, movement-based or in other formats – learning occurs while making, and via subsequent reflection on what was created, and throughout the process that led to certain outputs or outcomes (Gayá Wicks and Rippin, 2010; Grisoni, 2012). For instance, Brigitte Biehl-Missal and Claus Springborg (2015) explore the dynamics between dance and organizations through a special issue in *Organizational Aesthetics*, while Katharina Miko-Schefzig, Mark Learmonth and Robert McMurray (2020) investigate how film and moving images can provide significant contributions to organization studies. Taylor (2008, 399–400) identifies four main benefits of arts-based learning: (a) they draw on tacit and embodied forms of knowing or sensory experience; (b) they offer a holistic approach to experience rather than merely through logical, systematic processes; (c) they offer meaning-making through personal experiences; and (d) they provide lasting impacts because of their affective component.

Arts-based methods can be used to explore not only individual experiences, the inner world and its fluctuations, but also some broader macro phenomena that are of direct relevance for society and organizations, such as sustainability (Kastner and Wallis, 1998). There has been a strong current of work by scholars in management and organization studies advocating for the cross-pollinations between arts and business (see, for instance, Linstead and Höpfl, 2000; Austin and Devin, 2003; Witz et al, 2003; Ladkin, 2011; Meisiek and Barry, 2018; Guillet de Monthoux, 2020; Devin and Austin, 2012). Within a Black feminist framework, arts-based methods have been used in terms of both subversion and assertion of agency (Farrington, 2005). In an article stemming from arts-based experience of dancing and movement therapy and written as a dialogue, Pauliina Jääskeläinen and Jenny Helin (2021) discuss 'writing embodied generosity' as a way to be open toward the other, with curiosity toward the 'strangeness' in the other which becomes 'enabling' rather than marginalizing.

Poetic and narrative inquiry

The myopic investigation of organizing and organizations through narrow disciplinary and methodological templates and strict disciplinary boundaries fosters unnecessary 'epistemic gatekeeping' (Steger, 2019). The use of approaches and methods borrowed from other disciplines can instead allow different perspectives to come to the fore. In agreement with Steger (2019), I argue for the overcoming of dividing lines between disciplines in favour of a deep integration among fields of inquiry. At the moment, arts-based methods are increasingly becoming common in qualitative studies, albeit still considered somewhat 'alternative' (see earlier contributions on this by Knowles and Cole, 2008), and especially in management and organization studies, where these can be seen still as a form of writing differently. This type of interdisciplinary activity can be fostered through communities, research and education clusters that focus on a topic across fields of study and the use of particular methods.

Regardless of mainstream aversions towards this interdisciplinary cross-pollination, content-focused and methodological 'turns' have been increasingly visible during the past few decades, including the 'poetic turn' (Sparkes et al, 2003), joining a 'growing trend of [...] textual experimentation' (Ely, 2007, 571). Poetry has been used in many ways and from different approaches in qualitative research. For example, Poindexter (2002; 2006) rearranges her participants' stories as poems and notes, explaining that 'poems seemed to me to be embedded in the stories, just as the stories were embedded in the interviews, and when I extracted them, I felt a deeper sense of empathy and resonance with the caregivers' experiences' (2002, 709). Richardson (1992; 1997) used poetry as a way of producing evocative research texts; a process that Glesne (1997; 1999, 202) described as 'poetic transcription'. Patai (1993) used 'dramatic poetry' to present the stories of her participants in verse form. Notwithstanding the many critiques of poetry as a method of inquiry (see, for example, Silverman, 2007) and the need some have expressed to have an *ars poetica* (see Faulkner, 2007) dictating normative principles around poetry production and consumption, I believe that poetry (especially in its unleashed lyrical or evocative form) can also help the reader connect to a more instinctual and naïve way of knowing that is more prone to affective encounters. This is where poetry links with Feminism, inclusion and writing differently in its political potential. These are, to my mind, crucial when discussing inequality and experiences of marginalization, as highlighted by Audre Lorde: 'For women, then, poetry is not a luxury. It is a vital necessity of our existence. It forms the quality of the light within which we predicate our hopes and dreams toward survival and change, first made into language, then into idea, then into more tangible action' (Audre Lorde, 1984b, 37). As such, poetry becomes a powerful tool to express oppression. Esther Ohito and Tiffany Nyachae (2019) investigate the experience of Black girls and women from a feminist perspective through the use of poetry as a method within critical qualitative research to 'open possibilities for [de- and re-] constructing understanding' (Leggo, 2004, 30).

Poetic practices have also been investigated in terms of their potential in teaching and learning by scholars in management and organization studies (see Kostera, 1997; Grisoni, 2008, 2009; Taylor and Ladkin, 2009; Darmer and Grisoni, 2011). Poetry allows the organizing mind to wonder, wander and seek asylum in resonating spaces of meaning. As suggested by

Lorde's words above, poetry can ignite political action against inequality. Through poetry we can explore the echoes between text, emotions and embodiment that may create connections, rupture and arresting moments of understanding. It is a form of slow intensity, of revelling into instinctual as well as cognitive reflexivity. It's a way to *feel* and *listen* to what people think and feel, rather than to just read a conventional academic text. Stein (2003) shows how poetry can be used to identify and address issues in the workplace. Poetry can be deployed not only as a form of self-expression but also as a means to interpret narratives and texts produced by others. For example, in her study focused on experiences of disability in education, Angela Ward (2011) shows how poetic re-presentation can be used to address research dilemmas and employed as an alternative way of re-presenting participants' stories. Methodologically this is achieved through a careful and relational approach to the researcher's intervention on interview transcripts and other data, reordered and crafted as poetry in a way to 'foreground [...] stories, create verisimilitude and focus on the essence of the experiences, [to] create coherent storylines, and create evocative text' (Ward, 2011, 355).

The power of poetry and its social value also gained visibility beyond academia during the 20 January 2021 presidential inauguration of Joe Biden in the US, when Amanda Gorman, the nation's first-ever Youth Poet Laureate, read the poem entitled 'The Hill We Climb'. Sutherland (2013, 37) suggests that reflexive work can generate 'memories with future resonance and momentum', which can raise awareness and instigate action or ignite agency in the reader. In *The Words of Selves* (2000), Denise Riley argues that the self is multiply constituted, since many people speak through and 'as' us. Her writing is political, as she highlights how conflict and separatist agendas are informed by and sustain nationalist and racist sentiment. This multivoiced layering implies multiple conscious and unconscious responses, as well as resonances, since 'there is always another breath in my breath, another thought in my thought, another possession in what I possess, a thousand things and a thousand beings implicated in my complications' (2000, 184, citing Deleuze [1969] 2013). Riley calls this 'polyvocality' (2000), which becomes a key character in evocative forms of writing (such as poetry, narratives, autoethnography) used in feminist writing and writing differently. Language moves through and despite us, defining people through intrinsic and extrinsic processes, creating 'monuments of selves' (2000, 3) in our writing. As such, language is a mechanism of researching and writing differently in its potential both to open up possibilities and disrupt the status quo. Poetic language in management and organization studies is uncommon, although it allows the dialogic iterative process of polyvocality in understanding and (re)imagining the self and others in organizations, through the discursive dynamic that relies upon and implicates others through each poetic expression.

Located in the proximity of evocative or interpretive autoethnography, poetic inquiry (see, for instance, Prendergast, Leggo and Sameshima 2009; van Amsterdam and van Eck, 2019b) can be a way to write differently about trauma and violence in organizations. For example, Noortje van Amsterdam (2020) explored the issue of silence and sexual violence through five poems that contribute to discussions in organization studies regarding #MeToo (see Ozkazanc-Pan, 2019) and writing differently (see Grey and Sinclair, 2006; Fotaki, Metcalfe and Harding, 2014; Phillips, Pullen and Rhodes, 2014; Meier and Wegener, 2017; Gilmore, Harding, Helin and Pullen, 2019). Heather Höpfl considered narrative approaches to organizing as fundamental ways to understand organizing and organizations (1994), especially in the case of poetics, which she deemed key to unlock imagination and discourse (2000). This methodological approach allows the advancement of theoretical understandings of the concept of inclusion through an investigation of everyday practices and workplace experiences of in/exclusion. Dide van Eck's work is also a good example of writing differently – focusing on workplace diversity, organizational inclusion, power and inequality explored through organizational ethnography and arts-based research in the form of poetic inquiry. In addition to her methodological choice, she also focuses on gender and body size, an intersection often silenced in studies of organizing. Her collaboration with Noortje van Amsterdam is not only materialized through publications and joint projects (see van Amsterdam and van Eck, 2019a) but also through the sharing of their work beyond academic audiences through a website, 'Poetry at Work'.[1] Dirty writing (Höpfl, 2007; Pullen and Rhodes, 2008; Pullen, 2018) and writing differently often stem from writing that is personal and not intended for the academic public, which then finds itself shared at a late stage.

A lot has been written on the power of narratives in management and organization studies over the past three decades: Bochner and Riggs (2014) explored the increase in narrative inquiry across disciplines starting from the 1980s, and the 'narrative turn' (Denzin and Lincoln, 2002, 2005). Here I am particularly interested in the experience of writing itself, although this book will not focus explicitly on how writing differently can be done (this is addressed in an edited book by Kostera, 2022). This form of researching and writing differently is both embodied and affective, in terms of how we write and what we write. Acknowledging that scholars are situated in specific spaces that need recognition, we can discover ourselves and new meanings as we write. The writing process has also been investigated, for example, by Janet Sayers and Deborah Jones (2015, 104), who were inspired by Cixous's work:

Writings — inscribed black marks on blank things — are symbols or abstractions representing artefacts, actions and experiences, which through their very nature create a space between thought and words; between thought and body. There is a gap between the thought and the word on the page (or the screen). In the space and time between individual thought and its shareable representation in becoming the word, it is moderated through the political, social and cultural knowledge regimes that decide and organize what is known, what can be said, how it can be said, and to whom. Two relevant points are developed in the next two paragraphs; the medium for the black mark on the white page; and the interactive social process involved in words' becoming. (Sayers and Jones, 2015)

Narrative approaches to academic investigations allow research not to become trapped and squeezed within the confines of narrow academic writing praxis that turns embodiment, dynamic and moving experiences into static ones (Höpfl, 2010). Cixous warns:

It's perfectly possible to make a machine out of the text, to treat it like a machine and be treated by it like a machine. The contemporary tendency has been to find theoretical instruments, a reading technique which has bridled the text, mastered it like a wild horse with saddle and bridle, enslaving it. (Cixous, 1988, in Boulous Walker, 2017, 155)

The link between women's writing and their bodies has been discussed at length in feminist work, for example by Cixous (1976) and Kristeva (1987), who consider the abstraction of thought and how we can inscribe our bodies through writing or render it a stranger through language and writing, which become political statements. Through writing we can connect to our self and others, and inscribe ourselves onto text that denounces both inclusion and exclusion. Cixous writes:

I shall speak about women's writing: about what it will do. Woman must write her self: must write about women and bring women to writing, from which they have been driven away as violently as from their bodies — for the same reasons, by the same law, with the same fatal goal. Woman must put herself into the text — as into the world and into history — by her own movement. (Cixous, 1976, 875)

I maintain that poetry and evocative narratives – whether located within autoethnography or in other types of prose – lend themselves particularly well to the capturing of other people's imagination into our texts. Sensorial, affective and metaphorical writing can resonate with larger (even collective) experiences and reinscribe the feminine and the marginalized into narratives and academic publishing that have been dominated by masculine ways of researching and writing. Evocative narratives are found in various types of writing and genres, such as autoethnographic narratives, poetry, fictional stories and creative non-fiction (Gutkind, 2012). Lorri Neilsen also speaks of 'lyric inquiry' as an experience of 'expression and immersion' (2008, 96) and explains its value:

> Lyric inquiry draws upon non rationalist and nondiscursive ways of knowing in order to engage in inquiry practices and to produce written forms that have, up to now, been undervalued or ignored in scholarly discourses. Lyric inquiry is informed by aesthetic and philosophical principles of writing; it is based on a conviction that using expressive and poetic functions of language creates the possibility of a resonant, ethical, and engaged relationship between the knower and the known. [...] Characteristics [include] liminality, ineffability, metaphorical thinking, embodied understanding, personal evocations, domestic and local understanding, and an embrace of the eros of language. (Neilsen, 2008, 93)

These types of narrative are characterized by a sort of evanescence, a sense of vagueness, undetermined meaning, openness and interpretation that inhabits a particular feminine space in research. These texts are particularly relevant to researching and writing differently because they disrupt the masculine ways of understanding academic discourse and academic language.

Visual and performative methods

The link between narratives and visual or performative methods lies in the imagery and imagination, as well as in the movement in and of the text. Sayers and Jones (2015, 107) further pose that 'poems exist in the realm of making (mimesis) rather than knowing or doing.' Of course, art is used and exploited by organizations large and small to convey meaning and assign traits to their spaces – through artwork, architectural features, advertisements, colours and images. The distinction here between arts-based methods and 'visual' methods is purely caused by the structural needs of this text, as the latter overlaps with the former, and also with ethnographic methods. Leaders of organizations – as well as political leaders – use visual arts extensively to reinforce and sustain dynamics of power; for example, by commissioning the creation of art to justify their heroic self-narrative; running multimedia campaigns to reinforce messages that support their agendas; and even by commissioning the design of urban landscapes and buildings to support their propaganda. For instance, fascism in Italy used new imposing architecture that was inspired by visual symbols of power (such as the *fascio*) used in ancient Roman sites together with modern functionality. While drawing legitimacy from its Roman origins, the fascist architecture, especially in Rome, at the same time sought to disconnect itself from the past by looking for straight lines, repetitive shapes and patterns, hard corners and straight lines, through which the new regime promoted austerity in a combination of styles called *razionale* (rational). Entire neighbourhoods and towns were developed to support this agenda, often at the expense of existing historical relics and art that was wiped out or built over.

Visual arts – through photography, video and performative approaches – can be used as an interpretive lens or methods (see Sullivan, 2009) to understand organizations. Often, these approaches can foster the design of a study, and its data collection can constitute examples of researching and writing differently to surface sociopolitical struggle. Harriet Shortt and Samantha Warren (2019) developed grounded visual pattern analysis (GVPA) as a rigorous tool for analysing photos and visual patterns, combining both dialogic and archaeologic approaches to visual materials. Many embodied and handicraft methods 'of the hand' (such as knitting, crafting, collage, mixed methods creations) that are performative in nature merge with the purely visual methods such as photos and films. For instance, Harriet Shortt's work provides examples of integrating photoethnography in organization studies; her work on hairdressers shows how the material landscape of work can be used to create 'identitiscapes' around negotiated and re-created work identities (2015). I first met Harriet at the Standing Conference on Organizational Symbolism (SCOS) in 2010 where she presented her PhD research through a narrative centred around a beautiful quilt. I had never even imagined the possibility of doing something like that in an academic conference. In that same SCOS space of 'serious fun' and intellectual experimentation, over the years I have had the privilege to witness examples of embodied visual methods – for example, in Beatriz Acevedo's drawings that summarize academic presentations; Ann Rippin's embroidery and Lynne Baxter's knitting that surface historical and gendered relational dynamics. Another example of the use of visual methods both as still image and as film can be seen in an article by Eric Ping Hung Li, Ajnesh Prasad, Cristalle Smith, Ana Gutierrez, Emily Lewis and Betty Brown (2019), where the use of photo and video-voice campaigns was found to be useful for participants (and participant-led research) in considering issues around community building and in exploring sociopolitical dynamics of community belongingness. Further, Gudrun Skjælaaen, Arne Lindseth Bygdås, and Aina Landsverk Hagen (2020) explore the use of collaborative video research in organizational practices by combining ethnographic methods and intervention through film-elicitation. This approach, they pose, helps to reproduce the immediacy and vitality of lived experience by involving organizational members in capturing the multiplicity of organizational practices. The community relevance of this method is also present in Eric

Ping Hung Li and Ajnesh Prasad's study (2018), which looks at graffiti and social media as ideological and political acts of resistance.

These methods help bring together ethnographic and narrative approaches with embodied and sensorial understandings of organizations, which can be co-constructed and led with participants. This can be done by distinguishing the aims of visual inquiry – for example, whether the approach is one of *representation* or *enactivism*. Also, there is a fundamental difference in positionality of the researcher and the photographer, when these are not the same individual, to consider whether the scholar is best placed to discover 'hidden meanings' within the images to then be translated and analysed as text, or whether the aim is not to represent and unveil reality but instead to 'evoke, elicit and engage viewers in affective dynamisms that comprise physical phenomena and our sensuous perceptions' (Wood and Brown, 2012, 143). This is particularly linked to embodiment as the sense-making process is not simply carried out by the mind but is instead shaped by the actions and perceptions of those involved in it and their practices (Varela et al, 1993; Tsoukas, 2009). Film-elicitation as a method can also prompt embodied narrative performances where participants make their experiences and everyday practices sensible to themselves and others (Cunliffe and Coupland, 2012). Nik Taylor and Heather Fraser (2017) further explore how arts-based and visual methods (drawing from pictures, poems, stories and videos) can be used to recognize and value the work done by women and animals, thus linking post-human approaches to emotion and work. This responds to calls for research that resists speciesism and hegemonic masculinity, with the aim not just to be inclusive of women and other humans, but also of other agents that are considered and thus discriminated against for being too 'emotional' or feminine. Speciesism and masculinity stem from limiting and hierarchical ways of seeing the world (Kemmerer, 2011) that become normative in the practice and performance of social and organizational dynamics.

Performance and visual methods can also be considered ways to recentre the focus of research to include marginalized subjects, both human and non-human. This can be seen through a feminist and critical lens in the questioning of power and contribution. Indeed, organizing and work are commonly carried out not only by people, but by humans in dialogue with animals and artefacts. The medium of dance, film or theatre can help authors and participants communicate personal, rich, sensory knowledge which is related to the workplace or more 'concrete' episodes (Shotter and Tsoukas, 2014). This is done by combining experience and phenomena with different types of sensory stimuli (Madison, 2005), which may include but are not bound by language and text. The performance of everyday life (see Pelias, 1999), and performance as a way of knowing, have been increasingly used in management and organization studies. Specifically, research has considered theatre as a sense-making tool (see, for example, Mangham and

Overington, 1987; Kärreman, 2001; Beirne and Knight, 2007), and as a mechanism to reflect on organizational life *as* theatre, and on the use of theatre *in* organizations (see Schreyögg and Höpfl, 2004).

Theatre and performance-based inquiry are clearly linked to embodiment and sensuous understandings, which, as highlighted by Bell and King, can at times still be considered at odds with academic research

> Academics may be seen as a professional organizational group that is particularly reluctant to acknowledge or reflect upon the embodied aspects of their collective identity practices. The dichotomous and hierarchical opposition that exists between mind and body, intellect and emotion within academia presents the character of the ideal academic in a way which suppresses and subordinates the concept of the body through defining it negatively as unnecessary, intrusive or incidental. (Bell and King, 2010, 429)

In its resistance towards disembodied, masculine and normative understandings of research, this approach is then linked to feminist values and movement-based somatics which have the ability 'to transcend and challenge phallocentric societal structures' (Eddy et al 2014, 170). Resistance enacted through visual and performative methods can also bring together communities of practice, while highlighting marginalization and diffusing scholar–participant power dynamics.

Feminist approaches in researching and writing practices

I believe that a feminist approach to academic work (and to life more in general) must be pervasive and cannot be trapped within the specific confines of the theory, topic or method used in a study. As such, the feminist challenge to inequality and the status quo should be applied not only to the topic under inquiry and the way people interact with each other as co-authors, but to all aspects of academic work. This is why this book argues for the importance of both researching and writing differently, to consider feminist alternatives to processes and practicalities involved in academic research that are not merely limited to the writing itself. This means also critically engaging with taken for granted notions in one's field or in the day-to-day practice of research. This section provides two examples of feminist reflection on academic praxis that is common across various fields of inquiry: data and citations.

Feminist approaches to data

Data, and the use we make of them, are important. In line with my epistemological stance discussed earlier in Part III, I believe that data collection, coding and analysis cannot be objective and disembodied in their interaction with the researcher, as these activities are inevitably meshed with bias, interpretation and positionalities that imply the impossibility of neutrality. Although many articles are purely theoretical, in others there is a great variety of methods used to collect and analyse data. It can be various types of data (numerical, textual, visual) and can come from various sources (the author, individuals, groups of people or survey results). The potential of a feminist approach can be realized across different types of methods, and a combination of those. Staunæs and Brøgger (2020, 3) rightfully highlight that 'data and their mediated forms, such as visualizations, are neither neutral nor innocent, but agentic and performative'. As such, data can be problematized and their positionality critiqued, which has been a feature of post-qualitative inquiry (see St. Pierre, 2011; Gherardi, 2019b). Further, Angelo Benozzo and Silvia Gherardi (2020) reflect on 'not-yet data' or 'shadow data', thus probing the wonderous and disorientating fuzziness of illegible data and what it does to us as researchers.

Research superimposes the researcher, their body and intellect onto the data as 'in our work as researchers we weigh and shift experiences and make choices regarding what is significant, what is trivial, what to include, what to exclude ... by doing so, we craft narrative; we write lives' (Richardson, 1990, 10). Moreover, there is also the 'affective nature' of data, which is an important point in considering how researchers interact with the field, data and their findings. As doctoral students, academics are generally trained to think carefully about their data collection, what they want to gain from it, what the best method of collecting a certain type of data is, and the broad ethical impact the related data collection will have on the world. However, important considerations around data are both centred around the data we collect, generate and analyse, and the impact that data have on our professional selves – the metrics data generate and their implications. This complex web of meaning and consequences around data can be seen in a feminist context, whereby the word 'feminist', in Staunæs and Brøgger's words (2020, 5), can be taken to mean 'versions of thinking and acting that engage critically in analysis of and curious, creative and imaginative altering of conventional power relations and genealogies related to intersectional gender categories' to embrace ethics of care, affect and justice. Therefore, in considering, planning, collecting and using data, scholars need to ask themselves how these processes impact the creation, shaping and (re)configuring of affects, categories and practices (Staunæs and Brøgger, 2020).

The use of data and normative assumptions regarding what data can be deemed more acceptable than others in academic research are ways to belittle and manipulate feminist approaches, or marginalize studies that do not conform to masculine norms. McQueeney (2013) cautions against the 'reduction of feminist methodology to a conflict between politics and analysis' to avoid an oversimplification of feminist data and feminist ethnographers privileging participants' voices. So, instead of subjecting political beliefs and interpretations to a lower hierarchical level than analysis within the research process, feminists also explore who they are, what they feel, and their beliefs as tools for analysing data (Kleinman and Kolb 2012). Although research findings can at times be in conflict with feminist principles (Avishai, Gerber and Randles, 2013), this is also the case for non-feminist scholars who may find unexpected or challenging findings in their data. In particular, Kleinman and Copp (1993) note how feminist ethnographers should persevere in their questioning and explorations of politics, not to silence them from the data analysis and discussions, but instead to produce less biased, more original analyses. All research is political – not just in the data, but in the gaze we turn to a context and in the phenomena that we choose for investigation. When Feminism is depoliticized in the name of rigorous analysis and disembodied research methods, it becomes inextricably incorporated within dominant discourses and practices, therefore breeding new forms of patriarchal normative power (see Collins 2000; McRobbie 2009).

Data are not just about numbers and quotes: data hold meaning and power, can be leveraged and manipulated. Data are also used as a source of metric-driven instruments of power and oppression in academia. Staunæs and Brøgger (2020) explore alternatives to the metric-driven approach of contemporary neoliberal academic work and, in doing so, they start from an interesting premise: 'Data are not just representatives of something out there. When articulating the world, they generate the world' (2020, 1). Stemming from feminist new materialist concepts, and drawing from the use of tools from speculative feminist storytelling, Staunæs and Brøgger (2020) write through a 'critique beyond criticism' (Foucault, 1996), which aims to plant the seed 'for revolt and everyday utopias' (Staunæs and Brøgger, 2020, 2) and 'stays with the trouble' (Haraway, 2016) but is not devoid of hope. The way qualitative data are often belittled in mainstream positivist environments is once again a response to a masculine imprinting of the field, which aims to dissect, separate, structure and order data to avoid uncertainty, messiness and vagueness. This type of masculine understanding and manipulation of data finds comfort in sameness and assimilation, in pursuing paths carved by others before, in replicating, duplicating and comparing. The cutting-out of these qualitative and experimental data from the investigations of human experiences in the workplace and in organizing is a dismemberment of the (female) body at work, the gendered amputation of certain parts of academic work. As such, the neoliberal, masculine, rigid and patriarchal approach to methods and data is not only anti-feminist but also violent. And, sadly, it also renders data 'dumb matter' (Massumi, 2002) devoid of emotion, materiality and embodiment. Instead, the very value and 'wonder' of qualitative data lie in their ability to transcend the beaten path, to offer glimpses of individuality and exceptionality; it stems from the power data have to move and transform through surprise and critique. In researching and writing differently, we seek to unlock the potential of data by liberating them from silencing normative rules. Data are subjected to gendered hierarchies of power (Acker, 1990), so the challenging of the status quo needs to be implemented not only at the level of content, methodology and methods, but also at the level of the data. Writing differently and its kaleidoscopic sources of data can be considered as a feminist political project to bring the margins to the centre, to illuminate the experiences at interlocking nodes of oppressions, to unravel the dynamics of power between the individual, collective and systemic levels of organizing.

Data affect many people – the researcher, participants and academic networks; but also, in some cases, policy-making processes and social understandings. In considering this problem Staunæs and Brøgger (2020) propose the concepts of *affectivity* (intensities and tensions related to the process or processes of being touched and moved, which affect academic subjectivities, reading and writing) and *affect*s (affective intensities and tensions that can be named and coded semantically according to different registers) as two key factors to be related to data. Maggie MacLure (2013, 229) also shares the idea of affective data by considering how data are connected to different sensorial and affective registers, which can move the different stakeholders involved. Further, Maclure considers how wonder (in both its positive and negative affective connotation) is embedded within and radiates from data, which can cause disruption to academic epistemic certainty or to the comforts of data–related processes such as coding strategies and schemes. Wonder is a particularly fitting concept in researching and writing differently as it is relational, and it can be considered as a '*cognitive passion*, as much about knowing as about feeling', embodied and intellectual at the same time (Daston and Park, 2001, 14, my emphasis). And so perhaps researching and writing differently is also about agential wonder, or wondrous agency. The chiasmic poetics of wonder defined as cognitive passion avoid the hierarchical subjugations of one to the other, and suggest instead a dynamic iterative movement that *moves* both intellectually and emotionally.

Considered through these lenses, data can be understood as a feminist and political instrument, and not just as a means to reach an end within the mechanistic process of empirical research. Ahmed (2004) stresses how emotions as cultural politics can unite people, even at a distance. Similarly, words and signs have a responsive and emotional power to shape social behaviour, understanding and political actinon. Seen within this context, data, and the language we use to report on data, have the power to move and instigate change.

This potentiality can be felt on occasions where something—perhaps a comment in an interview, a fragment of a field note, an anecdote, an object, or a strange facial expression—seems to reach out from the inert corpus (corpse) of the data, to grasp us. These moments confound the industrious, mechanical search for meanings, patterns, codes, or themes; but at the same time, they exert a kind of fascination, and have a capacity to animate further thought. On other occasions I have called this intensity that seems to emanate from data, a 'glow'. (MacLure, 2013, 228)

Therefore, data should not be seen simply as results, findings or answers, but as a potential source of critique, disruption, challenge and change. The application of feminist ethics of care to data also brings to the fore resistance to the masculine understanding of the ideal 'scientist' or author, who superimposes their expertise and understanding onto the data, often obscuring the participant's voice – the crisis of representation (Lather, 1995; Denzin and Lincoln, 2000). It is important for all scholars, and especially those who are interested in researching and writing differently, to consider the ethical dilemmas around authorial voice and presence, the space and place occupied by the researcher, and the concomitant power dynamics which are inherent to the relationships established through data collection, interpretation and analysis. This is even more crucial in the case of research that focuses on people who are marginalized or oppressed.

Participatory research methods, some of which I outlined in the previous section, lend themselves to being considered feminist methods as these put the participants at the centre as leading the data creation or collation. These approaches can contribute to the development of deeper understandings by offering new or alternative points of view to ignite activism, agency and resistance, as well as solutions-orientated work (Brown et al, 2017). Arts based methods can provide opportunities to explore this type of participatory approach – for instance, through participant led photography, forum theatre and other forms of dramatic performance (Boal, 1995; Kaptani and Yuval-Davis, 2008). Page, Grisoni and Turner (2014) highlight how participatory research also enhances fairness and fosters equality, thus promoting 'aesthetic reflexivity' (Sutherland, 2013).

The relationship between Feminism and method is explored by Shulamit Reinharz (1992), posing that the integration of a variety of perspectives can be particularly useful to feminist inquiry. In an attempt to define what constitutes feminist research, Mary Dankoski (2000) builds on Reinharz's work (1992) to articulate some broad feminist research parameters:

In order to give some of these 'present but invisible' studies recognition, Reinharz's definition needs to be modified. I think that in addition to her criteria, (those methods used by self-defined feminists, award-winning feminist researchers, or seen in feminist publications), some of the other issues to be examined under criteria comprising feminist research include: (1) the types of research questions asked, (2) the theory or theories driving the research, (3) the methodology used, (4) the ethics of the researcher, and (5) the importance or significance of the results for advancing a feminist agenda. By 'feminist agenda' I mean a questioning and challenging of constructions of gender and power imbalances in many forms--based on race, socioeconomic status, sexuality and [...] power differences. [...] (Dankoski, 2000, 7)

This includes the participant's perspectives highlighted in participatory research, which is pertinent also to research that considers a variety of primary categories of experience that are often discriminated against (such as disability, gender, race and so on). It would be reductive to consider feminist research merely as antagonistic to positivist approaches, as marginal to mainstream experiences, or simply as a form of resistance. It is instead a valuable approach (and practice) in its own right, through its ethical stance, the plurality of its perspective, the reflexivity of its positionality and its inclusive character. Although there may not be methods that are exclusively feminist as such, there are methods of inquiry that are more appropriate or more frequently used in feminist studies and research. For example, Sherryl Kleinman (2007) offers a way to translate feminist principles into fieldwork practices, and suggest ways to articulate feminist sensibility into qualitative research more broadly. She does this by assigning a guiding feminist principle to each section of her book, to show exemplars of how the principle is researched in action, and which research questions and approaches can be used in relevant studies. Also, adopting a feminist and critical theory framework, Linda Tuhiwai Smith's book *Decolonizing Methodologies* (2013) highlights the need to question the Western paradigm of research and knowledge production, and to uncover the underlying assumption and taken-for-granted values and positions of research that discriminate against indigenous communities.

Feminist approaches to citation

Another way of embodying a feminist approach in research is to consider not only the methods used, the way we discuss our findings, which data and theories we enter into dialogue with and how we use them, but also how we cite them. This has been the topic of many feminist discussions, and it is often addressed in online academic communities.[2] Sara Ahmed recognizes the importance of citation practices both in building feminist theory and paying tribute to other scholars, but also in relation to memory and reproduction of knowledge:

Citation is how we acknowledge our debt to those who came before; those who helped us find our way when the way was obscured because we deviated from the paths we were told to follow. In this book, I cite feminists of color who have contributed to the project of naming and dismantling the institutions of patriarchal whiteness. (Ahmed, 2017, 17)

Citations are also the custodians of historic memory for an idea or a term, helping us trace back the steps of its development and usage across geographic locations and fields of inquiry. As such, approaches to researching and writing differently here are highlighted again not only in the content and output of *what* we write, but also in the process and approach to *how* we engage with our writing through feminist ethics.

Gendered citation practices are present in many fields. For example, Michelle Dion, Jane Lawrence Summer and Sara McLaughlin Mitchell (2018) show the gender gap in citations in political science, sociology and economics, whereby articles written by men tend to cite men scholars rather than women in the same field. This is dependent on the so-called 'Matthew effect' (the presence of male-dominated networks with few women academics) and the 'Matilda effect' (Rossiter, 1993) whereby women's research is less recognized or attributed to male scholars. Networks dominated by men tend also to promote and share work done by men – we see the negative repercussion of this more broadly on women and people racialized as Black or people of colour, who are less likely to be invited as guest seminar speakers or keynote speakers at conferences (see Nittrouer et al, 2018). This makes their work less visible, which also affects their citation rates. Early work by Marianne Ferber (1988) suggests that gendered citation patterns could become more equal with the development of a critical mass of women in the field; and so we can see how this may also be relevant in the case of Black scholars and those who identify with groups that are marginalized. Diversity of representation within a field influences citation metrics (Dion et al, 2018), but it is not the only answer to the challenging of gendered citation practices. The relational, political and systemic dynamics of citation indexes and metrics seem to be ignored in the use of citation indexes. Where such metrics are used to judge the quality of academic work, hinder promotion and career success, or to amplify some voices to the detriment of others, the political and discriminating character of the system becomes more apparent.

In a review of factors affecting the number of citations on academic papers, Iman Tahamtan, Askar Safipour Afshar and Khadijeh Ahamdzadeh (2016) identify three general categories (paper-related factors, journal-related factors and author-related factors), with 28 subfactors; they found that the quality of the paper, journal impact factor, number of authors, visibility and international cooperation are stronger predictors for citations. Although these may seem more 'objective' measures that are not connected to individual discrimination, a feminist perspective can help understand how one's citation index score is actually intertwined with nodes of oppression and discrimination at the individual, organizational and systemic level. The magnitude of this domino effect is rarely made clear in doctoral training and should be given more visibility. In *Invisible Women*, Caroline Criado Perez (2019) analyses data on six main themes (daily life, the workplace, design of the everyday, medical care, public life, and war and natural disasters) showing how deep-rooted bias produces a knowledge gap rooted in masculine norms, which become a source of systemic inequalities and discrimination against women. Clearly, inequality and exclusion are intimately connected to issues around the subject of inquiry and sociocultural gendered practices in academia. For example, if men are given workloads that involve more research, fewer pastoral and administrative tasks, they are likely to publish a higher volume of outputs, which generates more opportunities to capture citations. Another important issue in contemporary research practices is the conflation of metrics with a notion of 'objective' assessment of quality and meritocracy; this then implies that quality can be easily quantified through numbers, and that the highest scores provide a just assessment on merit, thus dictating who should get rewarded or published or hired. Research shows that algorithms in new technologies and indexing databases can be biased (see Lindebaum, Vesa and Den Hond, 2020), and constitute discrimination both for individuals (women being ranked lower) and at the group level (search engines favouring men – see Chen, Ma, Hannák and Wilson, 2018). If top-level institutions hire academics based on their performance shown through metrics, particular groups are excluded, thus creating a technology-enabled totalitarian system that reinforces discrimination and exclusion under the pretence of objectivity and quantitative evidence. Also, top-tier institutions tend to have larger pools of resources for academics to conduct research, present their work at conferences, take time off to complete their studies and increase the visibility of their research, which affects the quantity, quality and dissemination of research.

Citation practices have power, drawn from various sources and spaces. One source of power comes from the metrics used in many academic contexts, which I have mentioned before. In promotion applications, job recruitment and probation agreements the number of citations per article is often checked against an average 'acceptable' number, or against a citation index. Therefore, the so called *h*-index is used to measure in a quantitative manner the productivity and impact of a particular scholar. Specifically, it calculates the number of published papers (*h*) having the same (minimum) number of citations across journals, and it is heavily influenced by outliers. These indexes can be found on databases generally used for dissemination and archiving of research outputs, such as Scopus, Web of Science and Google Scholar. Interestingly, different databases can provide different values as some types of publications are excluded, and they use different ranges of years, which modify the h-index result. In addition, citations are also bound by dynamics of power, not only with regards to gender (Mitchell, Lange and Brus, 2013) but also in terms of the language used in the output – I would speculate that the number of international citations for papers written in English tends to be higher than those in Spanish or Arabic or French and so on. One's work and identity are then delegitimized by considering papers not written in English as research that 'does not count', or counts less, in the UK or other English-speaking contexts. This then already excludes or limits data, theories and contributions developed by indigenous cultures and those who do not operate in Anglocentric environments. Another citation-related index is altmetrics, which captures the number of mentions of an academic output on media and social media (like Twitter, Facebook, and online and newspaper articles). It goes without saying that people with larger or more widespread networks are likely to have their posts shared more widely, which may have a stronger impact on early-career researchers, those who do not have high representation in academic networks, and others who are unable to take part in conferences or events due to conflicting commitments.

Another implicit power dynamic of citation processes resides in the fact that, by publishing 'niche' articles, creating experimental work and using new methodologies, it may be more difficult to get published in mainstream top journals. These journals are read, and thus cited, by many scholars. As researchers tend to cite work from current conversations in the journal they are submitting to, or work written by members on the editorial board, the volume of citations increases exponentially. Then, this can be further exacerbated by reviewers who impose citations of their own work on authors, and authors who self-cite even when the topic does not warrant it. The perceived 'masculinity' level of the authorial team and the research topic itself can affect how 'scientific' and academically sound research is considered to be – thus going back to gendered hierarchies and the ideal academic as embodying masculine traits. These dynamics have also been considered in terms of recruitment policies whereby the same curriculum vitae was assigned a male or female name, and then an English or foreign surname, which highlighted discriminating practices. However, a similar experiment was also conducted on academic papers, whereby Knobloch-Westerwick, Glynn, and Huge (2013) investigated the Matilda effect by assigning male or female names to article abstracts submitted to a communication studies conference; they found that the perceived academic quality of the abstract assessed by 243 male and female graduate students scored higher for the abstract assigned to fictitious male authors, and also if the topic of the research outlined in the abstract was more 'masculine', showing how systemic, social and individual bias can contribute to the gendering of academic knowledge and practice.

Citing behaviours are important but are rarely taught or discussed in doctoral training, which tends to focus on the mechanics of finding and citing resources rather than the principles and values underpinning these practices. In my experience, *when* these topics are discussed, the focus is on getting better at playing the academic game and increasing one's citations – or avoiding plagiarism – rather than on critical and ethical approaches. In a study of 1.5 million JSTOR articles published between 1779 and 2011, Molly King and her colleagues (2016) found that men cite their own papers 56 per cent more than women do. Taking a historical perspective highlighted that this gap widened over time, as in the last two decades men were 70 per cent more likely to self-cite. This trend has been recognized as accountable for some of the gaps observed in citation deficits in various fields (see, for instance, Dion et al, 2018 across the social sciences; Hutson, 2006 in archaeology; Maliniak, Powers, and Walter 2013 in international relations). This instrumental behaviour also influences younger generations as their learning is premised on reading lists that are less focused on work from a diverse pool of scholars (we can think in terms of various characteristics like gender and race). For example, research on syllabi in the international relations field by Jeff Colgan (2017) has shown that women include more research by other women academics and self-cite less than their male counterparts.

While inclusion is important, practices of 'conscious selection' can also be a feminist act of resistance against unethical and masculine behaviours. In a world where citing somebody's work is also a metric gift, or the addition of a name to an authorial team can make a financial and progression difference, selective membership can be a way to challenge inequality and privilege. Some people may not warrant the benefit of inclusion – academic bullies, heroes of the egotistic masculine patriarchy, and people who belittle and erase others through their power. Reclaiming the theft of that space through feminist ethics of care and collaboration means resisting against institutional fatalism and the reinforcing of masculine structures of relationality and power. In agreement with Plotnikof and Utoft (2021), I see the inherent toxicity of masculine and neoliberal ways of researching as a fundamentally relational issue rather than a matter of pure individualization. As such, a regenerative way forward can be seen in how we work together and research through care and feminist values. It also means rejecting the norms deciding how, and by whom, that space remains occupied. This approach demands consideration of collective action and responsibilities over time, of the traces we leave of ourselves and others in our work, and also of the enabling dynamics implemented at the individual, institutional and systemic level. Equally, the dismantling of privilege and masculine norms in writing and researching also needs attention, to notice and problematize who is being excluded that should be present and heard, because they critique and challenge.

Names are also important, and the way we cite them makes a difference. Usually, authors are asked to conform to referencing requirements imposed by the publisher. Generally speaking, in bibliographies and reference lists, journals use only the initial of people in the authorial team. In-text references are generally based on surnames. Some journals, like *Culture and Organization*, have started reporting the full author's name in the bibliography to mitigate against gendered practices. When a paper is co-authored by more than three people, it is common to use the first author's surname followed by the abbreviation 'et al' (from the Latin expression *et alia*, meaning 'and others'), which reinforces games of power and competition in becoming first author as other names become erased. However, citation protocols vary greatly across fields of inquiry – for example, in scientific papers (like in the hard sciences) we tend to find more authors as data are shared across members of a laboratory, principal investigators and so on. In my authoring experience within the field of management and organization studies, rules and guidelines around authorship and the ordering of authors can be rather vague – some people have the data 'owner' as first author, others the person who has contributed the most. This topic can become very controversial as various power dynamics come into place – are more junior people always placed last? Should supervisors who have not contributed to the paper be included in somebody's doctoral research outputs? Again, I think that considerations based on feminist ethics of care (which I have explored before in this book) are important here.

Foreign names are also often avoided or misspelled – mine continues to be written incorrectly by colleagues after over a decade of working in the same institution. More importantly, even when cited, some have flagged that misspelling of their surnames is often missed by copy editors and writers, which can then result in skewed citation entries with multiple authors, which are not all pooled together in databases and then create multiple entries with fewer citations. Power dynamics are also enacted through the use of titles, which is something I have considered myself when citing colleagues in this book.[3] Women are often stripped of those titles by colleagues, managers and students while their male counterparts seem to retain the ability to be identified as Doctor or Professor in correspondence, during panels, speaker introductions and other professional interactions. Indeed, I have myself been at the end of a 'title drop' incident a few times.

Practical implications of researching and writing differently

This last chapter will consider a number of practical ways in which scholars who are interested in researching and writing differently can engage with it from the very beginning of their research journey. First, the chapter provides some reflection on the meaning of failure in the context of academia, researching and writing differently. Caring spaces and collective practices around writing differently will be presented as ways to foster growth and community building. I will also outline a number of practical aspects that are especially relevant for doctoral students and early-career researchers, starting with reflections on writing a doctoral study differently and publishing (journal articles, chapters and books). Finally, I address the impact that researching and writing differently can have on scholars themselves, before offering some concluding thoughts on the key points discussed in the book.

Embracing failure and creating caring spaces

Failure is an inevitability of academia, and one that I feel we are not prepared enough for as doctoral students or early-career researchers. I do not mean to be unnecessarily negative, but failure is something that needs to be accepted as an integral part of the process of working in today's academia. What is deemed to be 'failure' in contemporary neoliberal academia, and from whose perspective? Failure to get published, to get our texts accepted; failure to attract funding, or to get promoted; failure to be able to truly experience academic freedom; failure to enable ourselves and others to break away from unhealthy workplace dynamics; failure to find the time to read and think among a myriad of administrative tasks. The management and leadership literature itself, together with practitioner training and motivational speakers, have thrived on lessons based on the rejection of failure, strategies to avoid it and ways to mask it. Even in academia, somehow failure seems to only be embraced when it turns into a heroic narrative – like an academic entrepreneur who failed but never gave up on her idea and finally became a billionaire; a scientist who dedicated her whole life to finding a cure, failed innumerable times but then succeeded; the novel writer who approached a hundred publishers and got rejected by every one before finding a way to release her beautiful stories into the world and become internationally acclaimed. However, very often in real life there is no redemption to failure. And that's OK.

The current definition of the term 'failure' from Merriam-Webster refers to the 'omission of occurrence or performance, specifically: a failing to perform a duty or expected action; a state of inability to perform a normal function; a falling short' and 'a lack of success' (Merriam-Webster.com Dictionary). There is an interesting reference to what is 'normal' here, and so failure can be measured against a normalized social backdrop that provides a reference point for judgement. The online Oxford dictionary provides a definition of 'failure' as 'lack of success; the neglect or omission of expected or required action; the action or state of not functioning'. So here we can also see a sense of failure being thought of as a *lacuna* – the absence of success – or as an individual agentic factor in the disregard or exclusion of something. Therefore, if failure is a socially understood and negotiated concept predicated on expectations, and possibly on non-compliance, can failure to comply with an expected and normative sociocultural or professional context be seen in turn as a form of agency and resistance, and as a feminist political act? I pose that it can.

One point that is important to consider is the meaning of failure and what it is measured against in today's academia. Why is something considered a failure? For whom? And is it a failure at the individual level for which the system is responsible? Maybe the individual responsibility is also induced by a systemic failure. Is it appropriate to talk about individual failure when success is predicated on a failing or unjust system? Catherine Rottenberg (2014), argues that neoliberal Feminism locates full responsibility for well-being, success, a good work–family balance on individuals, thus highlighting the need to be entrepreneurial and adjust oneself to fit the system. In her work, Rottenberg critiques the approach behind 'leaning in' as an illustration of neoliberal Feminism that departs from social and collective feminist principles by focusing on the individual. Further, as success and performance are conceived in terms of internalized masculine metrics, strategies and coping mechanisms aimed at winning the masculine game are forced to do so by assimilation. Rottenberg (2014, 419) states: 'the neoliberal feminist subject is thus mobilized to convert continued gender inequality from a structural problem into an individual affair'. Here the term 'subject' refers to individuals, not necessarily women. I pose that this is also true for other aspects that generate systems of oppression and discrimination, not only gender (see class, race and so on). In this professional and socially constructed panorama, who succeeds – and who does so more quickly – tends to be predicated on who conforms to a social or institutional expectation of who will progress, and how to do so in the normative confines of that environment. Many people can be considered 'successful' on paper, with long curricula vitae (CV) populated with illustrious publications, high citation score indexes and records of external funding. But what if they have achieved this at the expense of ethical behaviour, or by neglecting their dear ones, stealing their students' ideas, dumping extra work on marginalized colleagues, and being included in publications they did not work on? Does that still count as success? Is a trajectory considered success only when linear and ascending?

In the field of management and organization behaviour, most top journals have a rejection rate between 70 and 95 per cent. So this already sets the context of a field that is extremely competitive – journals have a small number of issues published each year (usually around six, with additional sections, special issues, book reviews and so on), but top journals receive hundreds of article submissions every year, and often over a thousand. This hypercompetitive environment feeds a masculine approach to visibility, publication and interaction in the academic context, which David Knights (2006, 712) describes as 'the gladiatorial character of academic conferences, seminars and so on where discourses of masculinity are so dominant that subjects (not necessarily exclusively male) display their prowess in aggressively competitive conduct with one another. While appearing collegial, collaborative and cooperative, the cockfighting mentality generally prevails in most academic seminars.' In some countries, academics pursue the 'quantity' strategy, whereby they try to publish as many papers as they can, in whichever media and form they can achieve. This often generates long CV as a high number of publications is needed for promotion or profile-raising, regardless of their level or quality. In other countries, there may be national standards that control which types of outputs, journals or publishers should be pursued; in this case academics may prefer a strategy of fewer but targeted publications. The 'top' level international peer-reviewed outlets tend to have higher rejection rates, stricter measures of quality assurance and longer publication schedules. Having an article 'desk accepted' is extremely rare (I am not even sure if this expression exists, but I use it in contrast with its very common antonym 'desk reject'); and having a 'review and resubmit' decision outcome, or only going through one round of revisions, is often considered a positive editorial response.

Rejection and failure are intrinsic to the academic process of researching and writing. A similar dynamic to the one outlined for journal article publication is present in terms of grant applications, external funding, contracts with businesses and governmental units: there is a small pot of money and opportunities when compared to all the academics who need access to these. Academics often fail (excuse the pun) to disclose these instances of failure, because we have been told that we need to comply with masculine ideas of what an ideal worker looks like (Acker, 1990), what is considered to be 'successful' in academia – a notion that is often taken for granted, which needs deconstructing and problematizing – and what type of self-narratives we need to reinforce and perpetuate to be deemed 'proper' academics.

Within a mainstream context that predilects such masculine ideals of being an academic, which rejects failure, doubt, emotions and vulnerability, it is important to find communities, resources and alternatives to show that this is failure at the systemic and contextual level, not just at the individual level. As such, we should not be undermined and belittled by the relentless frequency of what can be seen as failure. Failure, or the perception of it, can become crippling and paralysing, especially in the early career stages. However, writing differently can provide a space where failure is not only recognized, but also critiqued and embraced. Helena Liu writes:

> This is a note about a companion of mine. It is the sharp pain seizing in my chest, the strangling of my throat and the vertigo of being swept under waves of hopeless despair. It is when my stomach mangles in a knot so that I can no longer keep food down, when my breath comes in short rasps and my shuddering heart threatens to crumble. The oppressive shadow of it lies in wait for me until my eyes flit open at quarter past three in the morning and I find it there in the stillness of the dark, leaning across the side of my bed. In moments of lightness and laughter, I forget it for a blissful moment. Then its hands clench around my shoulders again and all the suffocating sensations of my thundering heart, twisting stomach, rasping lungs, desperate broken hopelessness rush back. When I am most small, most alone, most fragile, it murmurs, 'You will fail'. 'You will lose everything'. 'You are worthless'. (2019, 865–66)

It is common to feel that failure is an individual problem, while everyone else 'gets' the system, is successful, receives support and so on. This is often because failure is not shared as frequently as success through social media, presentations and online presence. One day, after having received yet another rejection for a paper I thought was worthy of publication, I saw a post on social media by a very senior colleague whom I admire, disclosing the same experience. Perhaps it is not a coincidence that this communication happened within a closed group frequented by many scholars who are writing differently, and people who tend to show support for each other. A stream of similar stories followed in response to the post, making me feel sad for the profession but a little less sorry for myself: someone's paper had been rejected after four rounds of revisions; someone's funding idea had been stolen by a supervisor; a doctoral student's conference presentation quickly turned into a single-authored paper by another experienced academic; a reviewer had rudely dismissed a book proposal without fully reading the manuscript, and so on. Communities of knowing and practice can provide great support for scholars who do not operate 'in the centre' of their field, and online communities can be invaluable for those who feel marginalized, or for people who simply do not have others nearby taking similar approaches or with similar interests. We can create and nurture caring communities that hold spaces to fail, share, experiment and question ourselves collectively, and at the individual level.

It is important that we create caring or safe spaces for our vulnerable writing and our writing differently, on various levels. Although, it should be noted, that not everyone may feel safe in the same way in these spaces, or at all; indeed, there are different starting points, nodes of privilege and positions around power, hierarchy, relations and so on even within feminist and caring communities. Caring spaces can be created within a community, a journal, a conference, with a colleague, or a friend. However, it is important for scholars to become aware of how we can also create safe and caring spaces for ourselves – either in the form of inner spaces, or spaces in places that can foster our experience of researching and writing differently. This is perhaps also connected to time, and with what Jenny Helin called the 'vertical time' of writing (Helin, 2020), which is 'poetic time' in Bachelard's terms (2013, 59) as 'it moves, it proves, it invites, it consoles – it is astonishing and familiar'. Creating caring spaces is very important, and homes for the mind, especially as an early academic but also later in one's career. This point is linked to what I discuss next regarding communities of knowledge and practice. I think it is important to 'find your people', in many ways. At the start of my research journey, I was not aware of the group of academics I would be more engaged with later in my academic journey. They were all names, titles, references and citations that I failed to recognize, let alone acknowledge as a group of people in conversation. I did not feel that I could be part of that conversation, or that my voice would even ever get access to that dialogue. However, this happened – albeit slowly and over several years – through the work I published, the seminars I attended, and the conferences I joined. I started understanding what I was interested in studying – and I mean the broad area, not just a topic, as those have changed considerably over the past decade – and began following work in those strands of research more consciously and systematically. As my work started getting published, my visibility increased, and so I was asked to review articles for several journals. It is important that editors also help authors 'find their people' by approaching the right reviewers. This does not mean that different perspectives or challenges should not be sought, or that we should only surround ourselves with people who think like we do and write about the same topics, but that finding colleagues with similar interests (especially if those are not in the mainstream of one's field of inquiry) – even when their opinions are different but engaged with through openness and respect – can provide support, solidarity and motivation.

Communities of belonging and collective scholarship

One of the most engaging and satisfying aspects of Writing Differently is the sense of community, professional camaraderie and affective engagement that I perceive from its inhabitants. To me, this type of community is linked to feminist ethics of care, which are premised on a perspective of 'persons as relational and interdependent, morally and epistemologically', rather than focusing on individuals and their self-interest (Held, 2006, 13). In a neoliberal academic world that still values masculine ideals of what an academic looks like, the definition of being successful is entrenched in competitiveness and individuality (Lund and Tienari, 2018, 99). However, researching and writing differently offers the potential of an *agora* – a common space of collective gathering, a locus for intellectual exchange, a place of concerns for sociopolitical agendas and belonging. It also provides an emotional space of communion and emotion, as 'to care is to act not by fixed rule but by affection and regard' (Held, 2006, 24). This enabling environment challenges masculine ideas of failure and collaboration that are premised on calculations and instrumentalization, as well as metrics of input and output, and it is instead based on feminist ethics of care whereby 'central focus [...] is on the compelling moral salience of attending to and meeting the needs of the particular others for whom we take responsibility' (Held, 2006, 10). A community of belonging premised on feminist approaches provides opportunities to look *askance* and *athwart* (across, in an oblique direction) in relation to our fields, our communities and profession (see Khoo et al, 2020). As writing differently is still an alternative to the mainstream way of researching and writing in the field of management and organization studies, it is important to identify and join the community of scholars whose work we admire and are inspired by. The collective efforts and sentiment shared here can be both empowering and comforting: 'in changing academia from within, we cannot underestimate the need for such community building activities – safe inquiry spaces – offering resistance in solidarity.' (Helin, 2020, 13). There is also an important aspect of creating nurturing spaces for resistance-building, subversion and 'rocking the boat' (Liu and Pechenkina, 2016). Safe or caring spaces can be sustained to bring work and life together, aimed at nurturing and 'developing different ways of working and caring for others in the university.' (Pullen, 2018, 128). Rejecting masculine understandings of what it means to be an academic and being 'successful', exposing vulnerability, challenging sexist, racist and exclusionary behaviour (see Ahmed, 2017; Crimmins, 2019; Liu, 2019), can lead to failure as inability or unwillingness to comply. But, to my mind, that's positive failure.

Writing differently tends to be nested into storytelling in its resistance to assimilation and its imaginative way of understanding theories and processes of organizing (Boje, 2008; Gabriel 1995; 2000; 2008), often in the form of autoethnographic narratives. Reflecting on the interplay between the personal and the political, Tronto (1993, 118) highlights how ethics of care are entrenched in politics as a social practice rather than a personal disposition that becomes 'easy to sentimentalize and privatize'. As such, these stories help us connect the individual to the social, making sense of singular and collective struggle in an iterative manner. The French sociologist Maurice Halbwachs (1992) connects narratives and memory by posing that individual narratives are actually a reflection of a group's perspective, whereby the act of remembering is individual but drawing on the multiple sense-making, shared experiences, emotions and events to inform how and why these are remembered (Halbwachs, 1992; Middleton and Brown, 2005). As such, (re)told stories within a community (social, professional or international) that link the personal to the collective memory are 'shared, extra-individual representations of the past that resonate with members of a community at a certain point in time' (Mena et al, 2016, 9; see also Haug, 2008 on memory work). Helena Liu writes:

> I hold onto the belief that my writings are more than just a function of my job. I write to ease the pain I have endured and continue to endure as a woman of colour living and working in a patriarchal white supremacist settler-colony. I write to assert my humanity in a world that can often refuse to see me, my family, and my friends as fully human. (Liu, 2019, 868)

Researching and writing differently together is also a way to acknowledge the relationality of knowledge and research, and its value. In her beautiful chapter, Katie Beavan (2020, 102–3, emphasis in original) highlights this potential:

> What if knowledge isn't made by me or you, an act of imparting to our reader but, rather, is made in our *doing* together? Together scholar-to-scholar? Together with our readers? A temporal and spatially decentred experience sensing meanings rather than conceiving them from on high? [...] Textualised bodies, *feeling scholarship*, letting it seep into our skin and melt into the marrow of our bones, move in our blood, our borders bleeding. [...] *Knowledge*, a collective endeavour. Intersubjective. Flesh to flesh, emergings in the moments *between* us.

This togetherness is lived in the way research is designed, discussed, approached and carried out. Scholars can take advantage of many research methods to engage in this co-production and shared experience. For example, duoethnography or collective ethnography, arts-based methods and collective biography all provide a structured approach to explore collective researching and writing differently. Collective biography as a method is a way of building on memories and channel affect together. Davies and Gannon explain:

> In collective biography a group of researchers work together on a particular topic, drawing on their own memories relevant to that topic, and through the shared work of telling, listening and writing, they move beyond the clichés and usual explanations to the point where the written memories come as close as they can make them to 'an embodied sense of what happened'. (Davies and Gannon, 2006, 3)

Sara Dahlman, Jannick Friis Christensen and Thomas Burø (2020) show how the embodied and affective experience associated with the sharing of memories in collective biography does not require the phenomena to be shared by all authors to be done collectively. As such, these embodied methods – like affective ethnography (Gherardi, 2019a) and others that fall in with the sensory imperative (Juhlin and Holt, 2021) – can be used to support the creation and development of affective research important for experimentations in writing differently. Knudsen and Stage suggest:

> The development of methodologies for affect research should be regarded as an interesting zone of inventiveness, a zone raising reflections about what 'the empirical' produced tells us about the world and about the research setting, and a zone allowing us to generate new types of empirical material and perhaps to collect material that has previously been perceived as banal or unsophisticated. (Knudsen and Stage, 2015, 3)

Halbwachs also poses that individual reminiscences (stories, texts, visual ethnograhies, art exhibitions) are 'localized' within the thinking and sensibilities of the group they want to be part of, which individuals relate to either consciously or unconsciously (Halbwachs, 1992, 52). In this process of resonance, writing, sharing and recognition, collective frameworks and experiences serve to link individuals' 'most intimate remembrance to each other' (Halbwachs, 1992, 3). This dialogue can thus foster recognition and 'joint resonance' (Jääskeläinen and Helin 2021) through which sense-making and meaning creation is done collaboratively. Through this process of sharing and recognition, individual stories and memories become part of the shared collective as a polyphonic construct that moves writing differently into the Writing Differently movement. Alison Pullen notes:

> for writing to touch, we need to establish the affective sociality between writers and readers – it touches by promoting an ethico-political

relationship between us. This again seems quite simple until we remember the context in which we write, and when we remember women's place non-place, presence absence and abjection in the system. (Pullen, 2018, 124)

which is why writing from the body with resonance and fragility that expose the normatively silenced aspects of our work and life is so important and relational.

Affective encounters established through communities of research and professional practice can create multiple identity narratives, or help construct new ones. Foroughi (2020, 1349) explores how, being shaped by cultural practices or mnemonic products, multiple collective memories create and sustain multiple identities (Olick, 2008). In academia, these 'products' can be stories, co-authored articles, workshop experiences, messages of empathy and commonality. The more niche the academic interest and practice, the more camaraderie and sense of belonging to a collective is felt by the individuals. The sharing of writing differently experiences and memories becomes especially important when managing identity negotiations regarding the academics we are (and the ones we aspire to be), the positive influence we can have in our field of research, and through collaboration. Collective resonance reverberates and is deflected through affect and the bodies of the readers, at times coming back to the author through messages, online posts and words of solidarity. To me, these spaces are examples of feminist working that espouses feminist values and embraces vulnerability in the communities of scholars who organize often invisibly, to create caring spaces to work, live and write, and develop different ways of working and caring for others in the university (see Pullen, 2018, 128).

Researching and writing differently collaboratively

Over the past few years, I have found incredible support, intellectual growth, sense of belonging and camaraderie in some academic communities. Amanda Sinclair (2018) refers to connections and encounters with peers, colleagues and fellow scholars as 'gifts from feminism'. Another contemporary feminist writer, Sara Ahmed (2017, 3) writes that Feminism and other movements are ways to make connections as well as a shelter. Writing Differently can be that connective space for many scholars, a space where we can embrace feminist affective solidarity through dialogic reflective encounters (Vachhani and Pullen, 2019). Through these connections, exchanges and coalitions, we can share, delegate and hand over the agential potential to experience, take over and run with our ideas and fights. In this collective work lies our feminist potential for change. Marianna Fotaki (2013) highlights the importance for women of taking part in formal and informal academic networks, pointing out how they are often excluded from these events. This is echoed by Bell and King (2010) who also address the issue of women's bodies being ignored and silenced in conferences, which reinforces masculinity in academia. Engaging in 'networking' can contribute to career progression; however, events and more unstructured opportunities to encounter colleagues can also create ways to exchange knowledge about one's subject, and to develop better understandings of unwritten professional dynamics and taken-for-granted contextual circumstances. The chance to get in touch with colleagues through affective embodied communication (going beyond blind reviews or reading each other's scholarship from a distance) can create opportunities to get to know more people in the field (what some call 'increasing social capital') and create synergies that bring together researchers on grants, projects and publications (Howe-Walsh and Turnbull, 2016). This type of activity is essential within academia (Mavin and Bryan, 2002; Fotaki, 2013) – I would argue that this is the case not only in terms of career progression, but most importantly to enhance our individual well-being as academics, and to foster collective action.

Academic collaborations based on researching and writing differently, in my experience, have been permeated by a particular type of generative relationship between people that goes beyond traditional academic dynamics of power, hierarchy and privilege. With the aim to tackle nodes of oppression in our academic systems, colleagues across institutions and in different countries have come together with openness, respect, and a collaborative spirit to share and create knowledge together. Even though I have been lucky enough to forge new academic friendships and collaborations during the pandemic outbreak, perhaps also thanks to the availability of online modes of communicating and sharing, these relationships can be somewhat more challenging to establish online due to the affective, embodied and intimate character of much of the writing differently related work. Suvi Satama, Annika Blomberg and Samantha Warren (2021) discuss the embodied character of academic collaborations, posing that exploring and understanding the sensory microdynamics between oneself and colleagues is crucial for creative exchanges. In my experience, writing differently is linked to creativity understood as 'engagement in creative acts, regardless of whether the resultant outcomes are novel, useful, or creative' (Drazin et al, 1999, 287). This can be experienced as an internalized personal phenomenon or a collective one, emerging from an iterative approach to interpretation and ongoing negotiation of meanings and ideas at the cognitive, sensorial and affective levels (Koivunen and Wennes, 2011; Ryömä and Satama, 2019). It is therefore important to create spaces and opportunities to come together and collaborate in research and writing in manners that foster creativity, collaboration and collegiality.

As I mentioned earlier in this book, it is crucial to find and inhabit one's communities of knowledge and praxis, and to find 'your people' in the academic *mare magnum*. I cannot emphasize enough how important it is for academics, and especially early-career scholars whose network and collaborative relationships may yet to be fully developed, to find the right spaces for collegiate exchange. In my work, due to my current role and personal commitments, I have a very limited amount of time and financial resources to dedicate to seminars, research visits and conferences. This means being very selective with the events I am able to attend, and engaging with considerable advance planning.

Over the years, I have been able to explore workshops and presentations from various universities, and to better understand the difference among the various types of conferences, which I see as microcosms of academia. There are conferences which are mainstream, with thousands of people, where academics 'work the room' for positions or publications, where 'being seen' is equally as important – if not more so – than what you are there to present. Many of my friends and colleagues enjoy the variety of intellectual engagement and opportunities offered in those spaces. Within those large academic events, there are special interest groups, tracks or smaller sessions that can provide a conducive environment for academic exchanges. Other conferences are medium-sized and targeted to a more specific group, or academic approach or methodology, which I personally find more enabling and more attuned to my way of being in academia. Still, like most spaces, conferences large and small are populated by hierarchies, racism, sexism and the other dynamics we experience in everyday academia. As ideal loci of academic performativity, these can easily become spaces of marginalization or exclusionary practice (even when addressing topics of equality and social justice). However, these spaces can also be fulcra of community building, support stemming from different locations, intellectual growth and identification of a subcommunity of belonging. Many years ago, I found that space in the Standing Conference on Organizational Symbolism, at a time when I was a full-time lecturer and a weekend researcher, terrified about the mere idea of attending a conference, let alone presenting my own work. In that first experience I found colleagues who espouse a similar approach to scholarship and research, which allowed me to forge positive working relationships, and some friendships that are still ongoing after over a decade. It also allowed me to see examples of writing differently and researching differently, and gave me the confidence to attend other larger conferences. These shared events can also provide opportunities for 'defining moments' (Henderson, 2020; Khoo et al, 2020) that transform an individual micro-interaction or singular experience into a wider application to one's career or critical engagement with academia – for instance, I was able to recognize and become more consciously aware of the academic I did *not* want to turn into (the one asking questions about their own work in someone else's presentation, or hogging the mic; the one mansplaining on research; the one excluding doctoral students or using them as a power-magnifying clique; the one paraphrasing and recycling the same work for 20 years; the one talking only to 'the right people' such as high fliers, influential professors and editors). Inhabiting these collective academic spaces can be intimidating – walking into a room full of people who are different from you (Ahmed, 2012 in relation to whiteness); not seeing yourself represented in any of the keynote speakers or organizers; presenting in front of a large auditorium of invisible faces, or conversely in a small space that feels too intimate and encroaching on one's personal body. While conferences and professional gatherings can be important in finding a community of belonging, and especially as a doctoral student or an early-career scholar (Henderson and Burford, 2020; Kuzhabekova and Temerbayeva, 2018), they are also great opportunities for learning when to distance yourself from communities or groups that do not reflect who you are. Researching and writing differently, therefore, can also be seen as an approach to 'doing' academia together in a different way.

Researching and writing differently is also embodied in editorial choices, which need to be reflexive and ethical, dialogic and relational. These are the candelabra propping up the lights of our contributions to knowledge. For example, the selection of reviewers assigned to a paper should be thoughtful and appropriate, as it can make or break a potential publication (and its author) from the very start. Also, the choice of which articles are featured on a journal website, or which authors are interviewed and promoted on social media, are important ones, as these influence metrics, networks and, ultimately, individual performance indicators. Giving visibility to some papers, through publication but also spotlighting and open-access choices, also allows research to become more accessible. This may in turn prompt collaborations and connections that may have instead remained unexplored. A good example of this can be found in the journal *Organization*, where in 2020 Nancy Harding, Alison Pullen and Sheena Vachhani published the 'Editors' Picks: Feminism and Organization'. The very first paragraph of their introduction tells us:

> We read, reflected, discussed, paused and repeated this process. Selecting papers for inclusion reveals an academic bias for what 'should' be included, what we would 'like' to include, what debates 'need' to be revisited, and what papers 'open' up future discussion. Throughout the selection process, we acknowledged our biases and it is worth reflecting on that the three of us have talked, worked and published together. (Harding, Pullen and Vachhani, 2020, 1)

Finally, I'd like to make a special mention here of writing retreats, writing groups and bootcamps. These are sometimes organized before or after conferences, but can also be stand-alone events. I have always found the idea of a writing retreat greatly appealing, but I have never been able to justify untangling myself from work and personal commitments for three days or a week to do some writing[1]. For some people, the forced parenthesis away from meetings and other tasks warranted by a writing retreat is a blessed space in which to explore and unravel one's writing; for others, the forced timeline is off-putting. In some cases, these writing sessions can also be done in shorter sessions and at more regular intervals – for example, two hours on a weekly or monthly basis. While this type of coming together is often done by PhD students or scholars in the same field, this is not necessarily the case. The key point is in finding a space where writing has priority – whether it's done individually, as a pair or a group. Large portions of this book have been written in writing sessions I have held with a historian colleague of mine – we conduct our research on completely different topics and in different fields, but our weekly commitment to writing together motivated us to keep going, logging in on our online video platform to welcome each other and set our own goals for the session, then switching off camera and microphone to write, before finally reconvening to explore our writing. This colleague provided an empowering and supportive space for me to carve out time and motivation for writing, which I have come to treasure and really look forward to over the past year.

Researching differently for doctoral students

Researching and writing differently is a path that can start at the very beginning of an academic journey, or one that is developed later on instead of or in parallel to more traditional research. I started my doctoral studies while in the middle of my academic career at a time when I held the title of lecturer in business studies and the role of course/programme director. Although I had been living and breathing the higher education context as a student and then as a university teacher (first in Italy, then in China, and finally in the UK) I had never conducted academic research of the type that we conduct in the UK at the doctoral level. There were many things I did not know which researchers take for granted in this context: the nuances of difference in the type of research published across journals; the various ontological paradigms and epistemological approaches; the level of ethical concerns to be taken into account, and so on. Nobody had ever taught me how to read academic articles efficiently for a literature review, or how to write an academic paper to maximize my chances of publication – I learned by reading and doing, developing strategies 'on the go' that I later taught my students. Too often, doctoral students are not supported in the learning of this taken-for-granted knowledge, and academic practices and processes are obscured by keeping the focus on the resulting outputs. However, it is important that these are discussed and problematized, like in the beautiful work of Liela A. Jamjoom (2021), which is also a great example of writing differently, where she exposes the emotional journey of writing and presenting a conference paper within a system that is premised on colonialism. Through the use of autoethnography, she challenges othering and the conventions of academic writing, and connects with the reader at an affective and embodied level, as illustrated in the following extracts:

> The feelings of otherness all began when I was at the data collection phase of the study. Here I was searching newspaper texts to understand how articles wrote about Muslim bodies, how they were being represented, and what was being ignored. While I was aware of the misrepresentation of Muslims in the media, critically analyzing the texts was tedious and emotionally draining. I found myself questioning everyone and everything. (2021, 264)
>
> [...] As much as I am excited to send off the paper to conferences, I'm quite apprehensive as to how it will be received. At such critical times (Paris, San Bernardino, divisive Donald Trump) Islam is really the case everyone is against. So I wonder how it will be received, especially from me a Muslim author. I am willing to go ahead... yet I'm concerned. (2021, 266)
>
> After a series of exhausting questions, I was sad that I had presented my research at such a conference. I was tired from the incessant disregard of my work. I was also hurt by it all. I was not the only one who felt the angst and negativity in the room; my supervisor and two other management professors also stated that the comments were harsh and dismissive. I could not help but reflect on how power privileges some voices over others, and that my voice was being disqualified because it represented a 'marginal' perspective that did not represent most, if not all, the people in the room. (2021, 267)

In my experience, navigating the UK research system is rather tricky for those who come from different educational backgrounds where the practical ways of doing research can be considerably different and cause confusion. However, although my knowledge was limited to start with, I was lucky enough to be referred to a generous colleague for directions. I found myself in a lovely conversation with Heather Höpfl, who by the end of the meeting had decided to offer me a place on the PhD programme as one of her supervisees. I have provided elsewhere an autoethnographic account of our first encounter and our supervisory relationship in a co-authored article with Charlie Smith (Boncori and Smith, 2020). I remember vividly my anxiety, identity negotiations and desperate attempts at sense-making during the PhD journey, while my supervisor tried to get me to think out of the box and embrace 'non-standard' ways of thinking and writing. Although the PhD completion often culminates in the production of a thesis written according to certain standards aimed at evidencing an original contribution to knowledge creation, it is important that students do not focus only on the output. The real learning is in the journey itself, and in trying to understand who you want to become as an academic – unfortunately, I feel that the latter is often an aspect that becomes marginalized in the process of meeting milestones and deadlines, writing a certain number of words, and covering a significant amount of literature. As an external examiner of doctoral theses, I try to always ask this question: 'What next? What do you want to do and who do you want to be as an academic?'

Not all doctoral students have the privilege of being able to choose a supervisor, or to find one who fosters enabling environments for learning and experimentation. Many academics and their institutions still favour a mainstream approach to studying for a PhD and the production of its outputs (whether as a thesis or in the form of articles). While this may be due to preference or lack of expertise, it is sometimes also motivated by the student's best interest, in that a more traditional take on doctoral research may provide better access to a broader pool of jobs and publications upon completion. The 'Anti-editorial' by Olivier Germain (2020, 102), written differently for a special issue of *M@n@gement*, speaks to this tension:

> As the director of a doctoral programme in business administration, I sometimes wonder if I do anything but reproduce or even accelerate the shitshow. The PhD is a liminal space where learning prepares a student's transition to an academic role. However, we have collectively naturalised a set of institutional pressures, as if the typical experiences an academic will go through during his or her career were to be considered normal. We kindly and elegantly say that there are 'codes' or 'tricks of the trade' or 'routines' to be learnt – rites of passage. Academic language, when used to collectively narrate ourselves, is coupled with muted violence. Thus, it seems to be desirable to internalise certain socially accepted practices to avoid a shock upon entering academic life, between natural selection and an evolutionary approach.

In addition to the editorial, this special issue of *M@n@gement* also includes some great pieces that outline the personal, private, emotional and professional journey or identity-making during the PhD process, which is being considered in a growing body of literature (see Sawir et al 2008; Aitchison and Mowbray 2013). However, there is still some reticence in encouraging students to craft a thesis by writing differently due to the possible risks associated with it. Much of the doctoral student's journey is dictated by their supervisory team, the funding available to support their research, and the opportunities they are given to develop as scholars and academics. When I worked on my own thesis over a decade ago, I decided to use autoethnography (which at the time was rarely encountered in management and organization studies publications) and qualitative interviews. I tried to balance out a risky and rather experimental way of investigating organizations with a more common qualitative approach, and I also sneaked in some photos and titles in Chinese (the thesis was focused on understanding the experience of expatriates in China, see Boncori, 2013; Boncori and Vine, 2014). While my supervisor pushed me to embrace a researching differently approach, my circumstances, the professional context I operated in and the field of inquiry I had chosen were less than enabling. In some cases, students have to wait until after the successful defence of their thesis to explore different ways of researching and writing in academia.

Luckily, around the world today's doctoral students are taking more chances with their doctoral work and, thanks to technology, can often access different types of research. The increasing volume of interest in researching and writing differently at the beginning of one's journey as a researcher is evidenced, for example, in the great popularity gained by Ruth Weatherall's article (2019) 'Writing the doctoral thesis differently', and in a recent paper by Vince (2020) exploring the emotional aspect of conducting doctoral research. It is worth considering for a moment how PhD students nowadays are taught abought writing and publishing, and whether these different options of style, approach and content are even presented to them. PhD candidates are not only students, but academics and researchers in becoming, and I think that we – colleagues, supervisors, doctoral programmes, boards of examiners, external assessors, training schemes and so on – have a duty of care to show them and critically discuss different ways of researching and writing. Too often supervisors tend to impose their own journey and perspective on academia onto their doctoral students. Different academic contexts (including geographical ones) also have different perspectives on what 'counts' as a 'proper' publication – while the UK context is in principle focusing on fewer outputs of higher quality (albeit judged against masculine metrics), others look at quantity. To me, writing is a craft and not just a skill like every other skill. There are political and systemic dynamics behind how we research and write, which very often are not taught in formal doctoral training. There is a key difference between simply getting published and 'playing the academic game' on the one hand, and writing, writing well – possibly writing differently – or writing to make a difference, on the other. These choices have an impact on the way people inhabit academia and their livelihood. Exploring researching and writing differently may be challenging when operating in a foreign-language context, like I have been doing for most of my academic life, but it is not an insurmountable obstacle.

Considerations of future publications that could stem out of doctoral research are important for career purposes. In addition to addressing how academic publishing works in the creation of an output, another point that students may need support with is the idea that (as I explored in the previous chapter) being rejected – in terms both of thesis decisions and subsequent outputs – is actually a measure of their worth or the quality of their work. Rejection and failure happen to all academics at every level. Admittedly, I have been very lucky with most of my reviewers so far, but as an editor, a reviewer and an author I know that sometimes people who are supposedly judging others' work 'impartially' are often self-absorbed (and unnecessarily self-citing) or even plain rude, and may try to impose the text they would have wanted to write rather than what was submitted. What is considered worthy of rejection in one journal may be published with only minor revision in another of equal academic reputation and stance. The reality, according to my limited experience and perspective, is that there are no foolproof guides to writing academic text and publishing. It is an exercise in risk taking. I did not know any of this before starting a PhD, but the type and ranking of a journal, the approach of the editor(s)-in-chief, and in some contexts even the time of year or academic cycle are all deciding factors in one's publication success (in the UK it tends to be more challenging to publish towards the end of the Research Excellence Framework cycle because more people are scrambling to get publications out in order to preserve their job/promotion/performance, so popular journals have an even larger imbalance between supply and demand). Valerie Anderson, Carole Elliott and Jamie Callahan (2021) have articulated the dynamics of power and marginalization for people and scholarship that go hand in hand with the current system of journal rankings. There is also the matter of topics or conversations that are more or less in vogue, as there are different channels and academic 'homes' for different ways of writing (and one person can engage in more than one style and have a very varied academic portfolio) both in terms of institutions and journals. The article I co-authored on negotiating identities in 'the student-lecturer limbo' (Boncori and Smith, 2020) was desk rejected three times, and then embraced by another journal quite quickly. There is another paper in which I have invested more time, work and emotional labour as third author than any of my other work; and it took *seven years* to find it a home, while other papers I have written were submitted, sent to review and published in three or six months. This is not even about scholarship written differently; it applies to all types of research (or at least mine). Would I send a poetic-based autoethnographic article to some mainstream management journals? Probably not. The same way that I wouldn't really send a quantitative keyword-based literature review to *Culture and Organization*, as it would get desk-rejected. Understanding the type of academic work we do and its ideal home is crucial.

For doctoral students and early-career researchers it is important to step back and ask themselves some key questions: What do I want to say? Who is the right audience for that conversation? Which channels do they inhabit? At what level am I able to engage with in terms of depth and complexity of exploration and argumentation? How can I communicate my message in the most appropriate way? Along the way, I have learned my preferred ways of writing (I usually write for a specific journal) and where I feel more confident (I prefer to respond to special issue calls that deal directly with my topic rather than a general submission), but others may have completely different approaches, and it is important for doctoral students to receive support throughout this journey.

Publishing in journals, books and edited volumes

As I mentioned in Part II of this book, some journals have been more embracing than others in publishing work that is written differently, like *Gender, Work and Organization*; *Management Learning*; *ephemera*; *Organization*; and *Culture and Organization*, which tend to be where my intellectual home is located, where I like to publish my work and engage in the highest volume of reviewing other people's research. Some journals and publishers are indeed actively encouraging research that is rooted in feminist studies or pursued in a manner that speaks to writing differently.

As a PhD student and an early-career researcher, it took me a long time to understand the nuances and differences between the various journals listed on the Chartered Association of Business Schools (ABS) ranking, and the meaning behind their quantitative measures of impact, citations and so on. I was not fully aware of how to publish and what the process involves. Also, I just did not have the sociocultural and educational matrix to sustain my initial steps and understanding of the academic world. This information is often taken for granted by academics and it can constitute a significant knowledge gap for those who are first-generation researchers or academics like me, and it requires time to be understood and navigated effectively. Sara Ahmed notes:

> Those of us who arrive in an academy that was not shaped by or for us bring knowledges, as well as worlds, that otherwise would not be here. Think of this: how we learn about worlds when they do not accommodate us. Think of the kinds of experience you have when you are not expected to be here. These experiences are a resource to generate knowledge. (Ahmed, 2017, 9–10)

As an editor, I often get questions around these issues from doctoral students and early-career researchers. When applying for an academic job, scholars are often required to produce a research plan underpinned by a publication and dissemination strategy some time before having developed this deeper understanding about the journals available. To a certain extent, being able to choose is a privilege that many do not feel is at their disposal – in the current neoliberal research environment, where and how much one publishes may be the difference between gaining permanency or promotion, being able to be employed in various institutions or internationally. So many researchers work their way down the journal rankings to find a home for their work, regardless of the ethos, approach and content of the journal, as choice is often an unattainable privilege, especially early on in one's career.

In many professional academic contexts linked to management and organization studies, publishing journal articles in top-level journals is still considered the best way to show and disseminate the quality of one's academic work. Other fields still favour academic outputs in the form of monographs and books. Alexandra Bristow (2021) offers a thoughtful and thought-provoking reflection on 'critical' academic journal publishing, proposing a more radical reimagining of journals. Personal access to mainstream publications (such as those published by Elsevier, Springer and Sage) can be very expensive if articles are not 'open access'; students and academics affiliated to universities, research institutes or other academic organizations can usually take advantage of their institutional subscriptions to journals and request additional resources via libraries. This level of access is not guaranteed worldwide and creates barriers to scholars and their work. Research published as 'open access', as the name would suggest, is open to all, without financial or legal requirement. This allows a larger pool of people to read online, download and use the knowledge shared via academic publication. Some independent open-access journals, like *ephemera*, offer an alternative to mainstream publishing – these are led by a particular ethico-political stance, require no fee for publication or access, are independent, collectively run, and not-for-profit. Other open-access publications (for example, MDPI journals) involve a monetary gain for the journal, which often links their reputation to predatory publishers. While some journals are fully open-access, others have a hybrid model whereby some articles are shared openly and others require membership or subscription. Open-access work and other types of publication in some fields can also be premised on financial contributions and fees to be paid to a publisher, which clearly fosters discrimination and marginalization.

Journal articles nowadays tend to be submitted via an online portal and are considered by editors or associate editors who follow the journey of each manuscript from submission to publication. The first decision point is made by the editor as to whether an article is sent to reviewers or 'desk rejected' (immediately sent back to the authors) if unsound (of poor quality or underdeveloped) or unsuitable (not the right fit for the journal based on its aims and scope). Most papers that are desk rejected, in my experience, belong to the second category. I find it very important to write and target a manuscript to a specific journal, considering the conversations that are ongoing in that publication, including methodological concerns. Most journal articles published in reputable journals are supported by peer review (usually between two and four reviewers), whereby other academics are selected for their subject expertise (theoretical, methodological or contextual) and are asked to provide feedback on the paper with the aim to assess its quality and suggest improvements. Different journals have different time frames for reviews, which are then considered by the editor and a further decision is made as to whether the paper can be accepted as it is (which is extremely rare in my field), rejected, or if the authors are required to make minor or major changes. The editorial and reviewers' feedback on a manuscript is collated and sent the authors, who will address the points raised (or query those that seem problematic if necessary) and eventually resubmit. Obviously, one can also decide to 'pull' the paper, meaning that the paper is taken out of the submission process by the authors and can be submitted to another journal (a manuscript should never be submitted to more than one journal at the same time). However, in most cases, the reviewers' requests can be accommodated or negotiated for resubmission. Although there may be reviewers who are difficult, focused on the paper they would have wanted to write rather than the one at hand, self-citing without reason and making unreasonable requests, generally speaking feedback from reviewers genuinely contributes to the enhancement of the paper, and can also offer some illuminating insights and considerable contributions. There can be various rounds of reviews, which do not always result in publication, that in most cases eventually turn into a paper being accepted for publication. The following stage of a manuscript publishing life then focuses on the editing of the text, whereby the copy editor checks language and formatting before producing proofs to be checked and approved by the author. Once the author's legal agreement is signed, the manuscript is added to the production line. Most of the main journals nowadays offer 'online first' versions of the article that allow dissemination before the paper is formally included in an issue.

Edited books and academic monographs are another way of disseminating academic research. Editors from publishers often have 'meet the editors' sessions at conferences or book launches, or a desk where there is a display of recent publications by the press. They are usually happy to discuss the characteristics of the volumes they choose and the markets of their business, but also ideas and potential collaborations for publishing. In my experience of writing monographs and curating edited volumes, publishing these can be time-consuming but very rewarding. There are two approaches to publishing books, which I have found have strengths as well as weaknesses. One could choose to write a book first and then look for a publisher; otherwise, one can write only a small portion of the book – or even just a proposal – and find a publisher thereafter. The advantage of the first approach is that the writing can happen in an organic way and without being constrained by deadlines (usually authors have one or two years to deliver a manuscript). This can be useful when writing a mainstream publication that can easily be positioned in several publishing houses. However, by writing an extended proposal or just a few initial chapters to be considered by a publisher – usually the process involves a senior editor and then a decision-making board – authors can offer flexibility in terms of content, structure and style to match the specific needs of the publisher and the market. I used the first approach for the monograph I crafted out of my PhD thesis (Boncori, 2013), which was published with Palgrave, and the second approach for this monograph and some of my edited collections. The requirements for book proposals may vary from publisher to publisher, but tend to always include the following information, which is useful to consider before approaching them:

- Title and subtitle: evocative or informative, pinpointing topic and focus.
- Authors/editors: names, affiliation and a brief biography of the authorial/editorial team, mentioning their roles and key expertise.
- Short summary, scope and indicative table of contents: this is all about what you want to say in the book, and will include an indicative word count.
- Audience(s): who is the book for? This will also influence your register, writing style and tone.
- Market: what has been already written on the topic that is in direct or indirect competition with your book? What is the gap you are trying to fill, or your unique selling point?

Most book proposals go through at least one round of reviews before approval, and then again once the typescript is ready as a full draft.

A gentler introduction to publishing may be offered by the opportunity to publish book chapters in volumes edited by others. In my experience, once academics and PhD students start to present their work at conferences and publish their work, their area of expertise becomes increasingly known, which is how I started being invited to write book chapters. However, writing in this medium is not necessarily dependent on conferences and personal connections: calls for contributions are often circulated online in professional academic networks, via conferences and journals or publishers' websites, so invitations are not always necessary. Admittedly, I love writing book chapters (even though they tend to take a while to get published) as I feel that these are less constraining in terms of format and formulaic language, or even content, compared to journal articles. These offer great opportunities for experimentation and for writing differently. It should be noted that in some professional academic contexts these outputs are not recognized as high-level contributions and so may be considered of less value.

One aspect of publishing that is often left unspoken is how to deal with 'predator publishers'. Predator publishers can manifest themselves in the form of journals or press agencies that will contact scholars and offer to publish their work. Usually these are not indexed in lists that include reputable publications, such as the Academic Journal Guide (AJG), which is reviewed and published every three years by the Chartered Association of Business Schools (ABS) and includes publications in various academic fields. Predatory publishing often involves authors being charged to publish their work – generally speaking, in the field of management and organization studies, and in most social sciences, there is no need to pay for publication. Predatory publishing is also premised on fewer checks for quality and academic rigour, so the editorial, review and publishing services normally associated with publications in reputable journals or publishing houses are notably absent or substandard. Authors are tricked by promises of fast publication, or by fraudulent claims regarding citation and impact index, and by famous names included on the editorial boards (frequently used without permission). This also means that work published in this manner tends to be considered less favourably in assessment exercises or academic profiles, which is another reason why graduates and early-career researchers should avoid these publication channels. The names chosen by predatory publishers for their journals or series tend to resemble some mainstream or established ones, even bearing university names without actually having any affiliation with those institutions. Articles or books published here tend to also have limited dissemination and few citations.

Concluding remarks

I hate writing conclusions in articles and books, because I see research and writing as an iterative process that never really comes to an end. Can anyone – and should they – put a full stop on knowledge creation, activism, equity and Feminism? So, instead, I would like to offer some concluding remarks to summarize the key themes of the book, its implications, and ways forward.

The framing for this book is anchored against two key points: the neoliberal and masculine dynamics in today's academia; and the political and feminist nature of researching and writing differently. These contextual discussions provide the backdrop for the argument promoted in this book, focusing on the potential of researching and writing differently at the individual and collective level to foster different ways of inhabiting academia that are premised on inclusion. As outlined in the introduction, this book aimed to discuss why researching and writing differently is important in today's academic context; to offer an exploration of the meanings of 'writing differently', together with some examples; to provide reflections on other academic processes that can be done differently in line with feminist approaches; to investigate some of the qualitative methods and approaches that can be used in researching and writing differently; and finally to discuss some practical aspects linked with researching and publishing differently. This text is purposefully both theoretical and practical in nature, written in a conversational style that reaches across academic genres.

The first part considered the contemporary academic context, with a particular focus on the British environment, to reflect on issues around masculine metrics and understandings of doing research. I then explored why I consider researching and Writing Differently as a political and feminist project in its aim to illuminate a range of experiences and intersections of oppression, silence and inequality against a backdrop of hegemonic normative praxis. After a brief excursus into Feminism and its articulation into Black and Queer Feminism, I discussed why it is important to reclaim our scholarship and engage in Writing Differently today. The second part of the book offers an overview of research written differently, with numerous examples that are not intended to provide a literature review of writing differently but rather a starting point for scholars who wish to look into this type of work. I also highlighted some key aspects of writing differently, considering individual, collective and macro experiences through time and movement, embodiment and emotion. Looking at the potential as well as the risks of researching and writing differently, I stressed the crucial role of connections, collaborations and communities of belonging that are premised on the creation of caring spaces for the individual and their research. The last part of the book focused on the practical processes and implications involved with researching differently. Rooted in qualitative inquiry, I discussed some epistemological and methodological issues before turning to an overview of some methods that lend themselves to researching and writing differently, such as ethnography and arts-based methods (both narrative and visual ones). I also provided a reflection on some processes linked to researching differently, particularly with regards to feminist approaches behind data and citation practices. The last part of this volume considered issues around failure and community of belonging, before sketching out how doctoral students can approach their scholarship differently from the very start of their journey as researchers. I then clarified some taken for granted knowledge regarding the publication process across various types of outputs, and suggested ways in which writing differently can be done collaboratively.

Feminism is not just about sex and gender, but also about power and privilege. Therefore, it is not just about and from women. Like Feminism, researching and writing differently is engaged with at the individual, institutional and systemic or societal level, by people of all genders and sexual orientations. It is not a simple system of binary discrimination and exclusion, and its complexity of experience and perspectives should be acknowledged and appreciated, including the addition of intersectional and interdisciplinary perspectives. Researching and writing differently can become ways to engage with others (individually and as groups) through ethics of care, without othering, through affective, embodied and cognitive conversations, the sharing of stories and experiences, and inclusion that does not require assimilation.

This book does not offer a deep dive into an exploration of every single topic or potential path in researching and writing differently, but I hope that the reader found some ideas interesting, took up some provocations, engaged with a new method, or resolved to give further consideration to researching and writing differently. My intension has been to bring together some theories, perspectives, examples and reflections that may inspire researchers to continue on in this journey of discovery.

In this book I hoped to raise awareness about researching and writing differently, and to show how this approach and way of writing and researching could be understood (though not exclusively) through a feminist lens. I highlighted how this, as a movement, can be considered as a counter-narrative to today's neoliberal academic context(s), which perpetuates normative masculine ways of being an academic and writing. This book is concerned about the valuing of metrics and quantifiable measures of assessing academic value, performance and research viability. This concern extends also to the impact this has on academics, our well-being and career, but also on the effects this has on our profession: the development of our fields of inquiry, the creation of knowledge, the teaching we engage with and the support we provide to students and colleagues. This book is committed to researching and writing differently in a theoretical way to challenge the status quo, but also practically to instigate change in terms of praxis, which is why it includes exemplars and discussions on methods and the practicalities of engaging with writing differently.

Feminist disobedience can be uncomfortable to those who thrive within systems of inequality and oppression, and it can be easily ridiculed. I believe that we can allow ourselves to be idealistic and dare to research and write differently. Change starts with awareness and sight – once the effect of neoliberal, masculine, white and heteronormative principles are seen for what these have created in the praxis of todays' academia, the impact cannot be unseen. And that is where we can push for change, both individually and collectively. This book has sought to address some of the often unspoken and taken-for-granted issues permeating today's academia, at least in the UK but increasingly so on a global basis: neoliberal approaches that foster individualism and competition, underpinned by hyper-performativity and metric-driven assessments of value; the rejection of vulnerability and failure; the normative research environment based on masculine understandings of being an academic and doing research; the still prevailing notion of the disembodied ideal academic, void of emotion and caring responsibilities; the interlocking systems of oppression that are the matrix on which macro and contextual systems are built, supporting everyday praxis such as authorial team dynamics, reviewing and citing practices, approaches to data and referencing. These underlying dynamics of the higher education context are often actively hidden, or something that academics lament privately during conference events and on social media. I believe that we also have a duty of care towards current and future doctoral students to name these issues, and to attempt change where it is needed. Competitiveness and othering are inculcated from the very early stages of doctoral training. In order to be competitive, to 'produce' more and faster, and to satisfy metrics and quantifiable measures of excellence, academic praxis is turning into a calculated, interest-based process of individual advantage. Patomäki (2019) highlights how rankings and various indicators of productivity, usually measured in terms of output, provide templates for academics to curate a profile that does not allow thinking and (un)doing of academic work outside of the box. In the quest to climb to a top position in the league tables, those who do not fit in the box or operate at the margins are excluded. Drawing attention to the futility of this practice, Patomäki (2019) highlights that these rankings are empty of collective purpose. I believe that to make a difference we have to create systems that allow collective purpose, share different voices and promote openness to alternatives. And although this resistance can be enacted at the macro level, I contend that it starts at the micro level, through the reimagining and redeveloping of everyday individual and collegial understandings and practices. Researching and writing differently is a way to take a step forward in this journey. To me, this book is also a small artefact of resistance towards these systems of oppression that confine writing and researching into mainstream masculine straitjackets. It's a book about connections, emotions, text, embodiment and writing. This is for me a small step into the reclaiming of our scholarship, research and writing. To some extent, this book is an academic indulgence that goes against the grain of today's academic 'publication game', and it is also my homage to *being* differently and *working* differently as an academic: I believe that we can trace our own path away from – or at least in parallel to – hegemonic masculine understandings of what it takes to be a 'good academic' and pursue an academic career. In order to make a difference and write about research and education in a meaningful way, our fields (and in particular management and organization studies) need to become more open and embracing of different disciplinary knowledge, sensitivities and methods. One hope I hold for the future, which perhaps is already here, is for writing differently and women's writing to be valued in its own space, rather than just as a mere alternative to or a rejection of masculine forms of writing. A closed disciplinary cast of mind serves to compartmentalize knowledge into boxes that do not correspond to the lived experience of societies and organizations, and serves to reinforce 'epistemic gatekeeping' (Steger, 2019). Feminist thinking, researching, working and writing can help us reimagine structures, futures and organizing.

And so, to me, researching and writing differently does not mean only doing so in terms of the crafting of publications, but also relating to and supporting each other differently, writing funding applications differently, inhabiting collaborations differently, organizing workshops differently and so on. It is about connecting to people, research, the self, alterity and otherness, in a different way. It's about feminist perspectives, equity, the development of connections and relationships that challenge the patriarchal order. It is about ways in which we can queer the text to make unequal structures disappear. It is about questioning and challenging different interlocking nodes of oppression, surfacing privilege, to make a difference and ignite change at the individual, the organizational and the systemic level. Researching and writing differently also means being critical of our own practice and community, recognizing when this label is used to perform a certain type of academic activity, which reinforces a calculating masculine strategic way of approaching research and scholarship. As such, researching and writing differently is as much about inclusion as it is about selection. It is also a way to challenge notions about who is allowed to speak about what and in which spaces, within and outside of the feminist circles. Writing differently is nested in the power of subversion that is held in the personal experience, in the sensing and disrupting of masculine notions of quality and excellence. For some people, writing differently is a journey of discovery and nurture; for some, it is the only way that academic work really becomes meaningful; for others it is an ancillary activity to ride a trend that is performed in addition to the more mainstream research that informs promotions and professional strategies.

In this book I have sought to illustrate the multilevel meaning and sense-making linked to researching and writing differently, and the various ways in which it can be thought of and done, without wanting to prescribe a way of going about it. Researching differently is not necessarily always intended and conducted through a feminist lens. This, however, is how I chose to approach it. To me, writing differently read through a feminist perspective needs to be explored theoretically, ethically and in practice, both in its main processes and its related ones, and as a way of being and of doing, which is just as important (if not more) as the written output. This echoes Sara Ahmed's words (2017, 14) in relation to Feminism:

Feminism is at stake in how we generate knowledge; in how we write, in who we cite. I think of feminism as a building project: if our texts are worlds, they need to be made out of feminist materials. Feminist theory is world making. This is why we need to resist positioning feminist theory as simply or only a tool, in the sense of something that can be used in theory, only then to be put down or put away. It should not be possible to do feminist theory without being a feminist, which requires an active and ongoing commitment to live one's life in a feminist way.

I hope that in this volume I have been able to illustrate the importance, the potential and value of researching and writing differently. As such, I have provided examples of writing differently as a practice, as a published academic artefact, as a movement of scholars that can challenge existing academic structures, and also as a mind frame that can help us approach our academic professional world differently.

Notes

Introduction

[1] As a scholar mainly interested in qualitative approaches and driven by a social agenda, my work over the past ten years has focused on the exploration of inclusion (or the lack thereof) and the management of diversity in various types of organizations. I see Feminism, researching and writing differently as spaces of recognition and inspiration that can provide a springboard for both individuals and fields of practice to reach a better social dynamic. As such, it is important to acknowledge my own positionality from the very start of this project. I write this book as a white, Western, now middle-class(ish) feminist. I write this while being aware of what Judith Butler calls 'the embarrassed etc. clause' where a list is offered that 'strives to encompass a situated subject, but invariably fail[s] to be complete' (1990, 143). I have a job in academia, which is in itself a site of privilege and oppression. I am conscious of the working-class roots of my family of origin, and of how my current family faces different dynamics of privilege and marginalization across different intersections. I strive to remain self-reflective and self-critical about the ways my understandings of Feminism and my activism may marginalize others – for example in terms of gender, race, disability, sexual orientation and class. I am also aware of the privilege that comes from being able to read, speak and think in multiple languages, one of which is English – a language that dominates the world of academic publishing. As a scholar, my ability to use Italian, Spanish, Chinese and English has unlocked opportunities to learn that I would not have had in my mother tongue (Italian), and also to publish my work in the English medium that is accepted and understood more widely. This text is written from a very specific position and a juxtaposition of experiences, some of which I will share in this book. My 'text emerges from the researcher's bodily standpoint as she is continually recognizing and interpreting the residue traces of culture inscribed upon her hide from interacting with others in context' (Spry, 2001, 711).

Chapter 1

[1] Altmetrics stands for 'alternative metrics' as these are used to complement or in contrast to more standardized metrics such as citation indexes and journal impact factors. Typically, altmetrics monitor the reach and impact of scholarly work through online interactions such as posts and comments on social media.

[2] This book will privilege the use of the terms 'women/men' rather than 'female/male' in line with feminist praxis. Further, this terminology is intended to be inclusive rather than to denote a binary view of gender.

[3] As indicated in the Introduction, Writing Differently in this book is capitalized when taken in its meaning of a movement and collective political project.

Chapter 2

[1] The '+' plus sign here is used to include, rather than obscure, other non-binary, agender and gender non-conforming identities, as well as other sexual orientations that are not captured in the inevitably limited acronym LGBT.

[2] In previous work (Boncori, 2017a; Boncori, Sicca and Bizjak, 2019) I have used the phrase 'gender identity'. However, here I will use 'gender' as the expression 'gender

identity' has been recently used to marginalize and denaturalize gender for transgender and gender non-conforming people.

3   Athena Swan is the name of a charter established in 2005 to promote, recognize and monitor organizational commitment to advancing women's careers in STEMM fields (science, technology, engineering, maths and medicine). In 2015, the charter was emended to also include other fields (for example, arts, humanities, social sciences, business and law – AHSSBL) for colleagues in academic and professional support roles as well as for students. In addition, the category of gender was made more inclusive and the work tasked changed to address gender equality more broadly.

4   Like Athena Swan, the Race Equality Charter (formerly the Equality Challenge Unit) is part of Advance HE (previously known as Higher Education Academy). Launched in 2014 as a pilot and more broadly in 2016, this charter is focused on improving the representation, progression and success of minority ethnic staff and students within higher education.

Chapter 4

1   For more information on 'The Body of Work' seminar series, visit the website: https://bodyofworkseminar.wordpress.com/

2   The video of the 'Embodying Methods in Management and Organization: before, during and after COVID-19' event is available on YouTube: https://www.youtube.com/watch?v=_z2vFSbvOps

Chapter 5

1   See the website 'Poetry at Work' https://www.poetryatwork.me

2   See, for example, the website for the Digital Feminist Collective: https://digitalfeministcollective.net/index.php/2018/01/13/the-politics-of-citation/

3   After much consideration, I decided not to include academic titles here as the spirit behind this book is one of collaboration and collegiality, rather than of hierarchy.

Chapter 6

1   I am currently employed on a contract focused on education and leadership, with no formal expectation or requirement to engage in research. This means that any research-related activity (see publications, conferences, writing retreats and so on) is somewhat of an addendum, extra workload or indulgence, in my professional life.

Bibliography

Abdellatif, A., Aldossari, M., Boncori, I., Callahan, J., Chatrakul Na Ayudhya, U., Chaudhry, S., Kivinen, N., Liu, S.S.; Utoft, E., Vershinina, N., Yarrow, E. and Pullen, A. (2021) 'Breaking the mould: Working through our differences to vocalize the sound of change', *Gender, Work and Organization*, 28(5): 1956–79.

Acker, J. (1990) 'Hierarchies, job, bodies: A theory of gendered organizations', *Gender and Society*, 4(2): 139–58.

Acker, J. (1992) 'Gendering organizational theory', *Classics of Organization Theory* (6th edn), 450–9.

Acker, J. (2006) 'Inequality regimes: Gender, class, and race in organizations', *Gender and Society*, 20(4): 441–64.

Acker, J. (2012) 'Gendered organizations and intersectionality: Problems and possibilities', *Equality, Diversity and Inclusion: An International Journal*, 31(3): 214–24.

Adams, T.E. and Holman Jones, S. (2011) 'Telling stories: Reflexivity, queer theory, and autoethnography', *Cultural Studies↔Critical Methodologies*, 11(2): 108–16.

Adichie, C.N. (2014) *We Should All Be Feminists*, New York: Vintage.

Adler, N. (2006) 'The arts and leadership: Now that we can do anything, what will we do?', *Academy of Management Learning and Education Journal*, 5(4): 486–99.

Advance HE (2018) 'Equality in higher education: statistical report 2018', Advance HE, [online] 6 September, Available from: https://www.advance-he.ac.uk/knowledge-hub/equality-higher-education-statistical-report-2018 [Accessed 12 January 2021].

Ahmed, S. (2004) *The Cultural Politics of Emotion*, New York: Routledge.

Ahmed, S. (2006a) *Queer Phenomenology: Orientations, Objects, Others*, Durham, NC: Duke University Press.

Ahmed, S. (2006b) 'The nonperformativity of antiracism', *Meridians*, 7(1): 104–26.

Ahmed, S. (2007) 'A phenomenology of whiteness', *Feminist Theory*, 8(2): 149–68.

Ahmed, S. (2012) *On Being Included: Racism and Diversity in Institutional Life*, Durham, NC: Duke University Press.

Ahmed, S. (2017) *Living a Feminist Life*, London and Durham, NC: Duke University Press.

Ahmed, S. (2018) 'Notes on Feminist Survival', feministkilljoys, [online] 27 March, Available from: https://feministkilljoys.com/2018/03/27/notes-on-feminist-survival/ [Accessed 14 February 2021].

Ahonen, P., Blomberg, A., Doerr, K., Einola, K., Elkina, A., Gao, G., Hambleton, J., Helin, J., Huopalainen, A., Johannsen, B.F., Johansson, J., Jääskeläinen, P., Kaasila-Pakanen, A.-L., Kivinen, N., Mandalaki, E., Meriläinen, S., Pullen, A., Salmela, T., Satama, S., Tienari, J., Wickström, A. and Zhang, L.E. (2020) 'Writing resistance together'. *Gender, Work and Organization*, 27(4): 447–70.

Aitchison, C. and Mowbray, S. (2013) 'Doctoral women: Managing emotions, managing doctoral studies', *Teaching in Higher Education*, 18(8): 859–70.

Al Arris, A., Özbilgin, M., Tatli, A. and April, K. (2014) 'Tackling Whiteness in organizations and management', *Journal of Managerial Psychology*, 29(4): 362–9.

Alarcón, N. (1990) 'Chicana feminism: In the tracks of "the" native woman', *Cultural Studies*, 4(3): 248–56.

Alexander-Floyd, N.G. (2012) 'Disappearing acts: Reclaiming intersectionality in the social sciences in a post-Black feminist era', *Feminist Formations*, 24(1): 1–25.

Allen, P.B. (1995) *Art Is a Way of Knowing: A Guide to Self-Knowledge and Spiritual Fulfillment through Creativity*, Boston, MA: Shambhala Publications.

Alvesson, M. (2013) *The Triumph of Emptiness: Consumption, Higher Education, and Work Organization*, Oxford: Oxford University Press.

Amrouche, C., Breckenridge, J., Brewis, D.N., Burchiellaro, O., Hansen, M.B., Pedersen, C.H., Plotnikof, M. and Pullen, A. (2019) 'Powerful writing', *ephemera: theory and politics in organization*, 18(4): 881–900.

Anderson, L. (2006) 'Analytic autoethnography', *Journal of Contemporary Ethnography*, 35(4): 373–95.

Anderson, V., Elliott, C. and Callahan, J.L. (2021) 'Power, powerlessness, and journal ranking lists: The marginalization of fields of practice', *Academy of Management Learning and Education Journal*, 20(1): 89–107.

Antoniou, M. and Moriarty, J. (2008) 'What can academic writers learn from creative writers? Developing guidance and support for lecturers in higher education', *Teaching in Higher Education,* 13(2): 157–67.

Anzaldúa, G.E. (1991) 'To(o) Queer the Writer—Loca, escritora y chicana', in B. Warland (ed) *InVersions: Writing by Dykes, Queers and Lesbians*, Vancouver: Press Gang.

Anzaldúa, G.E. (2015) 'Preface: Gestures of the body—Escribiendo para idear', *Light in the Dark/Luz en lo oscuro: Rewriting Identity, Spirituality, Reality*, Durham, NC and London: Duke University Press, pp 1–8.

Archer, L. (2008) 'The new neoliberal subjects? Young/er academics' constructions of professional identity', *Journal of Education Policy*, 23(3): 265–85.

Ashcraft, K.L. (2020) 'The pandemic shift: Vulnerability and viral masculinity', Presentation at *Gender, Work and Organization* virtual seminar on COVID-19, [online] 23 June, Available from: https://www.facebook.com/GenderWorkOrg/videos/gwo-virtual-seminar-on-covid-19-speakers-slides/313897759626884/ [Accessed 9 October 2020].

Ashworth, R.E., McDermott, A.M. and Currie, G. (2019) 'Theorizing from qualitative research in public administration: Plurality through a combination of rigor and richness', *Journal of Public Administration Research and Theory*, 29(2): 318–33.

Austin, R.D. and Devin, L. (2003) *Artful Making: What Managers Need to Know about How Artists Work*, Upper Saddle River, NJ: Financial Times Prentice Hall.

Averett, P. (2009) 'The search for Wonder Woman: An autoethnography of feminist identity', *Affilia*, 24(4): 360–8.

Avishai, O., Gerber, L. and Randles, J. (2013) 'The feminist ethnographer's dilemma: Reconciling progressive research agendas with fieldwork realities', *Journal of Contemporary Ethnography*, 42(4): 394–426.

Bachelard, G. (2013) *Intuition of the Instant*, translated by E. Rizo-Patron, Evanston, IL: Northwestern University Press.

Baldacchino, J. (2009) *Education beyond Education: Self and the Imaginary in Maxine Green's Philosophy*, New York: Peter Lang.

Barad, K. (2012) 'On touching – The inhuman that therefore I am', *Differences*, 23(3): 206–23.

BARC (Building the Anti-Racist Classroom) (2020) 'Principled Space', [online] Available from: https://barcworkshop.org/resources/principled-space/ [Accessed 9 October 2020].

Barnes, C. (1996) 'Disability and the myth of the independent researcher', *Disability and Society*, 11(1): 107–12.

Barone, T. (2000) *Aesthetics, Politics, and Educational Inquiry: Essays and Examples*, New York: Peter Lang.

Barry, D. (2008) 'The art of …', in D. Barry and H. Hansen (eds) *The Sage Handbook of New Approaches in Management and Organization*, London: Sage, pp 31–40.

Barry, D. and Meisiek, S. (2010) 'Seeing more and seeing differently: Sensemaking, mindfulness, and the workarts', *Organization Studies*, 31(11): 1505–30.

Bauman, Z. (2000) *Liquid Modernity*, Cambridge: Polity Press.

Bauman, Z. (2003) 'Educational challenges of the liquid-modern era', *Diogenes*, 50(1): 15–26.

Bauman, Z. (2005) 'Education in liquid modernity', *Review of Education, Pedagogy, and Cultural Studies*, 27(4): 303–17.

Bauman, Z. (2009) 'Education in the liquid-modern setting', *Power and Education*, 1(2): 157–66.

Bauman, Z. (2012) 'Times of interregnum', *Ethics and Global Politics*, 5(1): 49–56.

Beavan, K. (2020) 'Breaking with the masculine reckoning: An open letter to the Critical Management Studies Academy', in A. Pullen, J. Helin and N. Harding (eds) *Writing Differently* (Dialogues in Critical Management Studies, vol 4), Bingley: Emerald Publishing Limited, pp 91–112.

Beavan, K., Borgström, B., Helin, J. and Rhodes, C. (2021) 'Changing writing/writing for change', *Gender, Work and Organization*, 28(2): 449–55.

Beck, U. (2007) *Weltrisikogesellshaft*, Berlin: Suhrkamp.

Beirne, M. and Knight, S. (2007) 'From community theatre to critical management studies: A dramatic contribution to reflective learning?', *Management Learning,* 38(5): 591–611.

Bell, E. and King, D. (2010) 'The elephant in the room: Critical management studies conferences as a site of body pedagogics', *Management Learning*, 41(4): 429–42.

Bell, E., Meriläinen, S., Taylor, S. and Tienari, J. (2019) 'Time's up! Feminist theory and activism meets organization studies', *Human Relations*, 72(1): 4–22.

Bell, E. and Sinclair, A. (2014) 'Reclaiming eroticism in the academy', *Organization*, 21(2): 268–80.

Bell, E. and Thorpe, R. (2013) *A Very Short, Fairly Interesting and Reasonably Cheap Book about Management Research*, London: Sage.

Bell, M.P., Berry, D., Leopold, J. and Nkomo, S. (2020) 'Making Black Lives Matter in academia: A Black feminist call for collective action against anti-blackness in the academy', *Gender, Work and Organization*, 28(S1): 39–57.

Benozzo, A., Bell, H. and Koro-Ljungberg, M. (2013) 'Moving Between nuisance, secrets, and splinters as data', *Cultural Studies↔Critical Methodologies*, 13(4): 309–15.

Benozzo, A. and Gherardi, S. (2020) 'Working within the shadow: What do we do with "not-yet" data?', *Qualitative Research in Organizations and Management: An International Journal*, 15(2): 145–59.

Berg, M. and Seeber, B.K. (2016) *The Slow Professor: Challenging the Culture of Speed in the Academy*, Toronto: University of Toronto Press.

Berry, C. and Jagose, A. (eds) (1996) 'Australia queer', *Meanjin*, 55(1): 5–11.

Bhabha, H.K. (1994) *The Location of Culture* (2nd edn), New York: Routledge.

Bhattacharya, K. (2016) 'The vulnerable academic: Personal narratives and strategic de/colonizing of academic structures', *Qualitative Inquiry*, 22(5): 309–21.

Bhopal, K. (2017) *The Experiences of Black and Minority Ethnic Academics*, London: Routledge.

Bhopal, K. and Henderson, H. (2021) 'Competing inequalities: Gender versus race in higher education institutions in the UK', *Educational Review*, 73(2): 153–69.

Bhopal, K. and Pitkin, C. (2020) '"Same old story, just a different policy": Race and policy making in higher education in the UK', *Race Ethnicity and Education*, 23(4): 530–47.

Biehl-Missal, B. and Springborg, C. (2015) 'Dance, organization, and leadership', *Organizational Aesthetics*, 5(1): 1–10.

Biehl, B. and Volkmann, C. (2019) '"Spirits, dancing in the flesh": Choreography and organisation', *Culture and Organization*, 25(4): 284–99.

Black, Y. (2020) '"The play's the thing": A creative collaboration to investigate lived experiences in an urban community garden', *Management Learning*, 51(2): 168–86.

Bleijenbergh, I.L., van Engen, M.L. and Vinkenburg, C.J. (2013) 'Othering women: Fluid images of the ideal academic', *Equality, Diversity and Inclusion: An International Journal*, 32(1): 22–35.

Boal, A. (1995) 'Forum theatre', in P.B. Zarrilli (ed) *Acting (Re)Considered*, London: Routledge, pp 251–61.

Bochner, A.P. and Ellis, C. (2003) 'An introduction to the arts and narrative research: Art as inquiry', *Qualitative Inquiry*, 9(4): 506–14.

Bochner, A.P. and Ellis, C. (2016) *Evocative Autoethnography: Writing Lives and Telling Stories*, New York: Routledge.

Bochner, A.P. and Riggs, N.A. (2014) 'Practicing narrative inquiry', in P. Leavy (ed) *The Oxford Handbook of Qualitative Research*, Oxford: Oxford University Press, pp 195–222.

Boje, D.M. (2008) *Storytelling Organizations*, London: Sage.

Boulous Walker, M. (2017) *Slow Philosophy: Reading against the Institution*, London: Bloomsbury.

Boncori, I. (2013) *Expatriates in China: Experiences, Opportunities and Challenges*, London: Palgrave Macmillan.

Boncori, I. (ed) (2017a) *LGBT+ Perspectives – The University of Essex Reader*, Napoli: Editoriale Scientifica.

Boncori, I. (2017b) 'The salience of emotions in (auto) ethnography: Towards an analytical framework', in T. Vine, J. Clark, S. Richards and D. Weir (eds) *Ethnographic Research and Analysis: Anxiety, Identity and Self*, London: Palgrave Macmillan, pp 191–215.

Boncori, I. (ed) (2018) *Race, Ethnicity and Inclusion – The University of Essex Reader*, Napoli: Editoriale Scientifica.

Boncori, I. (2020a) 'The never-ending shift: A feminist reflection on living and organizing academic lives during the coronavirus pandemic', *Gender, Work and Organization*, 27(5): 677–82.

Boncori, I. (2020b) 'Book Review: *Writing Differently* – Alison Pullen, Jenny Helin and Nancy Harding (eds)', *Gender, Work and Organization*, 28(1): 443–5.

Boncori, I. (2022a) 'Learning and doing autoethnography: Resonance, vulnerability and exposure', in N. Sutherland, H. Gaggiotti and J. Pandeli (eds) *Organizational Ethnography: An Experiential and Practical Guide*, London: Routledge.

Boncori, I. (2022b) 'Writing the personal', in M. Kostera (ed) *How to Write Differently: A Quest for Meaningful Academic Writing*, Cheltenham: Edward Elgar Publishing, pp 22–33.

Boncori, I. and Vine, T. (2014) '"Learning without thought is labour lost, thought without learning is perilous": The importance of pre-departure training and emotions management for expatriates working in China', *International Journal of Work, Organization and Emotion*, 6(2): 155–77.

Boncori, I., Brewis, J., Sicca, L.M. and Smith, C. (2019) 'Carne – flesh and organization', *Culture and Organization*, 25(4): 249–52.

Boncori, I., Sicca, L.M. and Bizjak, D. (2019) 'Transgender and gender non-conforming people in the workplace: Direct and invisible discrimination', in S. Nachmias and V. Caven (eds) *Inequality and Organizational Practice: Work and Welfare*, Cham: Palgrave Macmillan, pp 141–60.

Boncori, I., Sicca, L.M. and Bizjak, D. (2020) 'Workload allocation models in academia: A panopticon of neoliberal control or tools for resistance?', *Tamara: Journal for Critical Organization Inquiry*, 18(1): 51–69.

Boncori, I. and Smith, C. (2019) 'I lost my baby today: Embodied writing and learning in organizations', *Management Learning*, 50(1): 74–86.

Boncori, I. and Smith, C. (2020) 'Negotiating the doctorate as an academic professional: Identity work and sensemaking through authoethnographic methods', *Teaching in Higher Education*, 25(3): 271–85.

Boncori, I. and Loughran, T. (eds) (2020) *Health and Wellbeing – The University of Essex Reader*, Napoli: Editoriale Scientifica.

Bordoni, C. (2016) *Interregnum: Beyond Liquid Modernity*, Bielefeld: Transcript Verlag.

Bothello, J. and Roulet, T.J. (2018) 'The imposter syndrome, or the mis-representation of self in academic life', *Journal of Management Studies*, 56(4): 854–61.

Bourdieu, P. (1977) *Outline of a Theory of Practice*, Cambridge: Cambridge University Press.

Bowes-Catton, H., Brewis, J., Clarke, C., Drake, D.H., Gilmour, A. and Penn, A. (2020) 'Talkin' 'bout a revolution? From quiescence to resistance in the contemporary university', *Management Learning*, 51(4): 378–97.

Bowring, M. and Brewis, J. (2009) 'Truth and consequences: Managing lesbian and gay identity in the Canadian workplace', *Equal Opportunities International*, 28(5): 361–77.

Boylorn, R.M. (2013) 'Blackgirl blogs, auto/ethnography, and crunk feminism', *Liminalities: A Journal of Performance Studies*, 9(2): 73–82.

Bramming, P, Hansen, B.G., Bojesen, A and Olesen, K.G. (2012) '(Im)perfect pictures: Snaplogs in performativity research', *Qualitative Research in Organizations and Management*, 7(1): 54–71.

Branch, S. and Murray, J. (2015) 'Workplace bullying: Is the lack of understanding the reason for inaction?', *Organizational Dynamics*, 44(4): 287–95.

Bränström Öhman, A. (2012) 'Leaks and leftovers: Reflections on the practice and politics of style in feminist academic writing', in M. Livholts (ed) *Emergent Writing Methodologies in Feminist Studies*, New York: Routledge, pp 27–40.

Brewis, D.N. and Bell, E. (2020) 'Provocation essays editorial: On the importance of moving and being moved', *Management Learning*, 51(5): 533–6.

Brewis, D.N. and Silverwood, S.T. (2020) 'Annotation', in A. Pullen, J. Helin and N. Harding (eds) *Writing Differently* (Dialogues in Critical Management Studies, vol 4), Bingley: Emerald Publishing Limited, pp 67–90.

Brewis, D.N. and Williams, E. (2019) 'Writing as skin: Negotiating the body in(to) learning about the managed self', *Management Learning,* 50(1): 87–99.

Bristow, A. (2012) 'On life, death and radical critique: A non-survival guide to the Brave New Higher Education for the intellectually pregnant', *Scandinavian Journal of Management,* 28(3): 234–41.

Bristow, A. (2021) 'What was, is and will be critical about journal publishing?', *ephemera: theory and politics in organizations*, 21(4): 23–55.

Brown, L. and Boardman, F.K. (2011) 'Accessing the field: Disability and the research process', *Social Science and Medicine*, 72(1): 23–30.

Brown, W. (2015) *Undoing the Demos: Neoliberalism's Stealth Revolution*. Brooklyn, NY: Zone Books.

Brown, K., Eernstman, N., Huke, A.R. and Reding, N. (2017) 'The drama of resilience: Learning, doing, and sharing for sustainability', *Ecology and Society,* 22(2): 8.

Bryan, B., Dadzie, S. and Scafe, S. (2018) *The Heart of the Race: Black Women's Lives in Britain*, London: Verso Books.

Bryman, A., Bell, E. and Harley, B. (2019) *Business Research Methods* (5th edn), Oxford: Oxford University Press.

Burrell, G. and Morgan, G. (1979) 'Anti-Organisation Theory', in *Sociological Paradigms and Organisational Analysis: Elements of the Sociology of Corporate Life*, London: Routledge.

Butler, J. (1990/2011) *Gender Trouble: Feminism and the Subversion of Identity*, New York: Routledge.

Butler, J. (1993) *Bodies That Matter: On the Discursive Limits of 'Sex'*, New York: Routledge.

Butler, J. (2004) *Undoing Gender*, New York: Routledge.

Butler, N and Spoelstra, S. (2012) 'Your Excellency', *Organization*, 19(6): 891–903.

Butler, N. and Spoelstra, S. (2020) 'Academics at play: Why the "publication game" is more than a metaphor', *Management Learning*, 51(4): 414–30.

Calás, M.B. and Smircich, L. (1996) 'From the "woman's point of view": Feminist approaches to organization', in S.R. Clegg, C. Hardy and W.R. Nord (eds) *The Sage Handbook of Organization Studies*, London: Sage, pp 218–57.

Calás, M.B. and Smircich, L. (2006) 'From the "woman's point of view" ten years later: Towards a feminist organization studies', in S.R. Clegg, C. Hardy and W.R. Nord (eds) *The Sage Handbook of Organization Studies* (2nd edn), London: Sage, pp 284–346.

Calafell, B.M. and Moreman, S.T. (2009) 'Envisioning an academic readership: Latina/o performativities per the form of publication', *Text and Performance Quarterly*, 29(2): 123–30.

Callagher, L.J., El Sahn, Z., Hibbert, P., Korber, S. and Siedlok, F. (2021) 'Early career researchers' identity threats in the field: The shelter and shadow of collective support', *Management Learning*, 52(4): 442–65.

Carr, A. and Hancock, P. (2003) 'Art and aesthetics at work: An introduction', *Tamara: Journal for Critical Organization Inquiry*, 2(1): 1–7.

Carrim, N.M.H. and Nkomo, S.M. (2016) 'Wedding intersectionality theory and identity work in organizations: South African Indian women negotiating managerial identity', *Gender, Work and Organization*, 23(3): 261–77.

Cavarero, A. and Restaino, F. (2002) *Le filosofie femministe: due secoli di battaglie teoriche e pratiche*, Milano: Mondadori.

Chang H., Ngunjiri, F. and Hernandez, K.-A.C. (2012) *Collaborative Autoethnography*, New York: Routledge.

Chen, L., Ma, R., Hannák, A. and Wilson, C. (2018) 'Investigating the impact of gender on rank in resume search engines', in *Proceedings of the 2018 CHI Conference on Human Factors in Computing Systems* (Paper 651, pp 1–14).

Chilton, G. and Leavy, P. (2014) 'Arts-based research practice: Merging social research and the creative arts', in P. Leavy (ed) *The Oxford Handbook of Qualitative Research*, Oxford: Oxford University Press, pp 403–22.

Cixous, H. (1976) 'The laugh of the Medusa', translated by K. Cohen and P. Cohen, *Signs*, 1(4): 875–93.

Cixous, H. (1993) *Three Steps on the Ladder of Writing*, New York: Columbia University Press.

Clegg, S. (2008) 'Academic identities under threat?', *British Educational Research Journal*, 34(3): 329–45.

Cloutier, C. (2016) 'How I write: An inquiry into the writing practices of academics', *Journal of Management Inquiry*, 25(1): 69–84.

Cole, E.R. (2008) 'Coalitions as a model for intersectionality: From practice to theory', *Sex Roles: A Journal of Research*, 59(5–6): 443–53.

Cole, E.R. and Luna, Z.T. (2010) 'Making coalitions work: Solidarity across difference within US feminism', *Feminist Studies*, 36(1): 71–98.

Colgan, J. (2017) 'Gender bias in international relations graduate education? New evidence from syllabi', *PS: Political Science and Politics*, 50(2): 456–60.

Collins, P.H. (1990) 'Black feminist thought in the matrix of domination', in P.H. Collins *Black Feminist Thought: Knowledge, Consciousness, and the Politics of Empowerment*, Boston, MA: Unwin Hyman, pp 221–38.

Collins, P.H. (2000) *Black Feminist Thought: Knowledge, Consciousness, and the Politics of Empowerment* (2nd edn), New York: Routledge.

Collinson, D.L. (1988) '"Engineering humour": Masculinity, joking and conflict in shop-floor relations', *Organization Studies*, 9(2): 181–99.

Combahee River Collective (1977) 'The Combahee River Collective Statement', Boston, MA: Combahee River Collective.

Conrad, D. and Beck, J.L. (2015) 'Towards articulating an arts-based research paradigm: Growing deeper', *UNESCO Observatory Multi-Disciplinary Journal in the Arts*, 5(1): 1–26.

Contu, A. (2014) 'Rationality and relationality in the process of whistleblowing: Recasting whistleblowing through readings of Antigone', *Journal of Management Inquiry*, 23(4): 393–406.

Contu, A. (2020) 'Answering the crisis with intellectual activism: Making a difference as business schools scholars', *Human Relations*, 73(5): 737–57.

Cooper, A.J. (1892/2017) *A Voice from the South: By a Black Woman of the South*, Chapel Hill, NC: University of North Carolina Press.

Corlett, S., Mavin, S. and Beech, N. (2019) 'Reconceptualising vulnerability and its value for managerial identity and learning', *Management Learning*, 50(5): 556–75.

Corlett, S., Ruane, M. and Mavin, S. (2021) 'Learning (not) to be different: The value of vulnerability in trusted and safe identity work spaces', *Management Learning*, 52(4): 424–41.

Council of Europe (2019) 'Sexism: See it. Name it. Stop it.' Human Rights Channel [online] 16 September, Available from: https://www.coe.int/en/web/human-rights-channel/stop-sexism [Accessed 8 March 2021].

Craig, R., Amernic, J., Tourish, D. (2014) 'Perverse audit culture and accountability of the modern public university', *Financial Accountability and Management*, 30(1): 1–24.

Crenshaw, K.W. (1989) 'Demarginalizing the intersection of race and sex: A Black feminist critique of antidiscrimination doctrine, feminist theory and antiracist politics'. *University of Chicago Legal Forum*, 1989(1): 139–67.

Crenshaw, K.W. (1991) 'Mapping the margins: Intersectionality, identity politics, and violence against women of color', *Stanford Law Review*, 43(6): 1241–99.

Crenshaw, K.W. (2017) *On Intersectionality: Essential Writings*, New York: The New Press.

Criado Perez, C. (2019) *Invisible Women: Exposing Data Bias in a World Designed for Men*, London: Penguin Random House.

Crimmins, G. (ed) (2019) *Strategies for Resisting Sexism in the Academy: Higher Education, Gender and Intersectionality*, London: Palgrave Macmillan.

Cruz, C. (2008) 'Notes on immigration, youth, and ethnographic silence', *Theory Into Practice,* 47(1): 67–73.

Cunliffe, A.L. (2002) 'Reflexive dialogical practice in management learning', *Management Learning*, 33(1): 35–61.

Cunliffe, A.L. (2003) 'Reflexive inquiry in organizational research: Questions and possibilities', *Human Relations,* 56(8): 983–1003.

Cunliffe, A.L. (2018) 'Alterity: The passion, politics, and ethics of self and scholarship', *Management Learning*, 49(1): 8–22.

Cunliffe, A.L. and Bell, E. (2016) '*Management Learning*: Legacies and future possibilities', *Management Learning*, 47(2): 113–16.

Cunliffe, A.L. and Coupland, C. (2012) 'From hero to villain to hero: Making experience sensible through embodied narrative sensemaking', *Human Relations*, 65(1): 63–88.

Cuomo, C.J. (1998) *Feminism and Ecological Communities: An Ethic of Flourishing*, London: Routledge.

Dahlman, S., Christensen, J.F. and Burø, T. (2020) 'The fact of the belly: A collective biography of becoming pregnant as a PhD student in academia', *M@n@gement*, 23(1): 125–30.

Dallery, A.B. (1989) 'The politics of writing (the) body: Écriture féminine', in A.M. Jaggar and S. Bordo (eds) *Gender/Body/Knowledge: Feminist Reconstructions of Being and Knowing*, New Brunswick, NJ: Rutgers University Press, pp 52–67.

Dankoski, M.E. (2000) 'What makes research feminist?', *Journal of Feminist Family Therapy*, 12(1): 3–19.

Dar, S. (2018) 'The Masque of Blackness: Or, Performing Assimilation in the White Academe', *Organization,* 26(3): 432–46.

Dar, S., Liu, H., Martinez Dy, A. and Brewis, D.N. (2020) 'The business school is racist: Act up!', *Organization*, 28(4): 695–706.

Darmer, P. and Grisoni, L. (2011) 'The opportunity of poetry: Report about poetry in organizing and managing', *Tamara: Journal for Critical Organization Theory*, 9(1–2): 5–13.

Darsø, L. (2004) *Artful Creation: Learning-Tales of Arts-in-Business*, Frederiksberg: Samfundslitteratur.

Daston, L.J. and Park, K. (2001) *Wonders and the Order of Nature, 1150–1750*, New York: Zone Books.

David, E.J.R. (2013) *Internalized Oppression: The Psychology of Marginalized Groups*, New York: Springer.

Davies, B. and Gannon, S. (2006) 'The practices of collective biography', in B. Davies and S. Gannon (eds) *Doing Collective Biography*, Maidenhead: Open University Press, pp 1–15.

Davis, A.Y. (1981) *Women, Race and Class*, New York: Random House.

Davis, K. (2008) 'Intersectionality as buzzword: A sociology of science perspective on what makes a feminist theory successful', *Feminist Theory*, 9(1): 67–85.

Davis, O.I. (1998) 'A Black woman as rhetorical critic: Validating self and violating the space of otherness', *Women's Studies in Communication*, 21(1): 77–90.

Davis, O.I. (1999) 'In the kitchen: Transforming the academy through safe spaces of resistance', *Western Journal of Communication*, 63(3): 364–81.

Deitch, E.A., Barsky, A., Butz, R.M., Chan, S., Brief, A.P. and Bradley, J.C. (2003) 'Subtle yet significant: The existence and impact of everyday racial discrimination in the workplace', *Human Relations*, 56(11): 1299–324.

Deleuze, G. (1969/2013) *Logic of Sense*, translated by M. Lester with C. Stivale, London: Bloomsbury.

DeNora, T. (2000) *Music in Everyday Life*, Cambridge: Cambridge University Press.

Denzin, N.K. (2003) *Performance Ethnography: Critical Pedagogy and the Politics of Culture*, London: Sage.

Denzin, N.K. (2014) *Interpretive Autoethnography* (2nd edn), Thousand Oaks, CA: Sage.

Denzin, N.K. and Lincoln, Y.S. (2000) 'Introduction: The discipline and practice of qualitative research', in N.K. Denzin and Y.S. Lincoln (eds) *The Sage Handbook of Qualitative Research* (2nd edn), London: Sage.

Denzin, N.K. and Lincoln, Y.S. (eds) (2000) *The Sage Handbook of Qualitative Research* (2nd edn), London: Sage.

Denzin, N.K. and Lincoln, Y.S. (2002) *The Qualitative Inquiry Reader*, Thousand Oaks, CA: Sage.

Devin, L. and Austin, R.D. (2012) *The Soul of Design: Harnessing the Power of the Plot to Create Extraordinary Products*, Palo Alto: Stanford University Press.

Dewey, J. (2005) *Art as Experience*, London: Penguin.

Dhamoon, R.K. (2011) 'Considerations on mainstreaming intersectionality', *Political Research Quarterly*, 64(1): 230–43.

Dicks, B. (2014) 'Action, experience, communication: Three methodological paradigms for researching multimodal and multisensory settings', *Qualitative Research*, 14(6): 656–74.

Dill, B.T. and Kohlman, M.H. (2012) 'Intersectionality: A transformative paradigm in feminist theory and social justice', in S.N. Hesse-Biber (ed) *The Handbook of Feminist Research: Theory and Praxis* (2nd edn), Thousand Oaks, CA: Sage, pp 154–74.

Dion, M.L., Sumner, J.L. and Mitchell, S.M. (2018) 'Gendered citation patterns across political science and social science methodology fields', *Political Analysis*, 26(3): 312–27.

Diprose, R. (2002) *Corporeal Generosity: On Giving with Nietzsche, Merleau-Ponty, and Levinas*, New York: SUNY Press.

Doharty, N. (2020) 'The "angry Black woman" as intellectual bondage: Being strategically emotional on the academic plantation', *Race, Ethnicity and Education*, 23(4): 548–62.

Drazin, R., Glynn, M.A. and Kazanjian, R.K. (1999) 'Multilevel theorizing about creativity in organizations: A sensemaking perspective', *The Academy of Management Review*, 24(2): 286–307.

Du Bois, W.E.B. (1939/2005) *Black Folk Then and Now: An Essay in the History and Sociology of the Negro Race*, The Oxford W.E.B. Du Bois, Volume 7, edited by H.L. Gates, Jr., Oxford: Oxford University Press.

Dunlop, R. (2001) 'Excerpts from *Boundary Bay*: A novel as educational research', in L. Neilsen, A.L. Cole and J.G. Knowles (eds) *The Art of Writing Inquiry*, Halifax, Nova Scotia: Backalong Books, pp 11–25.

Eddo-Lodge, R. (2018) *Why I'm No Longer Talking to White People About Race*, London: Bloomsbury.

Eddy, M., Williamson, A. and Weber, R. (2014) 'Reflections on the spiritual dimensions of somatic movement dance education', in A. Williamson, G. Batson and S. Whatley (eds) *Dance, Somatics and Spiritualities: Contemporary Sacred Narratives*, Bristol: Intellect, pp 159–94.

Eisner, E. (2008) 'Persistent tensions in arts-based research', in M. Cahnmann-Taylor and R. Siegesmund (eds) *Arts-based Research in Education: Foundations for Practice*, New York: Routledge, pp 16–27.

Eliasson, O. (2019) 'Abstract: The Art of Design', Netflix, [Accessed 22 December 2020].

Ellingson, L.L. (2017) *Embodiment in Qualitative Research*, New York: Routledge.

Ellis, C. (2004) *The Ethnographic I: A Methodological Novel about Autoethno-graphy*, Walnut Creek, CA: Rowman Altamira.

Ellis, C. (2020) *Revision: Autoethnographic Reflections on Life and Work*, New York: Routledge.

Ellis, C. and Bochner, A.P. (2000) 'Autoethnography, personal narrative, reflexivity: Researcher as subject', in N.K. Denzin and Y.S. Lincoln (eds) *Handbook of Qualitative Research* (2nd edn), London: Sage, pp 733–68.

Ellis, C., Adams, T.E. and Bochner, A.P. (2011) 'Autoethnography: An overview', *Forum Qualitative Sozialforschung/Forum: Qualitative Social Research*, 12(1) Article 10. https://www.qualitative-research.net/index.php/fqs/article/view/1589/3095.

Elm, D.R. and Taylor, S. (2010) 'Representing wholeness: Learning via theatrical productions', *Journal of Management Inquiry*, 19(2): 127–36.

Ely, M. (2007) 'In-forming re-presentations', in D.J. Clandinin (ed) *Handbook of Narrative Inquiry: Mapping a Methodology*, Thousand Oaks, CA: Sage, pp 567–98.

Ely, R.J. and Meyerson, D.E. (2000) 'Advancing gender equity in organizations: The challenge and importance of maintaining a gender narrative', *Organization*, 7(4): 589–608.

El-Tayeb, F. (2011) *European Others: Queering Ethnicity in Postnational Europe*, Minneapolis, MN: University of Minnesota Press.

ephemera collective (2021) 'Pasts, presents and futures of critical publishing', *ephemera: theory and politics in organization*, 21(4).

Ericsson, D. and Kostera, M. (2020) 'Alterethnography: Reading and writing otherness in organizations', *Gender, Work and Organization*, 27(6): 1402–17.

Erskine, S.E. and Bilimoria, D. (2019) 'White allyship of Afro-diasporic women in the workplace: A transformative strategy for organizational change', *Journal of Leadership and Organizational Studies*, 26(3): 319–38

Essed, P. (1991) *Understanding Everyday Racism: An Interdisciplinary Theory*, Newbury Park, CA: Sage.

Estrella, K., Forinash, M. (2007) 'Narrative inquiry and arts-based inquiry: Multinarrative perspectives', *Journal of Humanistic Psychology*, 47(3): 376–83.

Ettorre, E. (2017) *Autoethnography as Feminist Method: Sensitising the Feminist 'I'*, London: Taylor and Francis.

Etzioni, A. (1988) *The Moral Dimension: Toward a New Economics*, New York: The Free Press.

European Commission (2018) 'The gender pay gap situation in the EU', [online] 9 July, Available from: https://ec.europa.eu/info/policies/just ice-and-fundamental-rights/gender-equality/equal-pay/gender-pay-gap-situation-eu_en [Accessed 30 September 2020].

Farrington, L.A. (2005) *Creating Their Own Image: The History of African-American Working Artists*, New York: Oxford University Press.

Faulkner, S.L. (2007) 'Concern with craft: Using ars poetica as criteria for reading research poetry', *Qualitative Inquiry*, 13(2): 218–34.

Faulkner, S.L. (2017) 'Faulkner writes a middle-aged *Ars Poetica*', in L. Butler-Kisber, J.J. Guiney Yallop, M. Stewart and S. Wiebe (eds) *Poetic Inquiries of Reflection and Renewal*, Nova Scotia: MacIntyre Purcell Publishing Inc., pp 147–52.

Faulkner, S.L. (2018) 'Crank up the feminism: Poetic inquiry as feminist methodology', *Humanities*, 7(3): 85.

Ferber, M.A. (1988) 'Citations and networking', *Gender and Society*, 2(1): 82–9.

Finley, S. (2008) 'Arts-based research', in J.G. Knowles and A.L. Cole (eds) *Handbook of the Arts in Qualitative Research: Perspectives, Methodologies, Examples, and Issues*, London: Sage.

Finley, S. (2011) 'Critical arts-based inquiry: The pedagogy and performance of a radical ethical aesthetic', in N.K. Denzin and Y.S. Lincoln (eds) *The Sage Handbook of Qualitative Research* (4th edn), Thousand Oaks, CA: Sage, pp 435–50.

Flam, H. and King, D. (eds) (2005) *Emotions and Social Movements*, Abingdon: Routledge.

Fleming, P. (2021) *Dark Academia: How Universities Die*, London: Pluto Press.

Foroughi, H. (2020) 'Collective memories as a vehicle of fantasy and identification: Founding stories retold', *Organization Studies*, 41(10): 1347–67.

Fotaki, M. (2013) 'No woman is like a man (in academia): The masculine symbolic order and the unwanted female body', *Organization Studies,* 34(9): 1251–75.

Fotaki, M. and Harding, N. (2018) *Gender and the Organization. Women at Work in the 21st Century*, London: Routledge.

Fotaki, M., Kenny, K. and Vachhani, S. (2017) 'Thinking critically about affect in organization studies: Why it matters', *Organization*, 24(1): 3–17.

Fotaki, M., Metcalfe, B.D. and Harding, N. (2014) 'Writing materiality into management and organization studies through and with Luce Irigaray', *Human Relations*, 67(10): 1239–63.

Foucault, M. (1980) *Power/Knowledge: Selected Interviews and Other Writings 1972–1977*, edited by C. Gordon, New York: Vintage Books.

Foucault, M. (1991) *Discipline and Punish: The Birth of the Prison*, translated by A. Sheridan, Ringwood: Penguin.

Foucault, M. (1996) 'What is Critique?', in J. Schmidt (ed) *What is Enlightenment? Eighteenth-Century Answers and Twentieth-Century Questions*, Oakland, CA: University of California Press, pp 23–61.

Fraser, H. and Taylor, N. (2017) 'In good company: Women, companion animals, and social work', *Society and Animals*, 25(4): 341–61.

Freeman, E. (2010) *Time Binds: Queer Temporalities, Queer Histories*, Durham, NC: Duke University Press.

French, R. (2001) '"Negative capability": Managing the confusing uncertainties of change', *Journal of Organizational Change Management*, 14(5): 480–92.

Fuchs, T. and Koch, S.C. (2014) 'Embodied affectivity: On moving and being moved', *Frontiers in Psychology*, 5: 508.

Gabriel, Y. (1995) 'The unmanaged organization: Stories, fantasies and subjectivity', *Organization Studies*, 16(3): 477–501.

Gabriel, Y. (2000) *Storytelling in Organizations: Facts, Fictions, and Fantasies*, New York: Oxford University Press.

Gabriel, Y. (2008) 'Spectacles of resistance and resistance of spectacles', *Management Communication Quarterly*, 21(3): 310–26.

Gabriel, Y. and Griffiths, D.S. (2004) 'Stories in organizational research' in *Essential Guide to Qualitative Methods in Organizational Research*, London: Sage, pp 114–26.

Gayá Wicks, P.C. and Rippin, A.J. (2010) 'Art as experience: An inquiry into art and leadership using dolls and doll-making', *Leadership,* 6(3): 259–78.

Gerber, N., Templeton, E., Chilton, G., Liebman, M.C., Manders, E. and Shim, M. (2012) 'Art-based research as a pedagogical approach to studying intersubjectivity in the creative arts therapies', *Journal of Applied Arts and Health,* 3(1): 39–48.

Germain. O. (2020) 'Anti-editorial – Living the PhD journey… The life of Pi', *M@n@gement,* 23(1): 102–41.

Gherardi, S. (1994) 'The gender we think, the gender we do in our everyday organizational lives', *Human Relations,* 47(6): 591–610.

Gherardi, S. (2019a) 'Theorizing affective ethnography for organization studies', *Organization,* 26(6): 741–60.

Gherardi, S. (2019b) 'If we practice posthumanist research, do we need "gender" any longer?", *Gender, Work and Organization,* 26(1): 40–53.

Gherardi, S., Nicolini, D. and Strati, A. (2007) 'The passion for knowing', *Organization,* 14(3): 315–29.

Gilmore, S., Harding, N., Helin, J. and Pullen, A. (2019) 'Writing differently', *Management Learning,* 50(1): 3–10.

Giraldi, W. (2014) 'Internal Tapestries: A Q&A with Louise Glück', Poets and Writers, [online] 20 November, Available from: https://www.pw.org/content/internal_tapestries?article_page=2 [Accessed 8 October 2020].

Glesne C (1997) 'That rare feeling: Re-presenting research through poetic transcription', *Qualitative Inquiry,* 3(2): 202–22.

Glesne, C. (1999) *Becoming Qualitative Researchers: An Introduction* (2nd edn), White Plains, NY: Longman.

Goffman, E. (1959) *The Presentation of Self in Everyday Life*, Garden City, NJ: Doubleday.

Goodwin, J., Jasper, J.M. and Polletta, F. (eds) (2001) *Passionate Politics: Emotions and Social Movements*, Chicago, IL: Chicago University Press.

Education and Skills Funding Agency (ESFA) (2019) '16 to 19 funding: high value courses premium', GOV.UK, [online] 4 November, Available from: https://www.gov.uk/guidance/16-to-19-funding-high-value-cour ses-premium [Accessed 12 November 2020].

Gramsci, A. (2011) *Prison Notebooks* (three volumes), edited and translated by J.A. Buttigieg with A. Callari, New York: Columbia University Press.

Green, J. (ed) (2017) *Making Space for Indigenous Feminism*, Halifax, Nova Scotia: Fernwood Publishing.

Grey, C. and Sinclair, A. (2006) 'Writing differently', *Organization,* 13(3): 443–53.

Grosser, D.K. (2020) 'Gender, business and human rights: Academic activism as critical engagement in neoliberal times', *Gender, Work and Organization*, 28(4): 1624–37.

Grzanka, P.R. (ed) (2019) *Intersectionality: Foundations and Frontiers* (2nd edn), London: Routledge.

Grzanka, P.R. (2020) 'From buzzword to critical psychology: An invitation to take intersectionality seriously', *Women and Therapy*, 43(3–4): 244–61.

Griffin, R.A. (2012) 'I AM an angry Black woman: Black feminist autoethnography, voice, and resistance', *Women's Studies in Communication*, 35(2): 138–57.

Grisoni, L. (2008) 'Poetry', in M Broussine (ed) *Creative Methods in Organizational Research*, London: Sage, pp 108–27.

Grisoni, L. (2009) 'Flavouring organisational learning with poetry', in J. Kociatkjewicz and D. Jemielniak (eds) *Handbook of Research on Knowledge-Intensive Organizations*, San Francisco, CA: IGI Global, pp 98–115.

Grisoni, L. (2012) 'Poem Houses: An arts based inquiry into making a transitional artefact to explore shifting understandings and new insights in presentational knowing', *Organizational Aesthetics*, 1(1): 11–25.

The Guardian (2019) 'Mental health: A university crisis', [online] Available from: https://www.theguardian.com/education/series/mental-health-a-university-crisis [Accessed 11 August 2020].

Guarino, C.M. and Borden, V.M. (2017) 'Faculty service loads and gender: Are women taking care of the academic family?', *Research in Higher Education*, 58: 672–94.

Guillet de Monthoux, P. (2020) 'Curating management philosophy: Art and aesthetics for business education', in C. Neesham and S. Segal (eds) *Handbook of Philosophy of Management*, Berlin: Springer.

Gutkind, L. (2012) *You Can't Make This Stuff Up: The Complete Guide to Writing Creative Nonfiction from Memoir to Literary Journalism and Everything in Between*, Boston, MA: Da Capo Lifelong Books.

Halberstam, J. (2011) *The Queer Art of Failure*, Durham, NC: Duke University Press.

Halbwachs, M. (1992) *On Collective Memory*, edited and translated by L.A. Coser, Chicago, IL: University of Chicago Press.

Hall, S. (1997) 'Culture and power', *Radical Philosophy*, 86: 24–41.

Halley, J.O'M. (2012) 'And violence' in *The Parallel Lives of Women and Cows: Meat Markets*, New York: Palgrave Macmillan, pp 141–2.

Halperin, D.M. (1995) *Saint Foucault: Towards a Gay Hagiography*, Oxford: Oxford University Press.

Hamer, F.L. (1964) Testimony given to the Democratic National Convention Credentials Committee, 22 August, Audio available at https://blavity.com/blavity-original/nobodys-free-until-everybodys-free-fannie-lou-hamers-legacy-is-more-important-now-than-ever?category1=politics.

Hamilton, L. and Mitchell, L. (2017) 'Dignity and species difference within organizations', in M. Kostera and M. Pirson (eds) *Dignity and the Organization*, London: Palgrave Macmillan, pp 59–80.

Hamilton, L. and Taylor, N. (2017) *Ethnography after Humanism: Power, Politics and Method in Multi-Species Research*, London: Palgrave Macmillan.

Hancock, A.-M. (2015) *Intersectionality: An Intellectual History*, New York: Oxford University Press.

Handforth, R. and Taylor, C.A. (2016) 'Doing academic writing differently: A feminist bricolage', *Gender and Education*, 28(5): 627–43.

Haraway, D.J. (1988) 'Situated knowledges: The science question in feminism and the privilege of partial perspective', *Feminist Studies*, 14(3): 575–99.

Haraway, D.J. (2016) *Staying with the Trouble: Making Kinship in the Chthulucene*, Durham, NC and London: Duke University Press.

Harding, S. (1991) *Whose Science? Whose Knowledge? Thinking from Women's Lives*, New York: Cornell University Press.

Harding, S. (1993) 'Rethinking standpoint epistemology: What is "strong objectivity?"', in L. Alcoff and E. Potter (eds) *Feminist Epistemologies*, New York: Routledge, pp 49–82.

Harding, S. (ed) (2004) *The Feminist Standpoint Theory Reader: Intellectual and Political Controversies*, London: Routledge.

Harding, S. (2007) 'Feminist Standpoints', in S.N. Hesse-Biber (ed) *Handbook of Feminist Research: Theory and Praxis*, London: Sage, pp 45–69.

Harding, N., Ford, J. and Fotaki, M. (2013) 'Is the "F"-word still dirty? A past, present and future of/for feminist and gender studies in *Organization*'. *Organization*, 20(1): 51–65.

Harding, N., Pullen, A. and Vachhani, S. (2020) 'Editors' picks: Feminism and Organization', *Organization*, [online] Available from: https://journals.sagepub.com/page/org/collections/feminism [Accessed 25 October 2020].

Harquail, C.V. (2020) *Feminism: A Key Idea for Business and Society*, New York: Routledge.

Harris, T.M. (2007) 'Black feminist thought and cultural contracts: Understanding the intersection and negotiation of racial, gendered, and professional identities in the academy', *New Directions for Teaching and Learning*, 2007(110): 55–64.

Hatch, M.J. (1993) 'The dynamics of organizational culture', *Academy of Management Review*, 18(4): 657–93.

Haug, F. (2008) 'Memory work', *Australian Feminist Studies*, 23(58): 537–41.

Held, V. (2006) *The Ethics of Care: Personal, Political, and Global*, New York: Oxford University Press.

Helin, J. (2019) 'Dream writing: Writing through vulnerability', *Qualitative Inquiry*, 25(2): 95–9.

Helin, J. (2020) 'Temporality lost: A feminist invitation to vertical writing that shakes the ground', *Organization*, [online] 25 September, https://doi.org/10.1177%2F1350508420956322.

Helin, J. and Avenier, M.-J. (2016) 'Inquiring into arresting moments over time: Towards an understanding of stability within change', *Scandinavian Journal of Management*, 32(3): 142–9.

Helin, J., Kivinen, N. and Pullen, A. (2021) 'Until the dust settles', *ephemera: theory and politics in organization*, 21(4): 89–115.

Hemmings, C. (2012) 'Affective solidarity: Feminist reflexivity and political transformation', *Feminist Theory*, 13(2): 147–61.

Henderson, E.F. (2020) *Gender, Definitional Politics and 'Live' Knowledge Production: Contesting Concepts at Conferences*, London: Routledge.

Henderson, E.F. and Burford, J. (2020) 'Thoughtful gatherings: Gendering conferences as spaces of learning, knowledge production and community', *Gender and Education*, 32(1): 1–10.

Hennessy, R. (2009) 'Open secrets: The affective cultures of organizing on Mexico's northern border', *Feminist Theory*, 10(3): 309–22.

Hernández Castillo, R.A. (2010) 'The emergence of indigenous feminism in Latin America', *Signs: Journal of Women in Culture and Society*, 35(3): 539–45.

Hesse-Biber, S.N. and Leavy, P. (2006) *The Practice of Qualitative Research*, Thousand Oaks, CA: Sage.

Hesse-Biber, S.N. and Leavy, P. (2008) *Handbook of Emergent Methods*, New York: Guildford Press.

Hollis, L. (2017) 'Evasive actions: The gendered cycle of stress and coping for those enduring workplace bullying in American higher education', *Advances in Social Sciences Research Journal*, 4(7): 59–68.

Holman Jones, S. (2008) 'Autoethnography: Making the personal political', in N.K. Denzin and Y.S. Lincoln (eds) *Collecting and Interpreting Qualitative Materials* (3rd edn), Thousand Oaks, CA: Sage, pp 205–46.

Holmes IV, O. (2019) 'For diversity scholars who have considered activism when scholarship isn't enough!', *Equality, Diversity and Inclusion*, 38(6): 668–75.

hooks, b. (1981) *Ain't I a Woman: Black Women and Feminism*, Boston, MA: South End Press.

hooks, b. (1989) *Talking Back: Thinking Feminist, Thinking Black*, Boston, MA: South End Press.

hooks, b. (1991) 'Theory as Liberatory Practice', *Yale Journal of Law and Feminism*, 4(1): 1–12.

hooks, b. (2000) *Feminism Is for Everybody: Passionate politics*, London: Pluto Press.

hooks, b. (2003) *Teaching Community: A Pedagogy of Hope*, New York: Psychology Press.

Höpfl, H. (1994) 'Learning by heart: The rules of rhetoric and the poetics of experience', *Management Learning*, 25(3): 463–74.

Höpfl, H. (2000) 'On being moved', *Studies in Cultures, Organizations and Societies*, 6(1): 15–34.

Höpfl, H. J. (2003) 'Becoming a (virile) member: Women and the military body', *Body and Society*, 9(4): 13–30.

Höpfl, H. (2007) 'The codex, the codicil and the codpiece: Some thoughts on diminution and elaboration in identity formation', *Gender, Work and Organization*, 14(6): 619–32.

Höpfl, H. (2010) 'A question of membership', in P. Lewis and R. Simpson (eds) *Revealing and Concealing Gender*, London: Palgrave Macmillan, pp 39–53.

Höpfl, H. (2011) 'Women's writing', in E.L. Jeanes, D. Knights and P. Yancey Martin (eds) *Handbook of Gender, Work and Organization*, Chichester: John Wiley and Sons, pp 25–36.

Höpfl, H. and Linstead, S. (1997) 'Introduction: Learning to feel and feeling to learn: Emotion and learning in organizations', *Management Learning*, 28(1): 5–12.

HoSang, D.M., LaBennett, O. and Pulido, L. (eds) (2012) *Racial Formation in the Twenty-First Century*, Berkeley, CA: University of California Press.

Howe-Walsh, L. and Turnbull, S. (2016) 'Barriers to women leaders in academia: Tales from science and technology', *Studies in Higher Education*, 41(3): 415–28.

Huopalainen, A.S. (2020) 'Writing with the bitches', *Organization* [online] 13 October, https://doi.org/10.1177/1350508420961533.

Huopalainen, A.S. and Satama, S.T. (2019) 'Mothers and researchers in the making: Negotiating "new" motherhood within the "new" academia', *Human Relations*, 72(1): 98–121.

Hurston, Z. N. (2000) 'How it feels to be colored me', in E.P. Stoller and R.C. Gibson (eds) *Worlds of Difference: Inequality in the Aging Experience*, Thousand Oaks, CA: Pine Forge Press, pp 95–7.

Hutson, S.R. (2006) 'Self-citation in archaeology: Age, gender, prestige, and the self', *Journal of Archaeological Method and Theory*, 13(1): 1–18.

Ifekwunigwe, J.O. (1998) 'Borderland feminisms: Towards the transgression of unitary transnational feminisms', *Gender and History*, 10(3): 553–7.

Ingold, T. (2008) 'Anthropology is not ethnography', *Proceedings of the British Academy*, 154: 69–92.

Irigaray, L. (1985) *Speculum of the Other Woman*, translated by G. Gill, New York: Cornell University Press.

Izak, M., Kostera, M. and Zawadzki, M. (eds) (2017) *The Future of University Education*, London: Palgrave Macmillan.

Jääskeläinen, P. and Helin, J. (2021) 'Writing embodied generosity', *Gender, Work and Organization*, 28(4): 1398–412.

Jaggar, A.M. (2015) *Just Methods: An Interdisciplinary Feminist Reader*, New York: Routledge.

Jago, B. (2002) 'Chronicling and academic depression', *Journal of Contemporary Ethnography,* 31(6): 729–57.

Jamjoom, L.A. (2021) 'A spectacle of otherness: An autoethnography of a conference presentation', *Qualitative Research in Organizations and Management,* 16(1): 261–77.

Janesick, V.J. (2001) 'Intuition and creativity: A pas de deux for qualitative researchers', *Qualitative Inquiry,* 7(5): 531–40.

Johansson, M. and Jones, S. (2020) 'Writing past and present classed and gendered selves', in A. Pullen, J. Helin and N. Harding (eds) *Writing Differently* (Dialogues in Critical Management Studies, vol 4), Bingley: Emerald Publishing Limited, pp 131–44.

Johnson, A.G. (2005) *The Gender Knot: Unraveling Our Patriarchal Legacy,* Philadelphia, PA: Temple University Press.

Jones, D.R., Visser, M., Stokes, P., Örtenblad, A., Deem, R., Rodgers, P. and Tarba, S.Y. (2020) 'The performative university: "Targets", "terror" and "taking back freedom" in academia', *Management Learning,* 51(4): 363–77.

Jones, J.L. (2003) 'sista docta' in L.C. Miller, J. Taylor and M.H. Carver (eds) *Voices Made Flesh: Performing Women's Autobiography,* Madison, WI: University of Wisconsin Press, pp 237–57.

Jones, S., Martinez Dy, A. and Vershinina, N. (2019) '"We were fighting for our place": Resisting gender knowledge regimes through feminist knowledge network formation', *Gender, Work and Organization,* 26(6): 789–804.

Jones, S.L.H., Adams, T. and Ellis, C. (2013) 'Introduction: Coming to know autoethnography as more than a method', in S.L. Jones, T. Adams and C. Ellis (eds) *Handbook of Autoethnography,* Walnut Creek, CA: Left Coast Press, Inc., pp 17–47.

Jørgensen, L. and Holt, R. (2019) 'Organization, atmosphere, and digital technologies: Designing sensory order', *Organization,* 26(5): 673–95.

Juhlin, C. and Holt, R. (2021) 'The sensory imperative', *Management Learning* [online] 9 December, https://doi.org/10.1177/13505076211062220

Just, S.N., Muhr, S.L. and Risberg, A. (2018) 'Feminism, activism, writing! Introduction to the special section', *ephemera: theory and politics in organization,* 18(4): 841–53.

Kallio, K.-M., Kallio, T.J. (2014) 'Management-by-results and performance measurement in universities – implications for work motivation', *Studies in Higher Education,* 39(4): 574–89.

Kaptani, E. and Yuval-Davis, N. (2008) 'Participatory theatre as a research methodology: Identity, performance and social action among refugees', *Sociological Research Online,* 13(5): 1–12.

Kärreman, D. (2001) 'The scripted organization: Dramaturgy from Burke to Baudrillard', in R. Westwood and S. Linstead (eds) *The Language of Organization,* London: Sage, pp 89–111.

Kastner, J. and Wallis, B. (eds) (1998) *Land and Environmental Art*, London: Phaidon.

Katila, S. (2019) 'The mothers in me', *Management Learning*, 50(1): 129–40.

Kelan, E.K. (2010) 'Gender logic and (un)doing gender at work', *Gender, Work and Organization*, 17(2): 174–94.

Kemmerer, L. (2011) *Sister Species: Women, Animals and Social Justice*, Chicago, IL: University of Illinois Press.

Khoo, T., Burford, J., Henderson, E., Liu, H. and Nicolazzo, Z. (2020) 'Not getting over it: The impact of Sara Ahmed's work within critical university studies', *Journal of Intercultural Studies*, 42(1): 84–98.

Kidron, C.A. (2009) 'Toward an ethnography of silence: The lived presence of the past among Holocaust trauma descendants in Israel', *Current Anthropology*, 50(1): 5–27.

King, M.M., Bergstrom, C.T., Correll, S.J., Jacquet, J. and West, D.J. (2017) 'Men set their own cites high: Gender and self-citation across fields and over time', *Socius: Sociological Research for a Dynamic World*, 3: 1–22.

Kiriakos, C.M. and J. Tienari (2018) 'Academic writing as love', *Management Learning*, 49(3): 263–77.

Kleinman, S. (2007) *Feminist Fieldwork Analysis*, London: Sage.

Kleinman, S. and Copp, M.A. (1993) *Emotions and Fieldwork*, Newbury Park, CA: Sage.

Kleinman, S. and Kolb, K.H. (2012) 'Traps on the path of analysis', *Symbolic Interaction*, 34(4): 425–46.

Knights, D. (2006) 'Authority at work: Reflections and recollections', *Organization Studies*, 27(5): 699–720.

Knights, D., Clarke, C.A. (2014) 'It's a bittersweet symphony, this life: Fragile academic selves and insecure identities at work', *Organization Studies*, 35(3): 335–57.

Knobloch-Westerwick, S., Glynn C.J. and Huge, M. (2013) 'The Matilda effect in science communication: An experiment on gender bias in publication quality perceptions and collaboration interest', *Science Communication*, 35(5): 603–25.

Knudsen, B.T. and Stage, C. (2015) 'Introduction: Affective methodologies', in B.T. Knudsen and C. Stage (eds) *Affective Methodologies: Developing Cultural Research Strategies for the Study of Affect*, New York: Palgrave Macmillan, pp 1–22.

Knowles, J.G. and Cole, A.L. (2008) 'Preface' in J.G. Knowles and A.L. Cole (eds) *Handbook of the Arts in Qualitative Research: Perspectives, Methodologies, Examples, and Issues*, Thousand Oaks, CA: Sage, pp xi–xiv.

Koivunen, N. and Wennes, G. (2011) 'Show us the sound! Aesthetic leadership of symphony orchestra conductors', *Leadership*, 7(1): 51–71.

Kostera, M. (1997) 'Personal performatives: Collecting poetical definitions of management', *Organization*, 4(3): 345–53.

Kostera, M. (2007) *Organizational Ethnography: Methods and Inspirations*, Lund: Studentlitteratur.

Kostera, M. (2020) *After the Apocalypse: Finding Hope in Organizing*, Winchester and Washington, DC: Zer0 Books.

Kostera, M. (2020) 'Managing for the common good', Keynote address (1 October) at In/Visible Conference, Designs of Social Experience, Kraków.

Kostera, M. (ed) (2022) *How to Write Differently: A Quest for Meaningful Academic Writing*, Cheltenham: Edward Elgar Publishing.

Kostera, M. and Harding, N. (2021) *Organizational Ethnography*, Cheltenham: Edward Elgar Publishing.

Kristeva, J. (1987) *Tales of Love* (translated by L.S. Roudiez), New York: Columbia University Press.

Krumer-Nevo, M. and Sidi, M. (2012) 'Writing against othering', *Qualitative Inquiry*, 18(4): 299–309.

Küpers, W.M. (2014) *Phenomenology of the Embodied Organization: The Contribution of Merleau-Ponty for Organizational Studies and Practice*, London: Palgrave Macmillan.

Kuzhabekova, A. and Temerbayeva, A. (2018) 'The role of conferences in doctoral student socialization', *Studies in Graduate and Postdoctoral Education*, 29(2): 181–96.

Ladkin, D. (2011) *Rethinking Leadership: A New Look at Old Leadership Questions*, Cheltenham: Edward Elgar Publishing.

Lather, P.A. (1995) 'The validity of angels: Interpretive and textual strategies in researching the lives of women with HIV/AIDS', *Qualitative Inquiry*, 1(1): 41–68.

Law, I. (2017) 'Building the anti-racist university, action and new agendas', *Race Ethnicity and Education*, 20(3): 332–43.

Law, J. (1994) *Organising Modernity: Social Ordering and Social Theory*, Oxford: Wiley-Blackwell.

Lawley, S. and Boncori, I. (2017) 'LGBT+ experiences of sport in educational settings', in I. Boncori (ed) *LGBT+ Perspectives – The University of Essex Reader*, Napoli: Editoriale Scientifica, pp 171–89.

Leading Routes (2019) 'The broken pipeline: Barriers to Black PhD students accessing research council funding', London: UCL/Leading Routes, [online] Available from: https://leadingroutes.org/the-broken-pipeline [Accessed 9 October 2020].

Learmonth, M. and Humphreys, M. (2011) 'Autoethnography and academic identity: Glimpsing business school doppelgängers', *Organization*, 19(1): 99–117.

Leavy, P. (2010) 'Poetic bodies: Female body image, sexual identity and arts-based research', *LEARNing Landscapes*, 4(1): 175–87.

Leavy, P. (2015) *Method Meets Art: Arts-Based Research Practice* (2nd edn), New York: Guilford Publications.

Leavy, P. (2018) *Handbook of Arts-Based Research*, New York: Guildford Press.

Leggo, C. (2004) 'The curriculum of joy: Six poetic ruminations', *Journal of the Canadian Association for Curriculum Studies*, 2(2): 27–42.

Liamputtong, P. and Rumbold, J. (eds) (2008) *Knowing Differently: Arts-Based and Collaborative Research Methods*, New York: Nova Science Publishers.

Li, E.P.H. and Prasad, A. (2018) 'From wall 1.0 to wall 2.0: Graffiti, social media, and ideological acts of resistance and recognition among Palestinian refugees', *American Behavioral Scientist*, 62(4): 493–511.

Li, E.P.H., Prasad, A., Smith, C., Gutierrez, A., Lewis, E. and Brown, B. (2019) 'Visualizing community pride: Engaging community through photo- and video-voice methods', *Qualitative Research in Organizations and Management: An International Journal*, 14(4): 377–92.

Lincoln, N.K. and Denzin Y.S. (2005) *The Sage Handbook of Qualitative Research*, Thousand Oaks, CA: Sage.

Lindebaum, D., Vesa, M. and den Hond, F. (2020) 'Insights from "The Machine Stops" to better understand rational assumptions in algorithmic decision making and its implications for organizations', *Academy of Management Review*, 45(1): 247–63.

Lingis, A. (2000) *Dangerous Emotions*, Berkeley, CA: University of California Press.

Linstead, S. and H. Höpfl (2000) *The Aesthetics of Organization*, London: Sage.

Liu, H. (2017) 'Redeeming difference in CMS through anti-racism feminisms', in A. Pullen, N. Harding and M. Phillips (eds) *Feminists and Queer Theorists Debate the Future of Critical Management Studies*, Bingley: Emerald Publishing Limited, pp 39–56.

Liu, H. (2017) 'Undoing Whiteness: The Dao of anti-racist diversity practice', *Gender Work and Organization*, 24(5): 457–71.

Liu, H. (2019) 'To be a hero and traitor: A reflection on truth-telling and fear', *ephemera: theory and politics in organization*, 19(4): 865–73.

Liu, H. (2020) 'What is Intersectional Feminism? A Definitive Guide', Disorient, [online] Available from: https://disorient.co/intersectional-feminism/ [Accessed 1 November 2020].

Liu, H. and Pechenkina, E. (2016) 'Staying quiet or rocking the boat? An autoethnography of organisational visual white supremacy', *Equality, Diversity and Inclusion: An International Journal*, 35(3): 186–204.

Loacker, B. (2021) 'Challenging thought at *ephemera*: Attempting to think and organize differently', *ephemera: theory and politics in organization*, 21(4): 143–62.

Lorde, A. (1984a) 'The master's tools will never dismantle the master's house', in A. Lorde (ed) *Sister Outsider: Essays and Speeches*, Trumansburg, NY: The Crossing Press, pp 110–13.

Lorde, A. (1984b) *Sister Outsider: Essays and Speeches*, Trumansburg, NY: Crossing Press.

Lorde, A. (2007) 'Learning from the 60s', Address given at Harvard University, February 1982, in A. Lorde (ed) *Sister Outsider: Essays and Speeches*, Trumansburg, NY: Crossing Press, pp 134–44.

Lorde, A. (2009) 'Poet as teacher – human as poet – teacher as human', in R.P. Byrd, J.B. Cole and B. Guy-Sheftall (eds) *I Am Your Sister: Collected and Unpublished Writings of Audre Lorde*, New York: Oxford University Press, pp 182–3.

Lorde, A. (2017) 'Age, race, class, and sex: Women redefining difference', in B.K. Scott, S.E. Cayleff, A. Donadey and I. Lara (eds) *Women in Culture: An Intersectional Anthology for Gender and Women's Studies* (2nd edn), Chichester: Wiley Blackwell, pp 16–22.

Lorde, A. (2018) *The Master's Tools Will Never Dismantle the Master's House*, London: Penguin.

Love, H. (2007) *Feeling Backward: Loss and the Politics of Queer History*, Cambridge, MA: Harvard University Press.

Lund, R. and Tienari, J. (2018) 'Passion, care, and eros in the gendered neoliberal university', *Organization,* 26(1): 98–121.

Lykke, N. (ed) (2014) *Writing Academic Texts Differently: Intersectional Feminist Methodologies and the Playful Art of Writing*, Abingdon: Routledge.

Mack, K. (2013) 'Taking an aesthetic risk in management education: Reflections on an artistic-aesthetic approach', *Management Learning*, 44(3): 286–304.

MacLure, M. (2013) 'The wonder of data', *Cultural Studies ↔ Critical Methodologies*, 13(4): 228–32.

Madison, D.S. (2005) *Critical Ethnography: Method, Ethics, and Performance*, London: Sage.

Mahmood, S. (2011) *Politics of Piety: The Islamic Revival and the Feminist Subject*, Princeton, NJ: Princeton University Press.

Maliniak, D., Powers, R. and Walter, B.F. (2013) 'The gender citation gap in international relations', *International Organization,* 67(4): 889–922.

Mandalaki, E. (2020) 'Author-ize me to write: Going back to writing with our *fingers*', *Gender, Work and Organization*, 28(3): 1008–22.

Mandalaki, E. and Pérezts, M. (2020) 'It takes two to tango: Theorizing inter-corporeality through nakedness and eros in researching and writing organizations', *Organization*, 29(4): 596–618.

Mangham, I.L. and Overington, M.A. (1987) *Organizations as Theatre: A Social Psychology of Dramatic Appearances*, Chichester: Wiley.

Mann, S.A. and Kelley, L.R. (1997) 'Standing at the crossroads of modernist thought: Collins, Smith, and the new feminist epistemologies', *Gender and Society*, 11(4): 391–408.

Marinetto, M. (2018) 'Universities' targets for research time are way off the mark', Times Higher Education, [online] 25 January, Available from: https://www.timeshighereducation.com/opinion/universities-targets-research-time-are-way-mark [Accessed 11 August 2020].

Martin, P.Y. (2006) 'Practising gender at work: Further thoughts on reflexivity', *Gender, Work and Organization*, 13(3): 254–76.

Massumi, B. (2002) *Parables for the Virtual: Movement, Affect, Sensation*, Durham, NC: Duke University Press.

Mavin, S. and Bryans, P. (2002) 'Academic women in the UK: Mainstreaming our experiences and networking for action', *Gender and Education*, 14(3): 235–50.

McCluney, C.L. and Rabelo, V.C. (2019a) 'Conditions of visibility: An intersectional examination of Black women's belongingness and distinctiveness at work', *Journal of Vocational Behavior*, 113: 143–52.

McCluney, C. L. and Rabelo, V. C. (2019b) 'Managing diversity, managing Blackness? An intersectional critique of diversity management practices', in L.M. Roberts, A.J. Mayo and D.A. Thomas (eds) *Race, Work, and Leadership: New Perspectives on the Black Experience*, Boston, MA: Harvard Business Review.

McIntyre, M. (2004) 'Ethics and aesthetics: The goodness of arts-informed research', in A.L. Cole, L. Neilsen, J.G. Knowles and T. Luciani (eds) *Provoked by Art: Theorizing Arts-Informed Research*, Halifax, Nova Scotia: Backalong Books, pp 84–99.

McMurray, R. and Pullen, A. (eds) (2020) *Gender, Embodiment and Fluidity in Organization and Management* (Routledge Focus on Women Writers in Organization Studies), New York: Routledge.

McNiff, S. (1998) *Art-Based Research*, London: Jessica Kingsley.

McNiff, S. (2011) 'Artistic expressions as primary modes of inquiry', *British Journal of Guidance and Counselling*, 39(5): 385–96.

McNiff, S. (2014) *Writing and Doing Action Research*, London: Sage.

McNiff, S. (2017) 'Philosophical and practical foundations of artistic inquiry', in P. Leavy (ed) *Handbook of Arts-Based Research*, New York: Guilford Press, pp 22–34.

McQueeney, K. (2013) 'Doing ethnography in a sexist world: A response to "The feminist ethnographer's dilemma"', *Journal of Contemporary Ethnography*, 42(4): 451–9.

McRobbie, A. (2009) *The Aftermath of Feminism: Gender, Culture, and Social Change*, Thousand Oaks, CA: Sage.

Meier, N. and Wegener, C. (2017) 'Writing with resonance', *Journal of Management Inquiry*, 26(2): 193–201.

Meikle, P.A. (2020) 'The right to breathe: a sociological commentary on racialized injustice, borders and violence', *Equality, Diversity and Inclusion: An International Journal*, 39(7): 793–801.

Meisiek, S. and Barry, D. (2018) 'Finding the sweet spot between art and business in analogically mediated inquiry', *Journal of Business Research*, 85(C): 476–83.

Meisiek, S and Hatch, M.J. (2008) 'This is work, this is play: Artful interventions and identity dynamics', in Barry, D, Hansen, H (eds) *The Sage Handbook of New Approaches in Management and Organization*, London: Sage, pp 412–22.

Melaku, T.M. and Beeman, A. (2020) 'Academia isn't a safe haven for conversations about race and racism', *Harvard Business Review*, [online] Available from: https://hbr.org/2020/06/academia-isnt-a-safe-haven-for-conversations-about-race-and-racism [Accessed 9 October 2020].

Mena, S., Rintamäki, J., Fleming, P. and Spicer, A. (2016) 'On the forgetting of corporate irresponsibility', *Academy of Management Review*, 41(4): 720–38.

Merleau-Ponty, M. (1962) *Phenomenology of Perception*, London: Routledge and Kegan Paul.

Merleau-Ponty, M. (1989) *Phenomenology of Perception*, translated by C. Smith, London: Routledge.

Merriam-Webster.com Dictionary, s.v. 'failure', https://www.merriam-webster.com/dictionary/failure.

Middleton, D. and Brown, S.D. (2005) *The Social Psychology of Experience: Studies in Remembering and Forgetting*, London: Sage.

Miko-Schefzig, K., Learmonth, M. and McMurray, R. (2020) 'A different way of looking at things: The role of social science film in organisation studies', *Organization*, 29(4): 653–72.

Mills, C.W. (1997) *The Racial Contract*, Ithaca, NY: Cornell University Press.

Mitchell, S.M., Lange, S. and Brus, H. (2013) 'Gendered citation patterns in international relations journals', *International Studies Perspectives*, 14(4): 485–92.

Minahan, S. and Wolfram Cox, J. (eds) (2007) *The Aesthetic Turn in Management*, Farnham: Ashgate.

Mittelman, J.H. (2018) *Implausible Dream: The World-Class University and Repurposing of Higher Education*, Princeton, NJ: Princeton University Press.

Mittelman, J.H. (2019) 'To risk or derisk the soul of the university? The peril in educational globalization', *Globalizations*, 16(5): 707–16.

Mohanty, C.T. (2003) *Feminism without Borders: Decolonizing Theory, Practicing Solidarity*, Durham, NC: Duke University Press.

Moraga, C. and Anzaldúa, G.E. (eds) (1983) *This Bridge Called My Back: Writings by Radical Women of Color* (2nd edn), New York: Kitchen Table: Women of Color Press.

Moraga, C. and Anzaldúa, G.E. (eds) (2015) *This Bridge Called My Back: Writings by Radical Women of Color* (4th edn), New York: SUNY Press.

Moreton-Robinson, A. (2000a) 'Troubling business: Difference and Whiteness within feminism', *Australian Feminist Studies,* 15(33): 343–52.

Moreton-Robinson, A. (2000b) *Talkin' Up to the White Woman: Aboriginal Women and Feminism*, St Lucia, QLD: University of Queensland Press.

Moreton-Robinson, A. (2006) 'Towards a new research agenda? Foucault, Whiteness and Indigenous sovereignty', *The Australian Sociological Association,* 42(4): 383–95.

Morrissey, J. (2015) 'Regimes of performance: Practices of the normalised self in the neoliberal university', *British Journal of Sociology of Education,* 36(4): 614–34.

Münch, R. (2014) *Academic Capitalism: Universities in the Global Struggle for Excellence,* London: Routledge.

Muñoz, J. (2009) *Cruising Utopia: The Then and There of Queer Futurity,* New York: New York University Press.

Najda-Janoszka, M. and Daba-Buzoianu, C. (2018) 'Editorial paper: Exploring management through qualitative research – Introductory remarks', *Journal of Entrepreneurship, Management and Innovation,* 14(4): 5–16.

Nash, J.C. (2019) *Black Feminism Reimagined: After Intersectionality,* Durham, NC: Duke University Press.

Neilsen, L. (2008) 'Lyric inquiry', in J. Knowles and A.L. Cole (eds) *Handbook of the Arts in Qualitative Research: Perspectives, Methodologies, Examples, and Issues,* Thousand Oaks, CA: Sage, pp 93–102.

Neumann, I.B. (1996) 'Collecting ourselves at the end of the century', in A.P. Bochner (ed) *Composing Ethnography: Alternative Forms of Qualitative Writing,* Walnut Creek, CA: AltaMira Press, pp 172–98.

Nittrouer, C.L., Hebl, M.R., Ashburn-Nardo, L., Trump-Steele, R.C.E., Lane, D.M. and Valian, V. (2018) 'Gender disparities in colloquium speakers at top universities', *Proceedings of the National Academy of Sciences of the United States of America,* 115(1): 104–8.

Nkomo, S.M. (1988) 'Race and sex: The forgotten case of the Black female manager', in S. Rose and L. Larwood (eds) *Women's Careers: Pathways and Pitfalls,* New York: Praeger, pp 133–50.

Nkomo, S.M. (1992) 'The emperor has no clothes: Rewriting "race in organizations"', *Academy of Management Review,* 17(3): 487–513.

Nkomo, S.M. and Al Ariss, A. (2014) 'The historical origins of ethnic (white) privilege in US organizations', *Journal of Managerial Psychology,* 29(4): 389–404.

Nkomo, S.M., Bell, M.P., Roberts, L.M., Joshi, A. and Thatcher, S.M. (2019) 'Diversity at a critical juncture: New theories for a complex phenomenon', *Academy of Management Review,* 44(3): 498–517.

Nussbaum, M.C. (2011) *Creating Capabilities: The Human Development Approach,* Cambridge, MA: Harvard University Press.

O'Shea, S.C. (2018a) '"I, Robot?" Or how transgender subjects are dehumanised', *Culture and Organization,* 26(1): 1–13.

O'Shea, S.C. (2018b) 'This girl's life: An autoethnography', *Organization,* 25(1): 3–20.

O'Shea, S.C. (2019) 'Cutting my dick off', *Culture and Organization*, 25(4): 272–83.

O'Shea, S.C. (2020) 'Working at gender? An autoethnography', *Gender, Work and Organization*, 27(6): 1438–49.

Office for National Statistics (2020) 'Gender pay gap in the UK: 2019', [online] Available from: https://www.ons.gov.uk/employmentandlabou rmarket/peopleinwork/earningsandworkinghours/bulletins/genderpaygap intheuk/2019 [Accessed 30 September 2020].

Ohito, E.O. and Nyachae, T.M. (2019) 'Poetically poking at language and power: Using Black feminist poetry to conduct rigorous feminist critical discourse analysis', *Qualitative Inquiry*, 25(9–10): 839–50.

Olick, J.K. (2008) '"Collective memory": A memoir and prospect', *Memory Studies*, 1(1): 23–9.

Olufemi, L. (2020) *Feminism, Interrupted: Disrupting Power*, London: Pluto Press.

Ottensmeyer, E.J. (1996) 'Too strong to stop, too sweet to lose: Aesthetics as a way to know organizations', *Organization*, 3(2): 189–94.

Owen, L. (2020) 'Innovations in menstrual organisation: Redistributing boundaries, capitals, and labour', PhD thesis, Melbourne: Monash University, Available from: https://doi.org/10.26180/5ed437df63c80

Oxford Dictionaries, s.v. 'failure', https://premium.oxforddictionaries.com/ definition/english/failure.

Özkazanç-Pan, B. (2019) 'On agency and empowerment in a #MeToo world', *Gender, Work and Organization*, 26(8): 1212–20.

Özkazanç-Pan, B. and Pullen, A. (2020) 'Gendered labour and work, even in pandemic times', *Gender, Work and Organization*, 27(5): 675–6.

Özbilgin, M. (ed) (2009) *Equality, Diversity and Inclusion at Work: Yesterday, Today and Tomorrow*, Cheltenham: Edward Elgar Publishing.

Ozturk, M.B. and Rumens, N. (2014) 'Gay male academics in UK business and management schools: Negotiating heteronormativities in everyday work life', *British Journal of Management*, 25(3): 503–17.

Page, M., Grisoni, L., Turner, A. (2014) 'Dreaming fairness and re-imagining equality and diversity through participative aesthetic inquiry', *Management Learning*, 45(5): 577–92.

Page, T. (2017) 'Vulnerable writing as a feminist methodological practice', *Feminist Review*, 115(1): 13–29.

Patai, D. (1993) *Brazilian Women Speak: Contemporary Life Stories*, New Brunswick, NJ: Rutgers University Press.

Parker, M. (2002) 'Queering management and organization', *Gender, Work and Organization*, 9(2): 146–66.

Patomäki, H. (2019) 'Repurposing the university in the 21st century: Toward a progressive global vision', *Globalizations*, 16(5): 751–62.

Patton, T.O. (2004) 'Reflections of a Black woman professor: Racism and sexism in academia', *Howard Journal of Communications*, 15(3): 185–200.

Pelias, R.J. (1999) *Writing Performance: Poeticizing the Researcher's Body*, Carbondale, IL: Southern Illinois University Press.

Pereira, M.D.M. (2017) *Power, Knowledge and Feminist Scholarship: An Ethnography of Academia*, London: Taylor and Francis.

Pereira, M.D.M. (2021) 'Researching gender inequalities in academic labour during the COVID-19 pandemic: Avoiding common problems and asking different questions', *Gender, Work and Organization*, 28(S2): 498–509.

Pérezts, M., Faÿ, E. and Picard, S. (2015) 'Ethics, embodied life and esprit de corps: An ethnographic study with anti-money laundering analysts', *Organization*, 22(2): 217–34.

Perry, M. and Medina, C.L. (eds) (2015) *Methodologies of Embodiment: Inscribing Bodies in Qualitative Research*, London: Routledge.

Phillips, A. (2004) 'Defending equality of outcome', *Journal of political philosophy*, 12(1): 1–19.

Phillips, M., Pullen, A. and Rhodes, C. (2014) 'Writing organization as gendered practice: Interrupting the libidinal economy', *Organization Studies,* 35(3): 313–33.

Phillips, N. (1995) 'Telling organizational tales: On the role of narrative fiction in the study of organizations', *Organization Studies,* 16(4): 625–49.

Pierazzini, M.E, Bertelli, L. and Raviola, E. (2021) '*Working with words: Italian feminism and organization studies*', *Gender, Work and Organization*, 28(4): 1260–81.

Pink, S. (2009) *Doing Sensory Ethnography* (2nd edn), Thousand Oaks, CA: Sage.

Plotnikof, M. and Utoft, E.H. (2021) 'The "new normal" of academia in pandemic times: Resisting toxicity through care', *Gender, Work and Organization*, 29(4): 1259–71.

Plotnikof, M., Bramming, P., Branicki, L., Christiansen, L.H., Henley, K., Kivinen, K., Resende de Lima, J.P., Kostera, M., Mandalaki, E., O'Shea, S., Özkazanç-Pan, B., Pullen, A., Stewart, J., Ybema, S. and van Amsterdam, N. (2020) 'Catching a glimpse: Corona-life and its micro-politics in academia', *Gender, Work and Organization*, 27(5): 804–26.

Poindexter, C.C. (2002) 'Research as poetry: A couple experiences HIV', *Qualitative Inquiry*, 8(6): 707–14.

Poindexter, C.C. (2006) 'Poetic language from a focus group with African American HIV-positive women over age 50', *Affilia: Feminist Inquiry in Social Work*, 21(4): 461.

Porschitz, E.T. and Siler, E.A. (2017) 'Miscarriage in the workplace: An authoethnography', *Gender, Work and Organization*, 24(6): 565–78.

Pow, K. (2018) '"Be Exactly Who You Are": Black Feminism in Volatile Political Realities', in A. Johnson, R. Joseph-Salisbury, B. Kamunge (eds) *The Fire Now: Anti-Racist Scholarship in Times of Explicit Racial Violence*, London: Zed Books, pp 235–49.

Powell, W.W. and DiMaggio, P.J. (eds) (1991) *The New Institutionalism in Organizational Analysis*, Chicago, IL: Chicago University Press.

Prasad, A. (2014) 'You can't go home again: And other psychoanalytic lessons from crossing a neo-colonial border', *Human Relations*, 67(2): 233–57.

Prasad A. (2016) 'Cyborg writing as a political act: Reading Donna Haraway in organization studies', *Gender, Work, and Organization,* 23(4): 431–46.

Prendergast, M., Leggo, C.D. and Sameshima, P. (2009) *Poetic Inquiry: Vibrant Voices in the Social Sciences*, Boston, MA: Sense.

Prichard, C. and Benschop, Y. (2018) 'It's time for Acting Up!', *Organization*, 25(1): 98–105.

Priola, V., Lasio, D., De Simone, S. and Serri, F. (2014) 'The sound of silence. Lesbian, gay, bisexual and transgender discrimination in "inclusive organizations"', *British Journal of Management*, 25(3): 488–502.

Pullen, A. (2018) 'Writing as labiaplasty', *Organization*, 25(1): 123–30.

Pullen, A. and Rhodes, C. (2008) 'Dirty writing', *Culture and Organization*, 14(3): 241–59.

Pullen, A. and Rhodes, C. (2015) 'Writing, the feminine and organization', *Gender, Work and Organization,* 22(2): 87–93.

Pullen, A. and Thanem, T. (2010) 'Editorial: Sexual spaces', *Gender, Work and Organization*, 17(1): 1–6.

Pullen, A., Harding, N. and Phillips, M. (eds) (2017) *Feminists and Queer Theorists Debate the Future of Critical Management Studies*, Bingley: Emerald Publishing Limited.

Pullen, A., Helin, J. and Harding, N. (eds) (2020) *Writing Differently* (Dialogues in Critical Management Studies, vol 4), Bingley: Emerald Publishing Limited.

Puwar, N. (2004) *Space Invaders: Race, Gender and Bodies Out of Place*, Oxford: Berg.

Rabelo, V.C., Robotham, K.J. and McCluney, C.L. (2020) '"Against a sharp white background": How Black women experience the white gaze at work', *Gender, Work and Organization*, 28(5): 1840–58.

Reed-Danahay, D. (ed) (1997) *Auto/ethnography: Rewriting the Self and the Social*, New York: Berg.

Rees, T. (2005) 'Reflections on the uneven development of gender mainstreaming in Europe', *International Feminist Journal of Politics*, 7(4): 555–74.

Reinharz, S. (1992) *Feminist Methods in Social Research*, New York: Oxford University Press.

Research Excellence Framework (2021) 'About the REF', [online] Available from: https://www.ref.ac.uk/about-the-ref/ [Accessed 28 September 2020].

Rhodes, C. (2015) 'Writing organization/romancing fictocriticism', *Culture and Organization*, 21(4): 289–303.

Rhodes, C. (2017) 'Academic freedom in the corporate university: Squandering our inheritance?', in M. Izak, M. Kostera, M. Zawadzki (eds) *The Future of University Education*, London: Palgrave Macmillan, pp 19–38.

Rhodes, C. (2019) 'Sense-ational organization theory! Practices of democratic scriptology', *Management Learning*, 50(1): 24–37.

Richardson, L. (1990) *Writing Strategies: Reaching Diverse Audiences* (Qualitative Research Methods Series, vol 21), London: Sage.

Richardson, L. (1992) 'The consequences of poetic representation: Writing the other, rewriting the self', in C. Ellis and M.G. Flaherty (eds) *Investigating Subjectivity: Research on Lived Experience*, Newbury Park, CA: Sage, pp 125–40.

Richardson, L. (1995) 'Writing: A method of inquiry', in N.K. Denzin and Y.S. Lincoln (eds) *The Sage Handbook of Qualitative Research* (1st edn), Thousand Oaks, CA: Sage, pp 516–29.

Richardson, L. (1997) *Fields of Play: Constructing an Academic Life*, New Brunswick, NJ: Rutgers University Press.

Riley, D. (2000) *The Words of Selves: Identification, Solidarity, Irony*. Stanford, CA: Stanford University Press.

Rippin, A. (2017) 'Writing with Eve: Queering paper', A. Pullen, N. Harding and M. Phillips (eds) *Feminists and Queer Theorists Debate the Future of Critical Management Studies*, Bingley: Emerald Publishing Limited, pp 171–94.

Roberts, L.M., Mayo, A.J. and Thomas, D.A. (2019) *Race, Work, and Leadership: New Perspectives on the Black Experience*, Boston, MA: Harvard Business Review Press.

Rolling, J.H. (2010) 'A paradigm analysis of arts-based research and implications for education', *Studies in Art Education*, 51(2): 102–14.

Rolling, J.H. (2013) *Arts-Based Research Primer*, New York: Peter Lang Publishing.

Rosenthal, L. (2016) 'Incorporating intersectionality into psychology: An opportunity to promote social justice and equity', *American Psychologist*, 71(6): 474–85.

Rossiter, M.W. (1993) 'The Matthew Matilda effect in science', *Social Studies of Science*, 23(2): 325–41.

Rottenberg, C. (2014) 'The rise of neoliberal feminism', *Cultural Studies*, 28(3): 418–37.

Rumens, N. (2012) 'Queering cross-sex friendships: An analysis of gay and bisexual men's workplace friendships with heterosexual women', *Human Relations*, 65(8): 955–78.

Rumens, N. (2013) 'Queering men and masculinities in construction: Towards a research agenda', *Construction Management and Economics*, 31(8): 802–15.

Ryömä, A. and Satama, S. (2019) 'Dancing with the D-man: Exploring reflexive practices of relational leadership in ballet and ice hockey', *Leadership*, 15(6): 696–721.

Salskov, S.A. (2020) 'A critique of our own? On intersectionality and "epistemic habits" in a study of racialization and homonationalism in a Nordic context', *NORA – Nordic Journal of Feminist and Gender Research*, 28(3): 251–65.

Sang, K., Al-Dajani, H. and Özbilgin, M. (2013) 'Frayed careers of migrant female professors in British academia: An intersectional perspective', *Gender, Work and Organization*, 20(2): 158–71.

Sang, K., Powell, A., Finkel, R. and Richards, J. (2015) '"Being an academic is not a 9–5 job": Long working hours and the "ideal worker" in UK academia', *Labour and Industry: A Journal of the Social and Economic Relations of Work*, 25(3): 235–49.

Sapir, E. (1961) *Culture, Language, and Personality: Selected Essays*, edited by D. Mandelbaum, Berkeley, CA: University of California Press.

Satama, S. (2020) 'Researching through experiencing aesthetic moments: "Sensory slowness" as my methodological strength', in A. Pullen, J. Helin and N. Harding (eds) *Writing Differently* (Dialogues in Critical Management Studies, vol 4), Bingley: Emerald Publishing Limited, pp 209–30.

Satama, S., Blomberg, A. and Warren, S. (2021) 'Exploring the embodied subtleties of collaborative creativity: What organisations can learn from dance', *Management Learning*, 53(2): 167–89.

Sawir, E., Marginson, S., Deumert, A., Nyland, C. and Ramia, G. (2008) 'Loneliness and international students: An Australian study', *Journal of Studies in International Education*, 12(2): 148–80.

Sayers, J.G. (2017) 'Feminist CMS writing as difficult joy: Via bitches and birds', in A. Pullen, N. Harding and M. Phillips (eds) *Feminists and Queer Theorists Debate the Future of Critical Management Studies*, Bingley: Emerald Publishing Limited, pp 155–70.

Sayers, J.G. and Jones, D. (2015) 'Truth scribbled in blood: Women's work, menstruation and poetry', *Gender, Work and Organization*, 22(2): 94–111.

Schreyögg, G. and Höpfl, H. (2004) 'Theatre and organization: Editorial introduction', *Organization Studies*, 25(5): 691–704.

Schüssler Fiorenza, E. (1993) *But She Said: Feminist Practices of Biblical Interpretation*, Boston, MA: Beacon Press.

Scott, J.W. (1986) 'Gender: A useful category of historical analysis', *The American Historical Review*, 91(5): 1053–75.

Seidman, S. (1995) 'Deconstructing queer theory or the under-theorization of the social and the ethical', in L. Nicholson and S. Seidman (eds) *Social Postmodernism: Beyond Identity Politics*, Cambridge: Cambridge University Press, pp 116–41.

Sellers, S. (ed) (2004) *Hélène Cixous: The Writing Notebooks*, New York: Continuum.

Sholock, A. (2012) 'Methodology of the privileged: White anti-racist feminism, systematic ignorance, and epistemic uncertainty', *Hypatia*, 27(4): 701–14.

Shore, C. and Wright, S. (2015) 'Audit culture revisited: Rankings, ratings, and the reassembling of society', *Current Anthropology*, 56(3): 421–44.

Shotter, J. and Tsoukas, H. (2014) 'Performing *phronesis*: On the way to engaged judgement', *Management Learning*, 45(4): 377–96.

Shortt, H.L. (2015) 'Liminality, space and the importance of "transitory dwelling places" at work', *Human Relations*, 68(4): 633–58.

Shortt, H.L. and Warren, S.K. (2019) 'Grounded visual pattern analysis: Photographs in organizational field studies', *Organizational Research Methods*, 22(2): 539–63.

Silva, C.R. (2021) 'Writing for survival (… and to breathe)', *Gender, Work and Organization*, 28(2): 471–80.

Silverman, D. (2007) *A Very Short, Fairly Interesting and Reasonably Cheap Book about Qualitative Research*, London: Sage.

Simmonds, F.N. (1999) 'My body, myself: How does a Black woman do sociology?', in J. Price and M. Shildrick (eds) *Feminist Theory and the Body: a Reader*, New York: Routledge, pp 50–63.

Simpson, R., Ross-Smith, A. and Lewis, P. (2010) 'Merit, special contribution and choice: How women negotiate between sameness and difference in their organizational lives', *Gender in Management: An International Journal*, 25(3): 198–207.

Sinclair, A. (2018) 'Five movements in an embodied feminism: A memoir', *Human Relations*, 72(1): 144–58.

Skjælaaen, G.R., Bygdås, A.L. and Hagen, A.L. (2020) 'Visual inquiry: Exploring embodied organizational practices by collaborative film-elicitation', *Journal of Management Inquiry*, 29(1): 59–75.

Śliwa, M. and Johansson, M. (2014) 'The discourse of meritocracy contested/reproduced: Foreign women academics in UK business schools', *Organization*, 21(6): 821–43.

Śliwa, M. and Johansson, M. (2015) 'Playing in the academic field: Non-native English-speaking academics in UK business schools', *Culture and Organization*, 21(1): 78–95.

Smith, L.T. (2013) *Decolonizing Methodologies: Research and Indigenous Peoples*, London: Zed Books.

Soroptimist International (2020) Soroptimist International, [online] Available from: https://www.soroptimistinternational.org [Accessed 22 September 2020].

Sparkes, A.C., Nilges, L., Swan, P. and Dowling, F. (2003) 'Poetic representations in sport and physical education: Insider perspectives 1', *Sport, Education and Society*, 8(2): 153–77.

Spry, T. (2001) 'Performing autoethnography: An embodied methodological praxis', *Qualitative inquiry*, 7(6): 706–32.

Spry, T. (2011) *Body, Paper, Stage: Writing and Performing Autoethnography*, Walnut Creek, CA: Left Coast Press.

St. Pierre, E. (2011) 'Post qualitative research: The critique and the coming after', in N.K. Denzin and Y.S. Lincoln (eds) *The Sage Handbook of Qualitative Research* (4th edn), Thousand Oaks, CA: Sage, pp 611–25.

Stanley, L. (1994) 'The knowing because experiencing subject: narratives, lives and autobiography', in K. Lennon and M. Whitford (eds) *Knowing the Difference: Feminist Perspectives in Epistemology*, London: Routledge, pp 132–48.

Staunæs, D. and Brøgger, K. (2020) 'In the mood of data and measurements: Experiments as affirmative critique, or how to curate academic value with care', *Feminist Theory*, 21(4): 429–45.

Steffan, B. (2020) 'Managing menopause at work: The contradictory nature of identity talk', *Gender, Work and Organization*, 28(1): 195–214.

Steger, M.B. (2019) 'Committing to cultures of creativity: The significance of transdisciplinarity', *Globalizations*, 16(5): 763–9.

Stein, H.F. (2003) 'The inner world of workplaces: Accessing this world through poetry, narrative, literature, music, and visual art', *Consulting Psychology Journal: Practice and Research*, 55(2): 84–93.

Stewart, K. (2007) *Ordinary Affects*, Durham, NC: Duke University Press.

Steyaert, C. (2015) 'Three Women. A Kiss. A Life. On the queer writing of time in organization', *Gender, Work and Organization*, 22(2): 163–78.

Strathern, M. (ed) (2000) *Audit Cultures: Anthropological Studies in Accountability, Ethics and the Academy*, London: Routledge.

Strati, A. (1992) 'Aesthetic understanding of organizational life', *Academy of Management Review*, 17(3): 568–81.

Strati, A. (1999) *Organization and Aesthetics*, London: Sage.

Strati, A. (2000) 'The aesthetic approach in organization studies', in S. Linstead and H. Höpfl (eds) *The Aesthetics of Organization*, London: Sage, pp 13–34.

Strati, A. (2007a) 'Aesthetics in teaching organization studies', in M. Reynolds, R. Vince (eds) *The Handbook of Experiential Learning and Management Education*, London: Oxford University Press, pp 70–86.

Strati, A. (2007b) 'Sensations, impressions and reflections on the configuring of the aesthetic discourse in organizations', *Aesthesis*, 1(1): 14–22.

Strati, A. (2007c) 'Sensible knowledge and practice-based learning', *Management Learning*, 38(1): 61–77.

Strati, A. (2009) ' "Do you do beautiful things?" Aesthetics and art in qualitative methods of organization studies', in D. Buchanan and A. Bryman (eds) *The Sage Handbook of Organizational Research Methods*, London: Sage.

Strati, A. (2010) 'Aesthetic understanding of work and organizational life: Approaches and research developments', *Sociology Compass*, 4(10): 880–93.

Strauβ, A. and Boncori, I. (2020) 'Foreign women in academia: Double-strangers between productivity, marginalization and resistance', *Gender, Work and Organization*, 27(6): 1004–19.

Styhre, A. (2013) 'Gender equality as institutional work: The case of the Church of Sweden', *Gender, Work and Organization*, 21(2): 105–20.

Sullivan, G. (2009) *Art Practice as Research: Inquiry in Visual Arts* (2nd edn), Thousand Oaks, CA: Sage.

Sullivan, N. (2003) *A Critical Introduction to Queer Theory*, New York: NYU Press.

Sunderland, N., Bristed, H., Gudes, O., Boddy, J. and Da Silva, M. (2012) 'What does it feel like to live here? Exploring sensory ethnography as a collaborative methodology for investigating social determinants of health in place', *Health and Place*, 18(5): 1056–67.

Sutherland, I. (2013) 'Arts-based methods in leadership development: Affording aesthetic workspaces, reflexivity and memories with momentum', *Management Learning*, 44(1): 25–43.

Suzack, C. (2010) 'Indigenous women and transnational feminist struggle: Theorizing the politics of compromise and care', *CR: The New Centennial Review*, 10(1): 179–93.

Suzuki, D. and Mayorga, E. (2014) 'Scholar-activism: A twice told tale', *Multicultural Perspectives*, 16(1): 16–20.

Swan, E. (2017) 'Manifesto for feminist critical race killjoys in CMS', in A. Pullen, N. Harding and M. Phillips (eds) *Feminists and Queer Theorists Debate the Future of Critical Management Studies* (Dialogues in Critical Management Studies, vol 3), Bingley: Emerald Publishing Limited, pp 13–37.

Szwabowski, O. and Wężniejewska, P. (2017) 'An co(autoethnography) story about going against the neoliberal didactic machine', *Journal for Critical Education Policy Studies*, 15(3): 105–44.

Tahamtan, I., Afshar, A.S. and Ahamdzadeh, K. (2016) 'Factors affecting number of citations: A comprehensive review of the literature', *Scientometrics*, 107(3): 1195–225.

Taylor, S.S. (2003) 'Knowing in your gut and in your head: Doing theater and my underlying epistemology of communication: Playwright and director reflections on "Ties that Bind"', *Management Communication Quarterly*, 17(2): 272–9.

Taylor, S.S. (2008) 'Theatrical performance as unfreezing: "Ties that Bind" at the academy of management', *Journal of Management Inquiry*, 17(4): 398–406.

Taylor, S.S. and Carboni, I. (2008) 'Technique and practices from the arts: Expressive verbs, feelings, and action', in D. Barry and H. Hansen (eds) *The Sage Handbook of New Approaches in Management and Organization*, London: Sage, pp 220–8.

Taylor, S.S. and Hansen, H. (2005) 'Finding form: Looking at the field of organizational aesthetics', *Journal of Management Studies*, 42(6): 1211–31.

Taylor, S.S. and Ladkin, D. (2009) 'Understanding arts-based methods in managerial development', *Academy of Management Learning and Education*, 8(1): 55–69.

Taylor, S.S., Fisher, D. and Dufresne, R.L. (2002) 'The aesthetics of management storytelling: A key to organizational learning', *Management Learning*, 33(3): 313–30.

Thanem, T. and Knights, D. (2019) *Embodied Research Methods*, London: Sage.

Thanem, T. and Wallenberg, L. (2016) 'Just doing gender? Transvestism and the power of underdoing gender in everyday life and work', *Organization*, 23(2): 250–71.

Tong, R. and Fernandes Botts, T. (2017) *Feminist Thought: A More Comprehensive Introduction* (5th edn), Boulder, CO: Westview Press.

Townley, B. (1994) 'Writing in friendship', *Organization*, 1(1): 24–8.

Tronto, J. (1993) *Moral Boundaries: A Political Argument for an Ethic of Care*. New York: Routledge.

Tsoukas, H. (2005) *Complex Knowledge: Studies in Organizational Epistemology*, Oxford: Oxford University Press.

Tsoukas, H. (2009) 'A dialogical approach to the creation of new knowledge in organizations', *Organization Science*, 20(6): 941–57.

Tuchman, G. (2009) *Wannabe U: Inside the Corporate University*, Chicago, IL: University of Chicago Press.

Twale, D.J. (2018) *Understanding and Preventing Faculty-on-Faculty Bullying: A Psycho-Social-Organizational Approach*, New York: Routledge.

Tyler, M. (2019) 'Reassembling difference? Rethinking inclusion through/ as embodied ethics', *Human Relations*, 72(1): 48–68.

Ulmer, J. (2017) 'Writing Slow Ontology', *Qualitative Inquiry*, 23(3): 201–11.

Vachhani, S.J. (2015) 'Organizing love: Thoughts on the transformative and activist potential of feminine writing', *Gender, Work and Organization*, 22(2): 148–62.

Vachhani, S.J. (2019) 'Rethinking the politics of writing differently through *écriture féminine*', *Management Learning*, 50(1): 11–23.

Vachhani, S.J. and Pullen, A. (2019) 'Ethics, politics and feminist organizing: Writing feminist infrapolitics and affective solidarity into everyday sexism', *Human Relations*, 72(1): 23–47.

Valtonen, A. and Pullen, A. (2020) 'Writing with rocks', *Gender, Work and Organization*, 28(2): 506–22.

van Amsterdam, N. (2015) 'Othering the "leaky body". An autoethnographic story about expressing breast milk in the workplace', *Culture and Organization*, 21(3): 269–87.

van Amsterdam, N. (2020) 'On silence and speaking out about sexual violence: An exploration through poetry', in A. Pullen, J. Helin and N. Harding (eds) *Writing Differently* (Dialogues in Critical Management Studies, vol 4), Bingley: Emerald Publishing Limited, pp 185–92.

van Amsterdam, N. and van Eck, D. (2019a) '"I have to go the extra mile": How fat female employees manage their stigmatized identity at work', *Scandinavian Journal of Management*, 35(1): 46–55.

van Amsterdam, N. and van Eck, D. (2019b) 'In the flesh: A poetic inquiry into how fat female employees manage weight-related stigma', *Culture and Organization*, 25(4): 300–16.

van Eck, D. and van Amsterdam, N. (2020) 'Affective engagement with airport security work: Wor(l)ding material agencies through poetry', *Organizational Aesthetics*, 10(1): 36–41.

Varela, F.J., Thompson, E. and Rosch, E. (1993) *The Embodied Mind: Cognitive Science and Human Experience,* Cambridge, MA: MIT press.

Vieta, M. (2014) 'The stream of self-determination and autogestión: Prefiguring alternative economic realities', *ephemera: theory and politics in organization*, 14(4): 781–809.

Vijay, D., Gupta, S. and Kaushiva, P. (2020) 'With the margins: Writing subaltern resistance and social transformation', *Gender, Work and Organization*, 28(2): 481–96.

Vince, R. (2020) 'Experiencing emotion in conducting qualitative research as a PhD student', *Journal of Management Education*, 44(4): 508–23.

Vitry, C. (2020) 'Queering space and organizing with Sara Ahmed's Queer Phenomenology', *Gender, Work and Organization*, 28(3): 935–49.

Walby, S. (2005) 'Gender mainstreaming: Productive tensions in theory and practice', *Social Politics: International Studies in Gender, State and Society*, 12(3): 321–43.

Ward, A. (2011) '"Bringing the message forward": Using poetic re-presentation to solve research dilemmas, *Qualitative Inquiry*, 17(4): 355–63.

Ward, J. and Shortt, H. (eds) (2020) *Using Arts-based Research Methods: Creative Approaches for Researching Business, Organisation and Humanities*, London: Palgrave Macmillan.

Warren, S. (2002) 'Show me how it feels to work here', *ephemera: theory and politics in organization*, 2(3): 224–45.

Warren, S. (2008) 'Empirical challenges in organizational aesthetics research: Towards a sensual methodology', *Organization Studies*, 29(4): 559–80.

Warren, S. (2012) 'Having an eye for it: Aesthetics, ethnography and the senses', *Journal of Organizational Ethnography*, 1(1): 107–18.

Weatherall, R. (2019) 'Writing the doctoral thesis differently', *Management Learning*, 50(1): 100–13.

Welsh, M.A., Dehler, G.E. and Murray, D.L. (2007) 'Learning about and through experience: Understanding the power of experience-based education', in M. Reynolds and R. Vince (eds) *The Handbook of Experiential Learning and Management Education*, Oxford: Oxford University Press, pp 53–69.

Whitfield, T.W.A. (2005) 'Aesthetics as pre-linguistic knowledge: A psychological perspective', *Design Issues*, 21(1): 3–17.

Wicks, P.G. and Rippin, A. (2010) 'Art as experience: An inquiry into art and leadership using dolls and doll making', *Leadership*, 6(3): 259–78.

Wilkinson, C. (2020) 'Imposter syndrome and the accidental academic: An autoethnographic account', *International Journal for Academic Development*, 25(4): 363–74.

Willmott, H. (1994) 'Management education: Provocations to a debate', *Management Learning*, 25(1): 105–36.

Witkin, R. (2009) 'The aesthetic imperative of a rational-technical machinery: A study in organizational control through the design of artifacts', *Music and Arts in Action*, 2(1): 56–68.

Witz, A., Warhurst, C. and Nickson, D. (2003) 'The labour of aesthetics and the aesthetics of organization', *Organization*, 10(1): 33–54.

Wood, M. and Brown, S. (2012) 'Film-based creative arts enquiry: Qualitative researchers as auteurs', *Qualitative Research Journal*, 12(1): 130–47.

Ylijoki, O.-H. and Henriksson, L. (2017) 'Tribal, proletarian and entrepreneurial career stories: Junior academics as a case in point', *Studies in Higher Education*, 42(7): 1292–308.

Yoo, J. (2019a) 'Learning to write through an awareness of breath', *Qualitative Inquiry*, 26(3–4): 400–6.

Yoo, J. (2019b) 'Exploring a timeless academic life', *Qualitative Inquiry*, 25(2): 192–9.

You Can't Beat a Woman (2017) 'Founding Women's Refuges: A Heritage Lottery project', [online] Available from: https://www.youcantbeatawoman.co.uk [Accessed 22 September 2020].

Yuval-Davis, N. (1998) 'Gender and nation', in R. Wilford and R.L. Miller (eds) *Women, Ethnicity and Nationalism: The Politics of Transition*, London: Routledge, pp 23–35.

Yuval-Davis, N. (2006) 'Intersectionality and feminist politics', *European Journal of Women's Studies*, 13(3): 193–209.

Zawadzki, M. (2017) '"The last in the food chain": Dignity of Polish junior academics and doctoral candidates in the face of performance management', in M. Izak, M. Kostera and M. Zawadzki (eds) *The Future of University Education*, London: Palgrave Macmillan, pp 63–84.

Zawadzki, M. and Jensen, T. (2020) 'Bullying and the neoliberal university: A co-authored autoethnography', *Management Learning*, 51(4): 398–413.

Index

References to endnotes show both the
page number and the note number (231n3).